D1478898

"Critical Race Theory can be used as an excuse to not talk about race, racial divisions, or systemic racial disparities. But we are called to the ministry of reconciliation. That requires us to talk honestly about the history of race in our country and the church. Part of that conversation is an accurate understanding of CRT: what it is, what it is not, and what we can learn from it. I have yet to come across anyone who leads that conversation with the same level of background, gospel-centered truth, and wisdom as Ed. This book is a vital part of engaging in the work of racial justice and reconciliation."
Schelli Cronk, chief operating officer of Transform Minnesota

"If you have questions about Critical Race Theory, Marxism, or social justice, *Untangling Critical Race Theory* has approachable, relatable answers. Ed unpacks scholarly frameworks in understandable terms, with essential context from Scripture, history, and present-day culture. This book is far from a dense academic read, and I was pleasantly surprised I couldn't put it down! If you want advice for navigating conversations on these topics with grace and intelligence, you will devour this book. If you're concerned about progressive ideology infecting society, you need to read *Untangling Critical Race Theory*."
Brooke Hempell, researcher and host of the *Race and Redemption* podcast

"As codirector of the Winsome Conviction Project, I can assure you there is nothing winsome about our current discussions of race. As soon as *Critical Race Theory, white privilege,* or *systemic racism* is uttered, walls go up and voices rise. While many books have been written on race and CRT, Dr. Uszynski—who I've known for over thirty years—is my most trusted source on how to have productive and honest conversations on difficult issues, especially race. Whether you agree or disagree with Dr. Uszynski, his insights will provoke, inspire, and help us communicate and not separate."
Tim Muehlhoff, professor of communication at Biola University and author of *End the Stalemate: Move from Cancel Culture to Meaningful Conversations*

"In recent years, few topics have delivered such heated opinions as Critical Race Theory. Still, many remain unclear of what it is, forming opinions based on popular catch phrases and political narratives. In *Untangling Critical Race Theory,* Ed Uszynski distills voluminous material to provide a truthful assessment of CRT that will both inform and challenge his readers. Specifically, Ed pleads for Christians who have dismissed CRT not only to reevaluate its contributions but also to understand why its concepts were developed in the first place. If you're looking for a theologically faithful, sociologically astute, and academically honest treatment of CRT, Uszynski's book is for you."
Eric Rivera, assistant professor of pastoral theology at Trinity Evangelical Divinity School and lead pastor of The Brook Chicago

"I wish I had read this book fifteen years ago! In an era where Critical Race Theory is weaponized by both the secular left and the secular right, and demonized by many Christians, Ed Uszynski intellectually, lovingly, and biblically calls Christians to more. The research, accessibility, and nuance of this book make it extremely helpful for people who are willing to ask what we should accept and what we should reject in the CRT conversation, and what impact that can have in our churches and communities."
Jim Davis, pastor of Orlando Grace Church, coauthor of *The Great Dechurching,* and host of the *As In Heaven* podcast

"In many ways, this book feels like a bunch of my chats with Ed Uszynski over the last few years, helping me make sense of inaccessible academic theories reduced to acronyms, ill-informed assumptions, and the real meaning of 'woke.' More importantly, Ed has challenged me that as a believer and leader, I can't sit on the sidelines of this conversation. He humbly models what it looks like to engage the tension of our own souls while seeking to understand and move toward those who might process their story through a different lens."

Brian Goins, speaker, creative strategist, and author of *Playing Hurt: A Guy's Strategy for Winning a Marriage*

"What a refreshing, absolutely necessary read Ed Uszynski has given us in *Untangling Critical Race Theory*. As I lament the state of our country and its growing antagonism toward biblical Christianity, I can't help but blame the American church at large. If we were united as we should be around the undeniable social ramifications of the gospel, society would see biblical Christianity as the answer, not the problem, to our stubborn racial divide. If we as American Christians have one last gasp at true unity across racial lines, salvaging our public perception, and perhaps sparking revival, reading *Untangling Critical Race Theory* is a critical first step."

Chris Broussard, sports broadcaster and founder of the K.I.N.G. Movement

"With great skill and care, Ed Uszynski untangles Critical Race Theory with the nuance needed for this controversial topic. He does so by interacting directly with the theory and not merely through critics of it. Yet there is a clear demarcation about both the value and limits of this approach to public space, honoring what should be heard in this conversation as well as what is problematic. If you read one book on this topic, here it is. You may hear things you have thought about reflected on with wisdom in this deep dive into this topic."

Darrell Bock, executive director for cultural engagement at the Hendricks Center and senior research professor of New Testament studies at Dallas Theological Seminary

"In this accessible yet thoughtful work, Dr. Ed Uszynski untangles fact from fiction about Critical Race Theory and settles the question of whether Christians (and anyone else) should accept or avoid it. With a rare combination of empathy, nuance and biblical fidelity, this book evaporates a haze of popular distortions about CRT, giving a fair assessment and presenting a way forward like never before. This work is a game-changer that brings clarity where there has been a lot of noise and confusion about the most controversial three letters of our time."

Rasool Berry, teaching pastor at The Bridge Church in Brooklyn, New York

"We hear 'Critical Race Theory' thrown around, and often in a negative light, but the vast majority of people have no real understanding of what these terms mean. Dr. Ed Uszynski is uniquely skilled and equipped to take this complex issue and make it accessible. Written with a deep love for God and the Bible, scholarly research, humility, and excellence, this timely book is one I highly recommend."

Vivian Mabuni, national speaker, podcast host, and author of *Open Hands, Willing Heart*

UNTANGLING CRITICAL RACE THEORY

WHAT CHRISTIANS NEED TO KNOW AND WHY IT MATTERS

ED USZYNSKI

FOREWORDS BY PRESTON SPRINKLE AND CRAWFORD LORITTS

An imprint of InterVarsity Press
Downers Grove, Illinois

FOR MY MOM, JOANNE MARIE USZYNSKI,

who has read more books than anyone I know

and taught me to love everything about them.

InterVarsity Press
P.O. Box 1400 | Downers Grove, IL 60515-1426
ivpress.com | email@ivpress.com

©2024 by Edward Thomas Uszynski

All rights reserved. No part of this book may be reproduced in any form without written permission from InterVarsity Press.

InterVarsity Press® is the publishing division of InterVarsity Christian Fellowship/USA®. For more information, visit intervarsity.org.

All Scripture quotations, unless otherwise indicated, are taken from The Holy Bible, New International Version®, NIV®. Copyright © 1973, 1978, 1984, 2011 by Biblica, Inc.™ Used by permission of Zondervan. All rights reserved worldwide. www.zondervan.com. The "NIV" and "New International Version" are trademarks registered in the United States Patent and Trademark Office by Biblica, Inc.™

While any stories in this book are true, some names and identifying information may have been changed to protect the privacy of individuals.

The publisher cannot verify the accuracy or functionality of website URLs used in this book beyond the date of publication.

Cover design: David Fassett
Interior design: Jeanna Wiggins
Image: Blocks abstraction - stock illustration / CSA Images, Getty Images

ISBN 978-1-5140-0481-4 (print) | ISBN 978-1-5140-0482-1 (digital)

Printed in the United States of America ♾

Library of Congress Cataloging-in-Publication Data
Names: Uszynski, Edward Thomas, 1968- author.
Title: Untangling critical race theory : what Christians need to know and
   why it matters / Ed Uszynski.
Description: Downers Grove, IL : IVP, [2024] | Includes bibliographical
   references.
Identifiers: LCCN 2024005008 (print) | LCCN 2024005009 (ebook) | ISBN
   9781514004814 (print) | ISBN 9781514004821 (digital)
Subjects: LCSH: Racism–Religious aspects–Christianity. | Critical race
   theory–United States. | BISAC: SOCIAL SCIENCE / Race & Ethnic Relations
   | SOCIAL SCIENCE / Sociology / Social Theory
Classification: LCC BT734.2 .U89 2024 (print) | LCC BT734.2 (ebook) | DDC
   261.8/3–dc23/eng/20240308
LC record available at https://lccn.loc.gov/2024005008
LC ebook record available at https://lccn.loc.gov/2024005009

30 29 28 27 26 25 24 | 13 12 11 10 9 8 7 6 5 4 3 2 1

CONTENTS

FOREWORD

PRESTON SPRINKLE

I KNOW OF NO OTHER WHITE EVANGELICAL CHRISTIAN who has devoted so many countless hours to studying race-related issues, from both books and people, than Ed Uszynski. Race-related questions are not simply intellectual or abstract for Ed. They are deeply personal and an integral part of his story. Any book on race relations must be just that—*relational*. If Ed were simply an academic who has read a lot of books on race, then I would not recommend this book.

And yet, Ed is an academic. I knew Ed before he started his PhD, and he was already thinking on a PhD level about race relations (or about anything, really). This is why I was thrilled when he decided to pursue a PhD in American culture studies at Bowling Green State University. His degree is basically a PhD in Critical Theory and Marxism, *not* by learning these ideas from their critics but from academics and fellow PhD students who passionately espouse them. Once you learn, in good faith, from the proverbial horse's mouth—rather than forming your opinions about a theory from those who only critique it—you realize that things are more complicated than they first appear.

So it is with Critical Race Theory (CRT). Ed is extremely clear in identifying aspects of CRT that conflict with a Christian worldview, and he unapologetically condemns these aspects in an intellectually responsible manner. And having read extensively from the works of Karl Marx and actual Critical Race theorists—who are in no way monolithic, as I came to know from reading Ed's book—Ed shows that there are aspects of these theories that can be appreciated by Christians, even aspects that *do* resonate with a Christian worldview.

Ed's book is not only a responsible, fair, and honest evaluation of CRT and its Marxist roots, it is also a model of what evangelical scholarship should look like. If you want an intellectually lazy approach to CRT that takes a binary—"CRT is evil!" or "CRT is 100 percent true!"— then stick to your favorite partisan pundit to spoon-feed you the "truth." But if you want an honest and responsible guide to help you think through the complexities of CRT and how it contributes to our understanding of race relations, then I cannot more highly recommend this book.

The thoughtful reader won't agree with everything Ed says. *I'm* not totally sure I agree with everything Ed says! But I don't recommend books simply because I agree with everything they say; I recommend books that are thoroughly researched and aren't afraid to curiously explore and evaluate complex ideas in good faith. Along those lines, *Untangling Critical Race Theory* is a masterpiece in what responsible evangelical engagement with a controversial idea should look like.

FOREWORD

CRAWFORD LORITTS

THIS IS ONE OF THE MOST IMPORTANT BOOKS I have read in recent years. I wish it had been written five years ago. The resurfacing of racial tension and polarization in the broader culture have affected and, sadly, infected many Christians. Relationships have been fractured, churches split, and parachurch organizations that have sought to address racial injustice have been accused of embracing cultural Marxism.

The culprit? Critical Theory and more specifically Critical Race Theory (CRT) have been identified as the source of racial tension and polarization. There are campaigns to purge society and Christian organizations and institutions of its contaminating influence. In some states, legislators are passing laws limiting and, in some cases, eliminating the teaching of Black history because it is viewed as divisive and a tool of CRT. Then there are the soundbites from the twenty-four-hour news channels, prominent social media influencers, bloggers, and Christian leaders all denouncing and condemning Critical Race Theory.

But what exactly is Critical Race Theory? What can we learn? What should we denounce and why? *Untangling Critical Race Theory* is a call to step back and take a close look at CRT (I think you will find chapter six especially helpful) and consider, as followers of Christ, how we should respond. These pages also underscore an appropriate caution: anger and fear have a way of clouding our perspective and pulling us toward misrepresentation. Fundamentally, to be Christian is to pursue truth. Throughout the pages of this book we are reminded that our critique of CRT must be honest and fair. And rightly so. This is a clear call and challenge for followers of Christ to seek to understand and to represent with integrity that with which we may disagree.

I have known Ed Uszynski for more than thirty years. Ed writes from the vantage point of a deep, abiding commitment to biblical orthodoxy; a personal commitment to evangelism and discipleship; deep, meaningful relationships and friendships across ethnic lines; and a comprehensive exposure to and study of Critical Race Theory. He is not an armchair theorist. He writes from this rich background and with compelling credibility. Both head and heart are in these pages. Perhaps you may not agree with all that Ed says or concludes, but I believe you will be drawn to his clarity and your thinking will be provoked.

I love the subtitle of this book, *What Christians Need to Know and Why It Matters*. This is a clear statement of the mission of the book, and in my view my dear friend more than delivers. I felt better equipped and even anchored after reading it. But in a wonderfully strange way I felt recommissioned, and I think you will too. Understanding what gave rise to Critical Race Theory should put the spotlight on compassion and motivate followers of Christ to do what should have been done. Thank you, Ed, for calling us to be portraits of the solution.

INTRODUCTION
WHY WE NEED ANOTHER BOOK ON RACE

In my entire adult life, I don't think America's dialogue about race has been as toxic as it is today. Extremists dominate, pushing us into ever-more-polarized ideological corners. If you live in right-wing space and spend time talking about contemporary racism or the ongoing, persistent consequences of centuries of slavery, Jim Crow, redlining, and segregation, extremists will quickly label you "woke." And no one should listen to anyone woke.

If you live in left-wing spaces and you push back against emerging "anti-racist" ideologies that sometimes declare the nation foundationally evil, engage in their own forms of gross racial stereotyping (including unremitting hatred for "whiteness"), and seek to defund and discredit policing itself, extremists will quickly label you "racist." And no one should listen to anyone racist.

DAVID FRENCH, "WHEN OUR FOREFATHERS FAIL"

"THE MESSAGES I SEE being pushed forward within our ministry have not been for oneness but are clouded with power and have caused separation and division."

"My radar goes up when I hear words like *oppressed, oppressor*, and *victim* when it comes to race. They are words of power and control with an agenda attached."

"Today it's not just white privilege, but amped up to white supremacy. It seems to me that there is nothing a white person can do to help fight racism."

"I'm concerned that we are slipping toward the heresy of liberation theology, if not in our statement of faith, then in our practice. We are moving toward a position and practice of the gospel only being the gospel if it moves us to action on the social justice front."

The above are all snippets of emails from white evangelical minister friends who are struggling to make sense of the racial rhetoric and discussions they encounter daily on campus, in their church, on social media, and with people in general.

They represent confusion about race and how to talk about it. They represent concern over theological drift and a fear that ideas expressed by the people they're engaging are unbiblical, especially when they suspect those ideas spring from secular ideologies. They represent feelings of inadequacy, since in their role they are expected to guide others in the race conversation but aren't even sure how to lead it for themselves.

For most, apart from the news or social media, they'd never think about race. It's not part of their daily experience. When nobody's looking, they're asking, "Why do I have to think about something that doesn't really affect me? And why should I prepare for conversations I don't really want to have?" These folks know they can't say it out loud, but they wish the whole matter of race would just go away so we could stop hearing about it altogether.

But we can't go on avoiding or ignoring it. As Christians, we *need* to talk about race because it concerns brothers and sisters who experience it as more than just a trending topic dropping into their social feed. They feel it every day of their lives, as either a person of color or a white person intimately connected to POC.[1] For them, not a day goes by when race isn't an issue on some level. It may be due to their work environment, where they live, or some other circumstance that keeps racial turmoil near the front of their consciousness. And guess what? They wish the whole matter of race would go away, too. But they know it won't happen until we talk about it *more*, not less.

People on both sides seem to be tired of the discussion. For those new to the subject, they're tired because they feel like it's forced on them by political agenda. For others who think about race all the time, they're tired because occasional "race quakes" give the impression of progress but never stick, and they don't believe more words and emotional energy will make a difference.

It's not the first time denominations have split, pastors were fired, or congregations were divided because of racial disagreement. Indeed, race never fully disappears from public discourse, but some epochs of American history seem more racially incendiary—and we're in one of those right now. The first decades of this century produced racial kindling vulnerable to a spark from any direction, and eager match lighters are everywhere.[2]

I appreciate the fatigue represented on both sides. I feel it, too. But now more than ever we need Christ followers to activate their minds and hearts and will to embrace this moment, especially those who've characteristically avoided the discussion, to heal within the church if not within our society. These conversations have been difficult enough in years past, but many feel even more overwhelmed today because so much race talk flows from another rather intimidating and unfamiliar body of work: Critical Race Theory.

WHAT IS "CRITICAL RACE THEORY"?

CRT originated as a formal discipline in the 1980s with a group of activist-minded law scholars who'd grown discouraged at the ongoing presence of disparities between white and black folks across society, even a decade after civil rights legislation made overt discrimination illegal. Their work defied the prevailing narrative at the time, that post-civil-rights America was now an equitable democracy whose treasures were always equally available to anyone who lived responsibly enough to receive them. Instead, they exposed how the legal system had embedded enough racially significant policies and patterns that disproportionate outcomes were almost guaranteed without ever appearing racist on the surface. Their work showed how racism could be present without racists, and it shook legal scholarship at its core.

But today CRT gets credited or condemned for conflicts happening all over the place. You hear about school curriculums teaching white kids to hate themselves: CRT. One-sided diversity seminars in the workplace: CRT. People being "canceled" on campuses and online: CRT. Athletes wearing justice slogans on their jerseys: CRT. It's not always clear what the three letters mean, but they seem to create problems between people wherever they show up.

In every lane of social life, a provocative lexicon confronts us with troubling ideas like "social justice," "white privilege," "white supremacy," and "intersectionality," disrupting concepts that sound vaguely familiar in some ways and radically new in others. We're being thrown into academic currents whose streams most of us rarely wade in, talking about subjects most of us intentionally avoid, with words and phrases whose meaning seems to change depending on who uses them. It feels like you're way behind in a complicated conversation with no obvious direction on how to catch up.[3]

Many in the evangelical Christian world have risen up to condemn CRT language and the ideas behind it, or at least what they perceive CRT to be based on social posts and media coverage. They warn that all of these concepts have roots in Marxism and Critical Theory—two other hastily condemned but little understood worlds—and are destructive to Christian faith. Disagreement about the relative danger of CRT has split churches, terminated pastors, and cost parachurch organizations staff and donors.

You hear the president of the United States condemn the use of Critical Race Theory in all government institutions, followed soon after by the presidents of major Southern Baptist universities doing the same on behalf of their own.[4] Christians aligned with these decisions affirm rejecting CRT wholeheartedly, but if you ask them what they mean by the phrase, you'll almost never hear the same definition twice.

But then you spend time with a Bible-believing, theologically robust, and culturally shrewd person who barely bats an eye at the language of CRT, who suggests that there's greater evil in ignoring the conditions prompting the language in the first place. They see CRT concepts as pointing out evils that have been ignored for generations, particularly in the church. They believe conversations stemming from CRT ideas can unite the church and help lead people to Jesus, but when you ask them, they rarely know the origins of many of the concepts.

One friend says CRT is of the devil, while another suggests not paying attention to the social realities behind CRT is the true demon. The red-meat commentary on either side produces a hysteria like medieval churches accusing heretics. The ugliness is real.

As Christians, how do we sort through all the rhetoric?

GETTING HELP TO MAKE SENSE OF IT ALL

When it comes to the topic of race, I regularly talk with Christians who are trying to understand terms circulating on social media, the politics behind policies, the history being cited or ignored, and the proper Christian response. It's not an overstatement to say that most people I encounter in the church are deficient in their theological thinking about race and ethnicity, especially white evangelicals. There's a vacuum when it comes to appreciation for the depth of our racialization as Americans and what the Bible has to say regarding questions pertaining to it. We can blame this illiteracy on many factors including age, social location, education, peer circle, vocation, entertainment, and media choices, but it's a reality. Not everyone has been exposed to the same level of experience or insight regarding "the race problem" in America.

As Michael O. Emerson and Christian Smith argued in their eye-opening analysis of race and the church, "racialization" is the unavoidable effect of living in "a society wherein race matters profoundly for differences in life experiences, life opportunities, and social relationships." It's the absorption of racial meaning into our psyche, a condition where "we are never unaware of the race of a person with whom we interact."[5] Within a racialized culture, some may place too much emphasis on race and others not enough, but let's not be distracted by the extremes. We need help thinking about the repercussions of living in a racialized culture—not by becoming more "woke" in the radical progressive sense, but by having our eyes opened in a "spirit-filled, mind of Christ" sense.

We need more people called to the racial mission field, people who not only intentionally seek and find common ground but also carefully steward others' different experiences instead of hunkering down behind battle lines assuming the worst about people they don't understand. Cultural competency was a theological and missiological goal long before it became the darling of secular HR departments.

Both inside and outside the church, racial tension receives fuel from many unresolved disagreements. Disagreement on whether a crisis actually exists. Disagreement on the origins of the division. Disagreement on the nature of the current race "problem" itself. Disagreement on definitions. Disagreement on the value of individual and collective experience. Disagreement on what constitutes a threat to the gospel. Disagreement on the relationship between gospel belief and gospel living. Disagreement on what counts as a "justice" issue.

Disagreement on where and how—if at all—race should be taught and discussed.

Our response to these disagreements can't be more hysteria. We don't need more simplistic soundbites. We need careful attention and purposeful reflection. We need more patience. We need tools to promote the kind of civil discourse that says, "I think I disagree, but help me see and understand your position." I want this book to aid that process.

I'm writing with a particular audience in mind, the one I most identify with due to my own background, the one that has raised the most concerns about CRT and its effect on the church. I'm writing for white evangelicals shaped by the expression of evangelicalism widely prominent in the last half of the twentieth century.

It's a pocket of evangelicalism shaped by Cold War politics, Religious Right social concerns, the rise of megachurch pastors, and the intensification of a consumerist-driven expression of Christianity. These evangelicals consider words like *race, racism, justice,* or *oppression* as important but secondary categories in Christian discipleship. They emphasize personal responsibility and individualism in their walks with God, and they lead others to Christ leaning heavily on the redemption aspects of the gospel. They tend to vote Republican if for no other reason than as a lesser of two evils, but also because conservative talking points align better with their version of evangelicalism. They've had some exposure to nonwhite cultures but mostly keep to their own. It's the Christianity I entered as a new Christ follower in 1988. There are plenty more distinctives we could plot, but you know if you fit what I'm describing.

I'm not writing to judge this group. I'm trying to fill a perceived gap. I know the concerns about CRT, but I see a different set of concerns that remain underexplored. Most evangelicals in the church that I'm in conversation with aren't trying to reconcile a neo-Marxist worldview with Christianity. They're trying to correct a Christianity that had *already* been syncretized with unbiblical thinking decades ago, but in ways many church folk don't recognize. Like blind men with their hands on different parts of the elephant, what we choose to focus on influences the examples we notice and our interpretation of them. Plenty of alarms have been set off by critics touching certain aspects of CRT. This book draws attention to other fundamental concerns being overlooked.[6]

I want to serve an audience trying to untangle the language and perspectives circulating about race right now, a Christian audience that wants understanding but finds itself vulnerable to rhetoric from the extremes. I appreciate people growing in racial *sensitivity,* but I also want to keep expanding racial *sensibility.* I'm writing for people with a heart for others, people who understand that while our citizenship and allegiance is fully vested in another kingdom, we're left here together for the time being to make sense of this one.

WHERE ARE WE GOING?

This is a book I wish had been written in the 1990s right when Critical Race Theory first came online. I wish I'd sounded an alarm then the way so many others are sounding alarms now, only from a different direction. I wish more Christians in my circle had asked, "What can we learn from these BIPOC scholars' work that will help us as the body of Christ? How can their concepts help us understand what we're missing and how to bridge racial gaps that still exist?" If we had thoughtfully interacted with it then, perhaps we'd be better equipped to discern our way through the confusion and hysteria today.

Are Christian critics really doing justice to CRT? I'm concerned when I see reductive summaries of concepts and ideas that surely require more context and nuance. Too many articles, videos, and podcasts reflect an inadequate understanding of the concerns behind CRT and what it's trying to accomplish. Frequently, I believe we're getting inaccurate representations of people condemned for referencing CRT ideas in the church. Too often Christian commentary denounces CRT while making light of the real problems it seeks to address. CRT strives for something considerably more sophisticated than "reducing all racial inequities to a struggle between oppressor and oppressed and presenting a worldview that is contrary to the Scriptures."[7]

Condemning it as *nothing* but an "oppressor/oppressed" framework or *just* a quest for an antibiblical version of "social justice" comes across as ridiculous to those who devote their vocational lives to it. By slowing down to consider words, their context, and the situations they have in mind, I hope to make the complex more understandable while adding nuance to topics often receiving only superficial treatment.

As for its association with Marxism, I know as nonradicals we're taught to reject anything associated with Marxism as evil, but I'm convinced that rejecting Marxian theorists without first taking their concerns seriously does more damage to Christian witness than good. Most people in my Christian world know enough about Marx to loathe him and everyone allied with him. Until recently, they'd never heard of Critical Theory or CRT, but in learning that they are both rooted in Marxist soil, they immediately assume the worst, accept the first condemnation they hear, and move on. I understand the antipathy toward Marx and his worldview, but this generation needs more Christians who will invest more time thinking theologically about his specific concerns and the conditions that produced them and less time rehearsing the evil done in his name.

The same is true for Critical theorists. I don't need most of their solutions, but I *do* need their observations. I need their concerns about the use of power, the way vulnerable populations get treated, the history of wealth and poverty, the ideology and implications of idolatrous consumerism—these are all under-theologized topics for many North American Christians. They expose corners of social life my conservative evangelical heritage too often ignores, pockets in desperate need of gospel solutions but left with mostly secular voices speaking into them.

Accordingly, this book sets out after three objectives: to provide a primer on CRT, a short history of the Marxism and Critical Theory from which it grew, and a practical investigation of what CRT's concepts mean for the church.

We'll examine the good and bad of crucial terms like *white supremacy*, *systemic racism*, and *social justice*. How do we navigate the competing responses to these words? How do we situate ourselves in the discussion and discern what others really want when using them? Most importantly, we'll discuss how a basic understanding of these concepts can improve conversations between Christ followers and between Christians and non-Christians. We'll explore why Critical Theory can be useful when thinking about popular culture and how it's alike and different from CRT. Finally, I'll respond to some common objections to racial questions springing from CRT as they're talked about in Christian spaces.

This book is not exhaustive by any means, but more than anything, I hope it produces *understanding*. The biblical word for understanding implies a God-given perception of the nature and meaning of things, hopefully resulting in sound judgment and decision making. It's tied to the power of comprehending and recognizing how parts of human experience fit together. We won't wind up with complete answers for every racial dilemma, but if we gain understanding regarding the cultural path CRT is paving today, I'll be encouraged.

Many Christians are concerned that allowing CRT into the church will invite God's judgment, but I'd counter that Christian silence in the face of injustice not only created a need for CRT in the first place but also continues to make its language attractive to many Christians today. The Bible offers the only real solution to racial cancer, but a proper representation of CRT acts like an MRI, exposing the toxic cells making the body sick. We need neither fear nor condemn CRT. We need to understand the truths behind its tenets and the gospel responses it calls forth.

GOOD NEWS AND BAD NEWS

The good news: I'm not writing this with an academic audience in mind. People devote their entire lives to studying the complicated topics in this book, but I'm trying to write in an accessible way for people who don't. That's my goal. You can decide whether I've succeeded. The bad news: it's still not going to be an easy read. Prepare for some challenging thinking on topics you probably don't dig into frequently. What you're about to read isn't the most technically rigorous option out there, but it's not a TED talk either.

When I showed a friend an initial proposal for this book, he said, "If someone picks up a book on Postmodernism, they don't want to read a bunch of chapters on the Enlightenment to get there. They want Postmodernism." This is true, but if you want a chance at *understanding* Postmodernism, what it's reacting against, and why its language works the way it does, a couple chapters on the Enlightenment help you move beyond the surface and into more discerning waters.

If you're holding this book, I'm assuming you want a deeper grasp of CRT. Critical Race Theory depends on Critical Theory, and Critical Theory grew out of Marxism—none of which are light reading. But it's also a mistake using those words interchangeably as though they're all the same thing. They're interrelated, share certain "familial" characteristics, and build on one another, but they're three separate bodies of thought arising in different contexts to serve different purposes. This book will help readers understand the distinction and show that while all three have problems, they can all be far more instructive for Christians than people realize. Nevertheless, if your reading stamina won't tolerate a journey through Marxism and Critical Theory, read chapter one, skip ahead to chapter five and jump right into CRT.

If you're considering the racial tension of our current moment and have to choose between a book on radical strategies and your Bible, study your Bible. But if you've got room for both, anyone seeking to live faithfully and missionally needs a generous understanding of all that gets called "radical" in this broken world. This book will take you in that direction.

I know it's easier to wade in superficial and politically charged soundbites and call it a day. But if we want to untangle the racial web in our cultural moment, we need to recognize not only what these academic disciplines sought to correct, but also why people are attracted to their ideas today.

But first, let me tell you how I got involved in this discussion in the first place.

1

A WHITE GUY'S JOURNEY INTO RACIAL CONTROVERSY

All I've ever wanted to do is tell (people) that I'm not trying to solve anybody's problems, not even my own. I'm just trying to outline what the problems are.

JAMES BALDWIN, "DOOM AND GLORY OF KNOWING WHO YOU ARE"

WHEN I FIRST STARTED THINKING about writing this book, I didn't envision devoting an entire chapter to my own life. But at a certain point I looked up and realized what an unusual combination of experiences I'm trying to steward. It's a strange mix of contrasts and contradictions. Sometimes I don't know how to put all the pieces together myself. Hopefully, this background will not only help readers understand my inspiration for stepping into this hurricane but also locate my current coordinates in it. If nothing else, it gives me an opportunity to explain my intellectual, biographical, and cultural motivations for being here.

This is a book about race and the church, but despite the social and ecclesial chaos marking the last decade, the triggering event that got me writing had nothing directly to do with race. Instead, a few years ago I read something that caused me to reinterpret my whole Christian life.

We'll start there.

WHICH CATASTROPHE SHOULD CONCERN US MORE?

It's 1947, a few years removed from the end of World War II and the beginning of unprecedented social prosperity for a significant slice of Americans. Carl Henry, a leading figure in what would become known as the New Evangelicalism, publishes a book called *The Uneasy Conscience of Modern Fundamentalism*.[1] Henry's intellectual and institutional leadership helped shape the evangelicalism so many of us embrace today, and his book presciently anticipates one of the reasons so many continue to leave it.

In the early 1900s, liberal-minded Christians began emphasizing care for the body at the expense of emphasis on the soul. "Fundamentalists" (forerunners of today's evangelicals) rightly rejected this version of a "social gospel" that left out sin and Savior. Instead, they began drawing lines of distinction that separated them from the apostasy they saw capturing some denominations.

But at the midpoint of the twentieth century, Henry grew concerned they'd overcorrected. By wisely separating from a cross-less social gospel, evangelicals drained away responsible social concern that historically accompanied the good news. To correct this imbalance, Henry urged, "Social justice is not . . . simply an appendage to the evangelical message; it is an intrinsic part of the whole, without which the preaching of the gospel itself is truncated. Theology devoid of social justice is a deforming weakness of much present-day evangelical witness."[2] He wasn't saying a person needed acts of social justice to acquire salvation but that new birth should produce a social consciousness that seeks justice wherever injustice exists. Not a "social justice" driven by political ideology but rather the struggle of a kingdom ethic brought to bear in real lives.

But in failing to develop the broad social implications of their own message, too few in the evangelical camp offered gospel-informed solutions to the problems of racism, war, poverty, misogyny, criminal justice, or other social inequities that developed as a result of sin. They'd created an unbiblical separation between the redemptive cross of Christ and the reforming social consciousness that should accompany discipleship. Henry argued that separating justification from justice not only undermined one of the intentions of gospel transformation but also created an artificial breach unknown to previous generations of Christians.[3] He warned that while "the church must reject trying to politicize an unregenerate world into the kingdom of God; it must also reject interpreting evangelical conversion devoid of active social concern as fulfilling Christian responsibility."[4]

In other words, Christian responsibility requires concern for what justice looks like in the world. It challenges isms, becomes sensitized to racial imbalance, watches out for those most vulnerable to mistreatment, stays alert to labor exploitation produced by both Capitalism and Communism, and other social abuses. It continually considers how to thoughtfully bring spiritual solutions to bear on social problems. Calling it "the most embarrassing evangelical divorce,"[5] Henry warned that "because many churches try to solve the social plight of the masses with individual evangelism as the only alternative, and avoid discussion of the duty and dangers of social involvement, *younger evangelicals are unprepared to confront the socioeconomic crisis [for example] except through socialist ideology*" (emphasis added).[6]

Catch that? When discipleship focuses on individual soul salvation at the expense of challenging a person to consider their Christian responsibility toward the social traumas of the day, it leaves them vulnerable to other non-Christian voices who *will* teach them how to engage those problems. Henry anticipated Christians entertaining secular language and thinking in nonbiblical, hybrid ways about race and other social problems *because their leaders either haven't developed or intentionally ignored what the Bible says about them.* This path creates two groups of Christians related to social issues: those unaware of the gaps in their preferred theological system when it comes to addressing social sin, and those who, in their desire to confront social sin, rely on secular language (and often secular solutions) to the detriment of their biblical anchor. The chickens Henry warned us about are most certainly coming home to roost.

We *should* be concerned when people in the church start leaning on secular language and secular solutions for spiritual problems, but why are they doing this in the first place? Could it be because we've failed to teach them substantive biblical language to address social sin like racism? Could it be that plenty of black pastors and theologians *were* doing this work from a biblical perspective across the last century, but those voices were never given a seat at evangelical leadership tables to make any difference?[7] Can we recognize where secular concerns and biblical concerns overlap, even if they propose different solutions? Or does every mention of a social issue like racism only trigger political alarms?

A paltry understanding of biblical social justice both precedes and predicts the current dustup about CRT. We're backfilling into a canyon created by our decades-long indifference toward problems the Bible plainly talks about but that get little attention in most white evangelical spaces. I'd argue that decades of denominational minimization of the race problem alongside shallow public evangelical responses to the plight and conditions of African American life in this country not only paved the way for the beginning of CRT in the 1980s but also continue to make its language attractive—and perhaps even necessary—in the face of anemic approaches to matters of race and ethnicity still present today.

So when I read a book by a Christian pastor subtitled *The Social Justice Movement and Evangelicalism's Looming Catastrophe*, I immediately thought of Henry. Which catastrophe should get more of our attention as Christ followers? Church people idolatrously attracted to secular ideas or church people who don't have biblical solutions for social concerns? If you say both, which catastrophe best represents most people in *your* congregation?[8]

I'm concerned that many of us embrace a form of evangelicalism that encourages us *not* to think substantively about race at all, and the entire church is suffering for it now. Henry was a godfather of modern evangelicalism, but if he wrote this book today, he'd be indicted for smuggling Marxist ideology into the church. That's a bigger problem than CRT.

I didn't meet Henry's writing until twenty-five years into my Christian life, but I understood the consequences of his warning long before I even knew what it meant to be a Christian. Here's how I got there.

MY ETHNICALLY DIVERSE, RACIALLY CHARGED ROOTS

I'm a white male who grew up in an ethnically diverse environment at the western edge of the greater Cleveland region. As a teen, I ran with a mix of working class black, Puerto Rican, and white folks, with rare but occasional exposure to the country club elite of our overlapping communities.

I lived in a conservative, middle-class home in a white neighborhood but went to high school with a racially diverse mix of kids coming from four sides of town and every stratum of socioeconomic reality. I had packs of both white and black friends, dated both, played basketball with both, partied with both. We all knew how to get along, but we also knew where the lines were drawn. It was unspoken but understood: We can all be friends, but there's safety in keeping to your own. Get sloppy making assumptions, and racial truth might unexpectedly appear in painful ways.

One example perfectly captures the bizarre nature of how racism would show up unannounced. I wanted to go to senior prom with one of my best friends who happened to be black and from the other side of town. I hung out at her house all throughout high school. Her mom and dad, solid Christian folks and neighborhood pillars, loved me and my family. A few weeks before prom, I went over to her house to ask her dad just as a formality. Zero stress. Thought I'd do it just to score some maturity points.

When I walked into the living room where everyone sat waiting, it was spooky quiet. Her dad looked at me and nodded over to her mom as if to say, "Talk with her." So I turned and asked her if I could take their daughter. She started crying and, between sobs, said, "Oh baby, I love you, but you can't take her to prom." Her reason? She couldn't have her daughter going to prom with a white boy. What would her church friends and others on the street say? Prom was forgettable, but I'll always remember the feeling in that room. Race is a *meaning* system, weighing on people in ways you can't always see. My assumption that there was no race problem among us didn't mean there wasn't one.

So ethnicity and race mattered greatly to the people I grew up around, and it became a source of collective identity, pride, and history as well as a way of drawing distinctions between "us" and "them." At the time, not knowing any better, I assumed this was the experience of most people in America, or at least those who lived in proximity to a major city.

But college exposed me to a different reality.

THE FIRST TWO YEARS OF MY UNDERGRADUATE EXPERIENCE

I became a Christian late in my freshman year, and it transformed the way I saw the world, including how I thought about both ethnic identity and the problems associated with it. I met white people from deep rural environments who had never interacted directly with a black person, and black people from deep city environments who'd had almost no contact with white people. I didn't know these categories existed, as I assumed everyone grew up like I did. It was my first realization that my experience was hardly the norm.

Two men exposed me to different but aligned highways of Christian experience. Bill Pugh, a white, former college-football-playing

Cincinnati suburbanite, led a ministry on campus called Athletes in Action. Bill was magnetic and charismatic, and he created an environment where people could speak openly, honestly, and directly from their background. Both white and black athletes came to his Bible studies and willingly brought friends. He attended a small, white country church that often gave us an opportunity to testify about what God was doing in our lives as athletes at Kent State University.

When not with Bill, I was with Cecil Shorts, an African American man from East Cleveland who led another campus ministry geared primarily toward black students called the ABCs of Salvation. He also organized a bus ministry that took students to a large church in Akron called the House of the Lord, an urban, black-led conservative church that was integrated, which I attended throughout my college years.

Both men taught me to prioritize the Word of God. Both taught me to think missionally. Both reached across the racial divide, believing the gospel to be every person's greatest need, and integrated the gospel message and concern for social issues as two sides of a coin. Ironically, Bill, who came from conservative political roots, operated as more liberal among his peers, bucking norms and reaching out to people most would ignore. Cecil, who came from the heart of the Democratic ghetto of inner-city Cleveland, sounded like any of the most conservative folks I would ever meet. Together they shaped my biblical, social, and political consciousness.

Freshman year I took a two-semester class called "Interpreting the Black Experience" taught by E. Timothy Moore, a non-Christian man who was nevertheless deeply spiritual and socially insightful. He and I spent hours together parsing the Reconstruction era, discussing debates within the black community about how to address Jim Crow segregation, learning about key figures and moments of the civil rights years, and absorbing the resistance that took place in the 1970s and 1980s. At the same time, I met Elder Gilbert Carter, a visiting pastor from Canton who taught an elective called "Evolution of the

Black Church in America," where I learned of the origin and evolution of the black ecclesial and theological tradition forged on American soil since the eighteenth century. Together we traced its development in slaveholding, segregated America right up through what was then the late 1980s, wrestling to understand the churches' role and response to all that Dr. Moore and I were also discussing.

All of this accelerated my understanding of the role race played in America as we entered the 1990s. I knew race mattered, but these studies helped me appreciate race as a far more pervasive and problematic subject than I had believed. For the first time, I understood how majority culture framed race in ways that didn't always do justice to historic realities.

MY LIFE WORKING IN A SPORTS MINISTRY AMONG POC

Since leaving Kent State, I've invested over three decades working as an evangelical minister, primarily using sports as a launching point into both black and white athletes' lives. The very nature of working among college and professional athletes makes race a constant subtext to thinking biblically about the world they inhabit, and I've entered those conversations as both a participant and facilitator.

I've attended events with predominantly white leadership and audiences and listened to the challenges they experience while trying to live their faith in a broken world. I've done the same at events with predominantly BIPOC leadership and audiences, observing where their concerns overlap and split in completely different directions, even under the same banner of relatively conservative evangelical Christianity.

I've taught the Bible in front of entirely black audiences, entirely white audiences, and evenly mixed audiences, gaining understanding into how their different subjectivities and social locations produce different questions and responses.

I've observed white leadership keeping "race" talk at arm's length, distancing themselves either because of discomfort or inadequacy or triggering beliefs that politicize or demonize the subject without discussion. I've listened to BIPOC brothers and sisters lament their lack of access to the leadership circle, and white folks' inability or unwillingness to recognize that the spaces we inhabit together are marked and guided almost entirely by Euro-aesthetics and Euro-concerns. I've listened to white folks trying to be reconcilers yet feeling that their best efforts will never be good enough and walking on eggshells in the presence of POC. And I've listened to black folks who are beyond weary in always playing the role of educator and feeling like they start all over again with each new encounter they have with white folks.

I've watched power plays, insecurity, backstabbing, and proud stubbornness get reduced and mislabeled as racism and seen concern for racially motivated prejudice and neglect reduced and mislabeled as Marxism, Critical Race Theory, and liberal Democratic posturing.

I haven't understood it all, and certainly don't have wise answers for it all, but across several decades these exposures gave me a degree in Christian BIPOC/white racial dynamics I don't take for granted.

THE RADICAL DIVERSITY AND UNEXPECTED
RELEVANCE OF MY GRADUATE STUDIES

I completed two master's degrees at Trinity Evangelical Divinity School. The first was a master of divinity in systematic theology, which grounded me in the history of primarily white conservative evangelicalism, a degree that for many decades existed as a gateway calling card into evangelical pastoral work.

At the same time, I completed a master's degree in Christianity and contemporary culture, which amounted to a "current issues in urban ministry" degree. It concerned itself with asking and answering how Christianity confronts questions related to both modernity and postmodernity, focusing attention on social ethics, how public policy affects the human condition in both history and real time, and the social crises that arise given the brokenness of the societies we create. We focused on biblical justice and considered its implications both for city life and for living in a technologically driven, post-Christian age, all from an orthodox Christian perspective. Racial dynamics played a significant role in these discussions, and we took field trips to places like Lawndale and Circle Urban Ministries in Chicago to understand how the gospel intersects the lives of people in settings of poverty and hopelessness.

A decade later, I entered a PhD program in American culture studies at Bowling Green State University, a degree focused on asking "eternal questions in new ways, and new questions using refined methods from a variety of disciplines." I wanted to dig deeper into the meaning of America, how it changes over time, and how we understand it from different perspectives depending on our gender, race, or class alignment. What I didn't anticipate was learning all of this through the lens of a Marxist worldview along with my baptism into the completely new and foreign language of Critical Theory.

Over the next five years, I was the politically conservative, white, male, hetero, evangelical Christian in classes where each of those labels was anathema. Through hundreds of hours of conversation and debate, I began to understand not only the thinking behind forms of radical progressivism but also the theory and application of Critical Theory and Critical Race Theory, two streams of thought I never imagined would become relevant in my future ministry.

TRANSLATING THE RACIAL DIVIDE

I present that background to establish that the subject of race has never been far from my consciousness. Between growing up in the ethnic melting pot of western Cleveland, receiving discipleship from both white and black folks, and pursuing graduate education in both conservative evangelical theology and Marxist Critical Theory, I've been in these conversations on all sides, among the progressive "woke" and regressive "unwoke," conservative and liberal, Christian and non-Christian. This book is my attempt to make some sense of it all.

People don't often take time to ask themselves, "Why do I think the way I think about people?" They haven't taken inventory of who and what shaped their belief system or reflected on how it's changed through the years or what caused it to change. But like submitting airport luggage to a customs agent for inspection, it's helpful to intentionally open our own bags and not only regularly scour the contents we find inside but also ask how they got there and whether they should stay.

As I assess my own life and consider how to steward the experiences God has given me as a white male, I have often played the role of translator on both sides of the racial divide throughout my time in ministry. To be clear, since I happen to be white myself, I'm writing primarily to help a white audience sort through the language and ideas circulating about race. But I'm writing as a translator from somewhere closer to the middle, meaning any Christian trying to understand what is happening in conversations around race—regardless of ethnic heritage—may benefit. I'm not lecturing either side, though I'd like to sound a few alarms that might be of Christian use, especially if those sirens point to exit doors we can all pass through safely.

WHY CHRISTIANS WINNING A CULTURE WAR ISN'T MY PRIMARY CONCERN

Before going any further, I need to put a few more cards on the table. If you try talking about race today—or really any social issue—you're stepping into a war zone. Two secular worldviews are at each other's throat. Right-leaning populist (i.e., conservative) movements see themselves as the final solution to preserving philosophical liberalism and democracy and the Western values supporting them. They're trying to prevent what they see as the destruction of American society. Meanwhile, leftist activists (i.e., progressive) believe the current ordering of society makes the language of democracy hollow. They desire revolutionary upheaval because the status quo maintains inequality and oppression in the lives of everyone not at the top.

I know Christians on both sides of this disagreement. I understand many of my friends' concern that radical Progressivism is taking over American institutions. I also appreciate other friends' arguments for why modern forms of Conservatism feel oppressive. I can even see why those committed to philosophical and social liberalism reject radical leftist solutions and wind up sounding like and siding with conservatives as a result. But understanding aside, I don't spend much energy fretting about which side is winning or losing the ideological war, and the reasons are an important foundation of this book.

First, for my Christian friends concerned we're losing the culture war, if progressive ideology "wins," it won't be because Christians failed at resisting it. Rather, it will be because God is using the spread of pagan ideology to discipline his church. It could be judgment for a flippant disregard regarding economic and political injustice, perhaps even for our treatment of immigrants, contempt for "the least of these," or our participation in all sorts of moral, sexual, and relational apostasy. I'd say the same thing to those few I know who are more concerned about radical Conservatism "winning." "It is time for judgment to begin with God's household" (1 Peter 4:17), and throughout the Bible God often uses people promoting godless ideology to deliver it.[9] But demonically fueled fascist movements never succeed without God's permission.

When do we reach the tipping point? When will God have had enough? I don't know, but I do know the tide of oppressive expressions of Progressivism or Conservatism won't be pushed back by shouting louder on social media or hosting conferences to fight with one another. The Bible recommends personal and corporate repentance as an antidote, not another social post to get the last word in.

Second, I refuse to be limited by binary-driven politics and their meager solutions. Unfortunately, we're living in an age where the political climate doesn't allow for a person to be labeled both "conservative" and concerned about capitalist excess or the mistreatment of immigrants. We don't have tidy labels for the person who is both against abortion and critical of structural and systemic sin patterns. We can hardly imagine a person being against promoting gender fluidity but also for racial justice. But Christians don't have to settle for that sort of reductionistic tyranny. We need more Christians who transcend binaries and not only see the brokenness in both camps but also apply a more sophisticated understanding of biblical praxis in the face of social evil. This won't happen if we've been discipled more by news networks than the Bible.

I'm not an advocate for putting our heads in the sand, but I see the futility of a world trying to fix itself without Jesus, and I'm not impressed with any of their solutions. So I don't align with the radical progressives, the philosophically liberal, or the staunchly conservative and don't care to spend much time arguing about any one of them as the "right" option. I want to be detached enough to discern what's wrong, what's right, and what's insightful in these worldviews, and I won't do that well if I'm coming to them as a partisan rather than as an "alien and stranger." The world desperately needs to see kingdom solutions as alternatives to those of secular progressives, secular liberals, and secular conservatives. When we start sounding too much like any of the three, we undermine our Christian witness. At the same time, all three have common-grace kernels of the kingdom, and Christians need discernment to sift them out.

Third, let's talk about "wokeism," perhaps the most politically loaded word of our day. I have vague recollections of African American kids using the word *woke* during high school in the 1980s, but I'm guessing none of them knew the source of its first use in the 1930s.[10] That's when blues singer Lead Belly wrote a song about the Scottsboro Boys, nine African American teenage boys accused of raping two women in Alabama in 1931, whose arrest and trial became one of the greatest miscarriages of justice in American history.[11] Belly said if you were black in Alabama in the 1930s, you needed to "stay woke," and the term has been a mainstay of black vernacular ever since. My west Cleveland classmates used it the way Lead Belly intended: to stay aware of what is really going on. Be careful. Keep your eyes open. Stay informed and don't get taken advantage of by anyone (especially white folks) who may not have your best interests in mind.[12] As far as I can tell, it's still a proactive, protective, and positive word in black culture today.

In 1962, perhaps prophetically, William Melvin Kelley highlighted "woke" in a *New York Times* essay about white people appropriating black slang terms and changing their meanings.[13] He died in 2017, but I'm guessing he wouldn't be surprised at what's happened since with the term *woke* outside black culture.

More recently, the term has been co-opted as a negative political buzzword, denoting a militant supporter of equality, diversity, and social justice issues.[14] It's a dog-whistle canopy for any identity-based social justice issues that Democrats and Progressives promote. Wokeism means blaming outcomes on systemic racism, affirming gay marriage, promoting transgenderism, canceling free speech, and focusing on victimization. That's probably how most evangelicals understand the word as it shows up now.

But in years of conversations with real Progressives, I've learned something important that goes beyond ideology: wokeism is primarily a retaliation. Political aggression that leverages race, gender, sexuality, and ableism is usually the inflamed response of human beings who've been deeply wounded by others. Politics aside, wokeism is an intentional overreaction weaponized for the purpose of reversing the pain of feeling mistreated or misunderstood. It's an ideological response to histories of real abuse, real domination, and real marginalization experienced in people's real narratives, a secular response to living amid the brokenness of the godless world we've created for ourselves as humans.

I know it's a poor fix. I'm not naive to the results. I'm just saying wokeism represents leftist solutions devised by hurting people who need gospel healing, not Christian judgment. Plenty of commentary exists on how to respond to the ideology, but are we giving attention to the pain behind it? I'm convinced that poorly lived Christianity plays a significant role in the formation of radical Progressivism. How we respond to hurting people matters.

So as I write this book, I'm not primarily interested in staking ground against one culture war ism or another. I won't align myself with any political side, though I am trying to correct inadequacies I've experienced in my own more conservative version of evangelicalism. And while I understand the political threat represented by the motives and results of wokeism, I'm more concerned with the brokenness of the people behind it. I'm driven by a desire for Christians to have more social empathy, a deepened understanding of the issues, and where necessary, an action-producing conviction regarding our current role in the race conversation.

2

WHAT DO WE NEED TO UNDERSTAND ABOUT MARXISM?

To see capitalism as a system that must be totally destroyed, to believe in international revolution, to see the working class as the only force that can lead such a revolution, to hate and fight against all forms of oppression and to organize now to make these ideas a reality—that's the essence of Marxism.

DANIEL TAYLOR,
"WHAT DOES IT MEAN TO BE A MARXIST?"

The vision of the left—and I think many conservatives underestimate this—is really a more attractive vision. The only reason for not believing in it, is that it doesn't work.

THOMAS SOWELL,
"COMMON SENSE IN A SENSELESS WORLD"

WE'RE STANDING NEXT TO EACH OTHER in the bathroom and I'm about to have a significant Marxist breakthrough. Justin and I are a year into our PhD program in American culture studies, and he stands out. He's rare, able to consume massive amounts of sophisticated information, coherently process and repackage it, then speak it back into the world in a way normal people like me can understand. We both want to dig into the cultural and intellectual traditions that have shaped and defined American identity, but we're coming from vastly different ideological directions. I'm a committed evangelical Christian trying to understand secular solutions to what I believe are ultimately spiritual problems. He's from a passively Catholic background and now fully committed to the philosophical tenets of Marxism. I find him almost intimidatingly articulate, surprisingly thoughtful, and exasperating in his commitment to a worldview whose end product always produces human misery.

Before the break he'd finished another impassioned explanation for why Marxist thought provided the only way to make things right socially, and I can't take it anymore. I follow him into the bathroom to ask one burning question: Why? I chase him to the wall and say, "Wherever Marx's ideas get taken seriously, the world suffers. How can you continue to argue for them?"

Without hesitating, he answers, "Because real Marxism hasn't been tried yet. Every time there's a chance for it to work, corrupt people hijack the moment and turn it into something evil. Marx—when his ideas are actually considered and taken seriously—values humans and provides a world where they can flourish. But people always screw it up. Communism isn't the socialism he envisioned." He finishes by saying Marx is misunderstood and misused, but if we would ever allow his ideas to really live, we'd all benefit.

Justin is no dummy. When I explain to him why my theological background not only gives me language to describe the fundamental problem behind "people screwing it up" but also convinces me that humanist utopias like the one Marx and so many others preach will never be possible, he listens. Human flourishing begins and ends with Jesus. Human solutions that leave him out are incomplete counterfeits despite their intentions to serve humanity.

We talk a little more before exiting the bathroom, and I can tell Justin is both perplexed by my matter-of-fact explanation of the gospel and still committed to ignoring it. He came into our cohort believing in a gospel-less utopia and it will take more than a singular bathroom confrontation to convince him otherwise.

I get this, but I also leave the bathroom recognizing something about myself: I want to better understand what attracts people to Marxism. I don't really know what Justin means when he says Marx needs to be "considered" and "taken seriously." As I walk out, I recognize I'm ignorant when it comes to a body of thought hundreds of millions are drawn to.

For the first time, I wonder to myself, *Instead of just reacting and rejecting Marx and his followers, what would it look like to actually try to understand why they think the way they think? Is there something I'm missing?* As a Christian from a conservative background, this will take some work.

WHY DOES A BOOK ABOUT CHRISTIANS AND CRT NEED TO START WITH MARXISM?

If you think it's hard having a conversation about race, try having one about Marxism! I remember being disturbed by the naive understanding my PhD cohort had regarding evangelical Christianity. Their version amounted to a sausage factory of negative anecdotes strung together, forming a hideous version of the "Christian" faith. The life of Jesus got completely lost in the woods of every abuse and mistreatment done in his name across two thousand years, and they couldn't bring themselves to see anything else.

But when it comes to Marxism, whether referring to its orthodox or more modern forms, Christians don't fare much better. I have little confidence in the average American Christian's ability to represent Marxist thought or, perhaps more importantly, sympathize with the conditions that prompted his words in the first place. Most Christians I know use his name like a cuss word, and among Christian friends in ministry, rarely can anyone accurately cite any specific thing he said or reproduce the underlying human problems and questions he was trying to solve. They react to a persona developed around only the worst parts of his effect on history and remain in the dark about the rest.

I know that was true for me. I was forty when I started my PhD program, and the only memory I had of talking about Marx in any of my previous schooling took me back to my junior year of college at Kent State. I had recently become a Christian and decided to take a Bible as Literature class. One day, the professor, a gentle man nearing retirement who genuinely identified with Jesus, said Christianity often resembles Marxism and cited a handful of verses to prove his point. I waited in line after class to confront him. I'd just been reading a book called *Seven Men Who Rule the World from the Grave*, and one of the chapters included a devastating portrayal of Marx.[1] Here I was, one chapter deep, standing in this man's face telling him he was wrong about Marxism and that it couldn't possibly have anything in common with Christianity. He graciously handled my arrogance and sent me on my way, and that's the only "conversation" I ever remember having about Marx as an undergrad. From my experience with Christians in my circle, not everyone shares my nineteen-year-old arrogance, but I don't think I'm alone in being thinly educated when it comes to Marx.

Most are familiar with the basics. He opposes Capitalism. He doesn't like private property. He considers any form of religion a pacifying drug—especially Christianity. We know he's been the philosophical justification for some of the worst horrors in human history and can name enemy governments still identifying with his name today. But it's become far too easy for Christians to simply dismiss an idea or a person by cursing them with the label "Marxist," knowing that doing so vilifies the target and effectively mic drops the conversation. I've found that it's always easier to condemn radicals by default rather than to try to understand why people become radical in the first place, especially if your personal roots grow in conservative soil. If you don't have social needs, it's easy to misunderstand the psychology of those who do. I believe the body of Christ can do better in this discussion.

Let me clarify up front: I am not a Marxist. I don't subscribe to either socialism or Communism. I don't desire to overthrow the United States economy or infiltrate the Christian church with Marxist ideology. I love owning property, selling on eBay, and changing jobs as I see fit. I'm not naive to the historic or present-day damage done by those using his words and ideas. Marx did a better job critiquing Capitalism than he did replacing it, and his solutions for the problems in his age only created worse problems in ours.

But because CT and CRT are swirling in public imagination, and because both trace their roots to Marxist economic, political, and social philosophy, I'd argue evangelicals need a deeper understanding and appreciation of the Marxian worldview now more than ever. We need understanding not so we can embrace it, but so we can empathize with people who do.

I'll go further. I think white evangelical Christians have something to learn from Marxism that anti-Marxist politics resists. Whether intentional or not, flippantly dismissing an idea as "Marxist" enables too many of us to avoid problems the gospel requires us to address. The world doesn't need more Marxists. It needs more Christians who see what Marx and his followers see, and who will courageously bring the gospel to bear on matters they'd rather ignore. We need appreciation for his ideas not because his solutions work, but because the questions his method prompts often shine light on dark corners of our own passivity and idolatry when it comes to people outside our normal circles.

And nowhere has a sloppy, knee-jerk rejection of ideas and people as "Marxist" done more direct damage than in the conversation around race. Indeed, what *does* Marxism have to do with race? Why did Marxist thought begin resonating with BIPOC intellectuals and black radicals in the early decades of the twentieth century?

HOW DOES KARL MARX BECOME "MARX"?

Pure "Marxism" is Karl Marx's thorough analysis and critique of the capitalist economic system. In works like *The Communist Manifesto*, *A Contribution to the Critique of Political Economy*, and most famously *Das Kapital*, he explained the history and "science" driving the capitalist approach to ordering economic life, how it sustains itself, and his theory on why it will quake every so often before it ultimately implodes. Marxism is part history (how the system came to be), part economic science (how the system actually works), and part social science (how people relate to one another within the system).

But, perhaps most controversially, Marxism also includes his solutions for how to fix the problems Capitalism inherently creates. Marx brazenly declared that "philosophers have only interpreted the world in various ways—the point is to change it," and people embodying his ideas definitely changed it.[2] Love him or hate him, Marxist thought reshaped the social and political landscape of the nineteenth and twentieth centuries, stimulating arguments in philosophy, history, politics, and, of course, economics, while acting as the backbone for radical action throughout the world.

We hear "radical" today and imagine opportunistic rabble-rousers blocking a busy Seattle intersection or setting fire to a Chicago storefront. But in 1840s Europe, "radical" meant standing up to monarchical rulers in the name of democracy. It meant pressing for freedoms we take for granted today. It meant political and social revolutionary tactics aimed directly at the sources of injustice.

We know details from the American Revolution and maybe something from the French Revolution, but do we know the uprisings of 1848–1849, also known as the "Springtime of the Peoples," the most widespread wave of transitional revolutionary activity in European history? These years mark a significant shift in European political and economic relations, when in more than a dozen countries, owners and workers rose up together against feudalistic hierarchies and fought for freedom from their control. In many cases they won, but unfortunately workers and the lower "classes" of people continued to suffer, only now at the hands of local business owners they'd just been fighting alongside instead of distant kings.

Why? Because these political revolutions were preceded by the Industrial Revolution of the previous century. New machines, textile production, and chemical processes significantly empowered owners of factories, mines, ships, and farms to replace kings in holding power over wage laborers. They became a new monarchy of sorts, a new controlling class, and collectively they began valuing profit over people. Working conditions were usually deplorable. There were no unions. No human resource departments. No policy books guiding accountability. People who previously received their living from the land or from employing a host of artisan skills now found themselves working in factories for double-digit hours before returning home to disease-infested slums. With revolution already in the air, these flammable conditions wait for someone's voice to strike the match.

Enter Karl Marx and his friends. Marx watches this exploitation and concludes the next revolution should overhaul the underlying economic system generating it. He argues that economic commitments create our politics and the way we relate with one another, not the other way around. With his friend Friedrich Engels, he publishes *The Communist Manifesto* in the middle of this political and economic turmoil and spends the rest of his life attacking Capitalism, teaching people not only his interpretation of how to understand the world, but also how to change it.

WHAT DID MARX ACTUALLY TEACH?

First, and this is critical to understand, Marxist thought assumes God doesn't exist. Marx was a materialist, which means all of life amounts to what can be seen or experienced through the senses—nothing more. There's no God or "Absolute Mind" or "Spirit" to aspire toward or worry about. Only conflicts arising out of material conditions that need to be resolved. Marxism is fundamentally an examination of life under the sun when there is no God, a rigorous attempt to explain what's wrong with the world, but without a spiritual dimension.

Second, his primary answer was Capitalism, specifically the class divisions created by an economic philosophy that encourages people to make products for profit instead of for usefulness or necessity. Marx wasn't against Capitalism as a purely philosophical idea. Rather, he hated what the mechanics of the capitalist social system did to everyone involved. Industrialization forced workers to leave agricultural and artisan work for soul-sucking jobs in factories, working long hours repeating mind-numbing tasks. Instead of making goods simply because they were needed for survival, people produced commodities for profit, and the products they made started to take on a mystical, fetishistic value of their own. In a quasi-spiritual way, products for mass consumption become personifications of competitive value, and in time they become more important than the humans who made them. Eventually, people experienced alienation in their relationship to the work of their own hands, to their coworkers, and even to themselves.

Marx compellingly described how people lost their authentic selves when their lives started revolving around products, when they started competing with other human beings for profit, when they stopped creating in their vocational world and instead worked like robotic machines. The estrangement people feel in their lives traces its existence to the social arrangements necessitated by Capitalism. From his perspective, on almost every level of our existence Capitalism doesn't serve human life; rather, it determines it in ways that inhibit human flourishing.

Third, Marxism assumes the economic system forms the base on which the rest of society develops. Marx believed that every component of society (superstructure) like schools, churches, media, and political organizations grew out of the way people ordered themselves in relation to the means of production (base). If you want to control the different aspects of society, he argued, get control of the underlying economic drivers (means of production), because everything else in society grows out of that space. Pure Marxist thought always believes what you see at the surface is being determined by the way we've structured ourselves economically below.

Fourth, it assumes someone benefits through the exploitation of someone else. Those who own the raw materials necessary to produce products are in a position to take advantage of those who turn the raw materials into products. People sell their labor to owners, but owners can pay them far less than the products they make will receive on the open market. This antagonism produces the most fundamental concern within a Marxian view of history: How is one group of people being taken advantage of or being exploited economically by another who has power over them? And what needs to happen to even out the playing field? Capitalism exacerbates social class struggle and social class divisions—the main forces driving history—and separates people based on "haves" and "have-nots." For Marx, Capitalism isn't inevitable, nor is the economic gap between groups accidental. It's the product of an economic system organized to privilege a few at the expense of the many.

Fifth, Marxism concludes that without intervention, Capitalism will inevitably implode. Marx warned that when people feel they're being taken advantage of, they will eventually rebel and that Capitalism, as a humanly created system rife with internal contradictions, would eventually collapse. At times he talked as though this would happen passively. At others, he argued it would happen as the exploited intentionally took measures to overthrow the current system. Power holders don't give up their power without a fight.[3] For Marx, the answer lay in the workers replacing their false consciousness (believing the way things are is the only way they could ever be) with a resolve toward revolution. Once workers truly understood their plight and rose up against the system together, then change would come. Human society, already broken beyond repair and getting worse under Capitalism, doesn't need renovation—it needs to be torn down to the studs and rebuilt.

Sixth, Marxism anticipates a socialist utopia, facilitated and controlled by the state, where everyone gets what they need to survive and people bring their best on behalf of the community. Marx became a light in people's darkness by asking, What if we could organize ourselves so that the physical needs of every member of society were met? What if we could do away with the evils produced by class division and fascist coercion and instead, through voluntary cooperation, people could develop every aspect of themselves in complete freedom?[4]

Seventh, Marx warned that formal religion was an "opiate," an effective tool used by power holders to hypnotize people and keep them in check. God talk teaches people to accept their lot in life, thereby allowing the status quo economic order to expand unchecked. For Marxist heaven to be realized, hope in a Christian heaven needs to go away. They are fundamentally at odds with one another and cannot coexist.[5]

SURPRISED BY MARX

Alongside the headlines of the past century, entire libraries exist not only to challenge the mechanics of Marx's science and philosophy but also as witnesses to the tragedy of his *Manifesto* being lived in real time. I don't pretend to be an economist, so I'll leave the details of financial analysis to others, but I can say after many class readings and discussions with people who practically worship him, I still saw him as a Christ-less villain. His words fueled some of the most tragic scenes known to history, and his solutions only replaced one broken ideology with a worse one. Justin was right in that the "all for one and one for all" sharing of resources and a state motivated by and committed to overseeing the best economic interests of its entire populace—not just the elite—has never truly been realized. Because of collective depravity—something we all *do* share in common—it never will be in this lifetime.[6] But reading Marx instead of his critics also surprised me. I found myself agreeing with many of his observations and insights about the way humans operate with one another in a capitalist system. Honestly, I wasn't expecting to learn anything from him. Turns out I was wrong.

I'd never thought at the level he does about how goods take on a quasi-"spiritual" magnetism and create false needs in people, or how capital would gravitate toward the formation of transnational monopolies instead of more democratic ownership. He surprised me by getting me to consider how the logic of Capitalism *does* require us to view one another as a means to an end. Profit does get pursued at the expense of people. Someone *is* always benefiting from the relative exploitation of someone else since labor benefits owners more than it compensates laborers, even if laborers are paid well. We may agree to it, but the class division between those at the top of the ladder and those at the bottom is real and not always the result of brilliance, harder work, or ingenuity. I never thought about the extent to which our schooling gets shaped by workforce demands, or the volatility of my entire retirement savings disappearing in one unpredictable market quake.

But perhaps most importantly, Marx forced me to pay closer attention to how people's lives are affected by the realities of the system we've accepted. He pointed out general truths about people's specific suffering that I'd grown complacent about, or worse, never cared about at all. He made me think about why I've come to accept what is as being the only way things could be, and how people ache because of it. Reading Marx didn't make me want to become a Marxist. It made me want to be a better Christian and caused me to wonder what else I wasn't giving attention to but should be. Reading Marx also triggered a long-buried memory whose significance wouldn't reveal itself until several years later during the racial turmoil that prompted this book.

In 1980, my dad got laid off from a foreman position at Ford. He'd only been there a year but was making many times over his previous salary as a teacher and coach, so he and my mom bought a bunch of stuff on credit. Within months of losing his job, they filed bankruptcy because he couldn't make payments. We had repo people ringing our phone and for a time depended on food stamps for our meals. My dad was devastated and humiliated.

On one hand, Marx would rightly blame the fallout on capitalist frailty: an oil embargo triggered a national recession, owners in the industry made bad decisions, and profit-driven financial professionals misread consumer cues. People at the top lost credibility and learned business lessons, but little else. People at the bottom lost their jobs and all that goes with them. The "haves" remained rich while the "have-nots" became poorer. On the other hand, no one told my parents to go into risky debt. They made a choice and had to take responsibility for it.

Invisible systemic realities created my parents' situation. So did their choice to go into debt. It should be obvious, but there's always an interplay between real systems and real choices. Some people emphasize one, some the other. More than anyone, Marx got me thinking about both.

Marx was both exasperating and illuminating, but he was nothing compared to those who picked up the tattered pieces of his philosophy and brought him into the twentieth century. Their radical introduction of "Critical" concepts onto the sociological playing field became a cornerstone for CRT.

3

THINKING CRITICALLY ABOUT CRITICAL THEORY

Fortunate is he who understands the hidden causes of things.

VIRGIL, "GEORGICS"

AFTER FINISHING TWO MASTER'S DEGREES in theology from a reputable evangelical seminary, a decade later I chose to stretch my mind in a different direction in a secular PhD program. It's not the normal next step taken by someone who's spent two decades in vocational ministry, but like Paul engaging Athenians and their "gods," I wanted a deeper understanding of America's "gods" and their operation among us. So in 2008 I was accepted to the American culture studies PhD program at Bowling Green State University.

I didn't expect the classes to be friendly to a Christian vision of the world, but I underestimated how radically different it would be from my conservative ministry "normal." For three years everything I read either came directly from Marx or was written by someone positively aligned with his view of the world. I arrived with a head full of C. S. Lewis, Francis Schaeffer, and G. K. Chesterton. I'd never heard of Max Horkheimer, Herbert Marcuse, or Michel Foucault, but reading them baptized me into a new way of thinking about the world. My relatively comfortable upbringing made it difficult to see the world through radical eyes, and the lenses they made me look through turned the world upside down.

For example, the word *progressive* got used as an adjective, verb, and noun. It showed up everywhere. We didn't discuss where to put moral lines but instead argued about the best ways to remove them entirely. Everyone kept referring to the problem of mass media being a "conservative" institution. Ronald Reagan was responsible for almost every current social problem. Beyond all that, I wore a trifecta of despised identity markers—white, male, hetero—and being a "Christian minister" wasn't exactly celebrated. It was like standing in a darkroom looking at negatives, squinting at blurry images trying to understand what I was seeing, and it took me almost a year to understand what was going on. I was being catechized into the world of Critical Theory.

Drinking from the well of CT always left me conflicted. This will sound like a contradiction, especially given what I wrote above, but the clashing sides I'm about to represent are important. We need to take the popularization of CT seriously, but for reasons that go beyond the critique of Christians currently sounding alarms.

I'll start by saying I agree that CT *should* be chastised for its illiberal, cynical, and unredemptive vision for the world. As a strategy to dethrone the ruling class and its values, it simply replaces one evil with another in the name of setting people free. It's not attempting to be a new Christian denomination. Stripped bare, Critical Theories offer a dense (but clever) twentieth-century recycling of common characteristics shared by all human-centered, godless ideologies throughout history. I usually arrived home after a day of haggling with my PhD cohort feeling dark and burdened, wanting a cleansing from all the cynicism and unhappiness it produced in me. I'm well acquainted with the pre-Christ chaos of living in a world without any hope other than the prospect of resistance, and I'm not at all attracted to it.

But what it's trying to help us see about the bondage created by rampant consumerism and oppressive forms of Conservatism, even if motivated by treacherous ideology, gets woefully underrepresented by Christians, and that posture of underrepresentation (and in some cases misrepresentation) carries over to Critical Race Theory. Pieced together, CT makes for a lousy set of beliefs to base one's life on, but like Marx's writing, its observations and the topics it forces us to consider are far more helpful than the conclusions it produces in its followers. I grew to admire what these theorists saw while shuddering at their response to it.

Most Christian critique specializes in rejecting its radical conclusions without ever taking its observations seriously or even considering how they came to those solutions in the first place. That's because most critics are convinced there *isn't* any benefit, or at least not much worth talking about. I disagree with that assessment and want to show why. If we're going to understand what CRT is trying to do and why, it will first be helpful to understand the same for CT.

THE RISE OF CRITICAL THEORY

In the first quarter of the twentieth century, European scholars influenced by the Marxist tradition faced a new social problem—where was the economic revolution and demise of Capitalism? Amid widespread global unrest and economic instability, the inevitable implosion Marx predicted didn't happen. After the Russian Revolution of 1917, fascist dictatorships became all the rage, and instead of utopia, people got the gas chambers of Hitler's Germany, the deadly despotism of Mao's China, and the iron fist of Stalin's Russia. Not exactly the heaven on earth Marxian loyalists anticipated.

It's in this cultural soil that an all-star cast of Jewish-German-Marxist scholars began working together to form the Institute for Social Research, more popularly known as the Frankfurt School. These intellectuals had been anticipating the establishment of the socialist government their namesake predicted. Instead, they began literally working in the seedbed of fascism that would soon grow into

Hitler's Holocaust. Perplexed by their misreading of history and their failure to anticipate the political tyranny characterizing their adulthood, they became suspicious that the underlying conditions protecting capitalist exploitation were also somehow empowering political dictatorship. They set out to understand how.

Why didn't the revolution happen the way it was supposed to? Why did people so easily allow one form of tyranny (economic) to be compounded by another (political) in the name of Communism, which was supposed to set everyone free? They no longer anticipated a revolution where workers rebel against exploitation but instead began exploring the cultural reasons why that would now probably never happen.

As a result, they developed a way of diagnosing and analyzing cultural ideas, trends, and behaviors called "Critical Theory," variously known as cultural Marxism, neo-Marxism, or Western Marxism.[1] Its goal was to understand and help overcome the social structures (i.e., ways of thinking, ways of organizing ourselves, ways of using language, ways of structuring institutions, etc.) through which people are kept in check, inviting their own domination. Like Marx, they still believed Capitalism created a class system, but they no longer believed it could be overturned without understanding ideological power and how it worked in social institutions. Freeing people from blindly accepting whatever presents itself as socially "normal" became their new objective.

UNDERSTANDING THE IMPORTANCE OF THE WORDS *CRITICAL* AND *THEORY*

What is a theory? In this context, "theory" refers to intentional, thoughtful human attempts to make sense of what's going on in society. In the hands of academic scholars, theories function as an interpretive lens, a way to describe how societies function, an educated attempt to explain why things are the way they are. Theories aren't worldviews in themselves, though they may be subsets of a worldview.

They are methods, singular lenses that produce and answer questions about specific social realities.

Traditional sociological theories focused on understanding or explaining what could be plainly observed, organized, and interpreted about society. But a *Critical* theory is suspicious. It assumes there's something more going on than what we plainly see. It refuses to blindly trust systems that require our submission, whether financial, educational, political, or religious. "Critical" doesn't believe in God, but it does believe in human depravity and the desire of the few to control the many. A Critical theory tries to see the ideological iceberg controlling people from beneath the water, expose it to everyone, and then hack at it until it loses its power.

In *The Matrix*, Morpheus confronts Neo to tell him that he's trapped in an artificial world, a prisoner in an elaborate deception created by an evil cyber intelligence. Neo's always been suspicious, certain something isn't right about the unfolding of his life, but he doesn't know what. Holding a colored capsule in each hand, Morpheus describes the choice facing Neo: "You take the blue pill—the story ends, you wake up in your bed and believe whatever you want to believe. You take the red pill—you stay in Wonderland, and I show you how deep the rabbit hole goes. Remember, all I'm offering is the truth. Nothing more."[2]

Like Morpheus, Critical theorists of the last century saw themselves as "red pill" dispensers, helping unmask and reveal the true nature of the late-capitalist world. They wanted to set people free from the machinery of the capitalist matrix and their perception of the conservative exploitation that comes with it. They no longer believed revolution would topple Capitalism as a system but instead turned their attention toward how to be more human within it.

That's why, as the last century developed, the tenor of neo-Marxist writing became less about the utopia of communism and more about the depravity of capitalist dominance and control within *all* social institutions and, most problematically, the subsequent need to erase the Conservative social categories and boundaries keeping people in check. For Critical theorists, Conservatism manifested itself through any political or organizational doctrine emphasizing the value of traditional institutions and practices, a craving for continuity and stability, and a reliance on political and cultural institutions leveraged to curb people's base and destructive instincts. Conservative dogma used as a social boundary maker was the vehicle giving power to the few so they could control the many.[3] It operated as a global tool for the privileged elite to protect the ongoing interests of the privileged elite against everyone else. Consequently, Critical Theory is a more recent stage of radical Marxian analysis inspecting how Capitalism (with its insatiable need for consumers) and Conservatism (with its dominant need for stasis) conspire to keep humans in a form of social bondage. For Critical theorists, Capitalism and Conservatism always come as a package, working together to keep people content in their grip. Within CT, Capitalism and Conservatism affect people's minds and what they do with their bodies. Thus, Critical Theory presents itself as an antidote, a remedy setting people free from the control of others, from mental and physical bondage, and from a variety of oppressions both real and perceived.

WHAT DOES "OPPRESSION" MEAN IN CRITICAL THEORY, AND WHY IS IT SO IMPORTANT?

A "critical" theory has a distinctive aim: to unmask the ideology falsely justifying some form of social or economic oppression and, in so doing, to contribute to the task of ending that oppression. It aims to provide a kind of enlightenment about social and economic life that is itself *emancipatory:* persons come to recognize the oppression they are suffering *as* oppression and are thereby partly freed from it.[4]

When I hear the word *oppression,* I naturally envision people being tied up, beaten down, mired in poverty because of tyrannical governments or marauding gangs. Oppression is almost always physical in my mind. Working under the gaze of fascist governments, early Critical theorists certainly witnessed, and in some cases, experienced physical brutality.

But they broadened oppression to include a poverty of spirit created by profit-driven, consumerist culture and the bondage of humans to social and moral norms dictated by others. They analyzed how and why the general masses not only gave their physical freedom to tyrants but with less obvious consequences also submitted their spirits to the machinery of Capitalism and other forms of what they considered Conservative control. It's important to understand this when it comes to how the word *oppression* gets used today, because for Critical theorists, oppression lives on a continuum with more physical forms of violence at one end and more psychological and emotional forms of violence at the other.

A Critical theorist sees it as the role of the scholar to unmask the not-always-obvious means through which interpersonal domination and inequality get established in society. In *The Truman Show*, Truman Burbank lives an ordinary life but doesn't realize his entire existence takes place on a large set populated by actors. His life is a reality show controlled by others. Everyone conspires to keep him trapped in the deception, not allowing him to see his reality or how those running the show determine the limits and boundaries of his existence. As Truman begins discovering what's happening to him, the host of a news show asks the director, "Why do you think that Truman has never come close to discovering the true nature of his world until now?" The director answers, "We accept the reality of the world with which we are presented. It's as simple as that."[5] Critical Theory wants people to stop accepting the world as it's presented and start thinking about how it came to be. How do ideological forces conspire to keep people in bondage to "norms" that keep the machine running while stifling human flourishing?

Think about it: if you've already decided there is no God's-eye view of the universe to be accessed, then it's true that every human interaction *is* relative, every decision truly subjective and dependent on context. Without believing in the involvement of a sovereign God, what else is history but a study in groups of people trying to dominate and control one another, and thus, groups of people also being dominated and controlled? With no God speaking from outside the system, whatever moral lines or social norms exist were put there by people in control of the power game, often resulting from a perverse mix of religion and politics. And why should we trust those people? How often do leaders with that kind of power die to themselves on behalf of others or use their power to benefit the most vulnerable in society?

Apart from spiritual intervention (a non-category in CT), that's not the way the world works. Critical theorists argue that whatever value system gets promoted by those with power should benefit or at least protect those most susceptible to control and manipulation, and too often it doesn't. The central problem, of course, becomes who gets to determine what values will become normalized. Who gets the power of being the privileged class? Who gets to decide where moral and social lines will be drawn?

Further, nearly all Critical theorists interpret the constraints of political and religious Conservatism as weapons of oppression, citing centuries of examples around the world of people being dominated by moral and social norms based on race, gender, sexuality, or other identity markers. However much the idea of oppression gets stretched today at the "psychological violence" end of the continuum, it's undeniable that in every society people *have* been targeted and trampled because of their skin color, biological gender, and sexual behaviors.

A history of abuse at the hands of power is woven into these groups' narratives, explaining why they're so predominant in discussions on social oppression. Norms don't magically appear. They're developed, nurtured, and massaged into existence as the conditions within society at a particular moment in time merge together to make them possible.[6] So CT dives into the "archaeology" of an idea and traces not only how social norms come into being, but also how some populations suffer more than others as a result, and hence, are oppressed.[7]

FOUR RECURRING THEMES CONFRONTED BY CRITICAL THEORY

Essays in Critical Theory are not bedtime reading. They're difficult, dense, often sprawling, and don't lend themselves to soundbite summaries. Complicating things more, they require thinking in a multidisciplinary way, needing some measure of competence in history, philosophy, sociology, economics, political science, and mass communication mediums of all sorts. But across these and other disciplines, four themes came up all the time in my studies, themes central to any "Critical" expression of theory, including the later birth of CRT: profit, power, politics, and Postmodernism.

The insatiable pursuit of profit. Critical Theory shares Marx's disdain for the way profit-driven Capitalism shapes human society, forcing us into a less humane, competitive posture toward one another both individually and collectively. Capitalism creates a society where the pursuit of profit transcends almost all other considerations. It determines what gets marketed. It shapes what becomes news. It influences how our schools and prisons and medical establishments function. It determines the length of workdays. It creates holidays. It's woven into every aspect of consumer society. But profit depends almost entirely on the success of the *culture industry*, an early CT concept developed by Frankfurt School leaders Theodor Adorno and Max Horkheimer.

The culture industry consists of all the producers of popular culture and their products: mass media, Hollywood, television, sports, advertising, and so on. It generates products that promise happiness, define the good life, and communicate a moral vision for how things should be. Thus, its messages are inherently political and relevant to power holders in society. The culture industry produces both imaginary and real needs, which induce shopping, which produces profit for the owners while soothing the soul of purchasers. This mutual interdependence gives the appearance of freedom and choice, but instead it creates a particular form of codependent bondage. It's strong language, but Critical theorists view the entire culture industry as a shiny tool of fascist control. Control increases as needs are created and products marketed based on their ability to generate profit. Everything else is secondary.

Further, CT despises the mass-produced, status-quo-preserving, conservative infection of "sameness" the culture industry creates in the name of profit. Why? Because believing in the status quo blinds people to their participation in their own exploitation as consumers. Over time, the passive consumption of prepackaged, mass-manufactured reproductions makes us less discerning about reality. CT asks, "What happens when material things and their appearance of value become more important than people? What happens when people become more concerned with buying than being?"[8]

The invisible influence of power. *Power* is a dirty word and can't be trusted unless you have it. On a micro level, CT is a study in individual, relational power dynamics. Power means advantage, the ability to coerce, to control, to bring change. The relative power scale gets tipped by gender, age, height, health, social class, perceived wealth, education, wisdom, family order, title, and race, but some form of power is always at work, whether consciously or not. So every social interaction gets assessed on a relational or social power continuum, followed by an investigation of how it's being leveraged.

On a macro level, CT studies groups with power. The power of elites, gatekeepers, financiers, or the military is always being used to bring about change or to keep change from happening. Power creates the status quo, then protects it. Power decides what public schooling looks like. Power decides what gets to be considered news for the day and what will be remembered as history tomorrow. Power puts political candidates in place. Power tries to establish what "is" versus what "is not" in people's minds.

CT is suspicious of bureaucratic power and assumes it will be used to protect privileged interests at the expense of common people. Critical Theory seeks to expose how it all works when acquisition and wielding of power become the endgame, and the domination of other humans its result. How does this get pulled off?

Through *ideology* and the effect of *hegemony*. *Ideology* is simply a mental framework—ideas, beliefs, images, and systems of representation—that groups of people use to make sense of the way society works. *Hegemony* is the ability to get people to willingly accept those beliefs as normal without coercion.[9] If whoever holds power can smuggle their desires into every content-based institution in society, and their ideas become the "cultural software" used to map the world for everyone else, they can control how people think and behave without them even realizing it's happening. Critical theorists recognize that whoever dictates the moral, social, and physical lines within which people are expected to operate controls lives. So they want to expose the invisible ideas that are driving behavior, show how they came to be accepted, and offer alternative ways of being.

The on-the-ground conflict of politics. Critical theorists are fond of saying, "Everything is political and politics is everything." Politics means more than what happens in Washington or the government operations on a state or local level, though they all play their role. Politics is embedded in our daily lives. It's in the food we eat, the clothes on our back, the transportation we take to school or work, the neighborhood we live in, our access to information as we wind down the day. Politics is about the power to make decisions about where boundaries get set, and it's behind the personal agency that violates or moves the boundary. No matter what we do, we are either passively accepting the current order of things or intentionally opting for another way of operating. Thus, everything is politics and politics is everything.

CT seeks to understand why we organize ourselves socially the way we do and the way those agreements play themselves out in everyday life. Hannah Arendt wrote, "Politics is based on the fact of human plurality,"[10] suggesting that people intersect one another while seeing the world through different lenses, and the contested nature of trying to work out those differences gives most every action a political dimension. Politics involves strategies to obtain positions of power or control in a situation among people so that their preferred way of seeing the world wins out.

"Critical" implies a desire to change society, not just interpret it, and change necessarily involves the shenanigans of traditional politics. So in keeping with their Marxist tradition, Critical theorists ask, "How does ideology prevent the emergence of 'everyday people' rising up against the established order? And how do we undermine those tactics?"

One reason Critical Theory appeals to so many people is that in rejecting the elite, it puts a premium on the perspective of "outsiders." What does the world look like through the eyes of the dispossessed? Outcast? Marginalized? Abused? Rejected? Uncool? What does history look like from the ground up, where common people living common lives make choices that shape everyday life? It advantages a "politics from below" and takes seriously the voice of common people.

CT derives positive energy from teaching people to resist, to reject socially declared norms and replace them with their own. Most Critical theorists live within a contradiction: they can be hopelessly nihilistic and endlessly deconstructive while stubbornly clinging to the possibility of change, a possibility that depends on destroying the current order of things. Society will have to get worse before it can get better, and that's okay. Upheaval, disruption, subversion—all life-giving, positive words for the Critical theorist because the current order oppresses anyone who lives outside the lines they had no say in drawing, borders usually established and enforced through some form of state-sanctioned force. Thus, looking through a lens where every behavior either affirms a passive acceptance of status quo or rejects it by swimming upstream, the worst form of political action is inaction.

The ubiquitous aroma of Postmodernism. In the middle of the twentieth century, the conceptual move from modernity to postmodernity among philosophers, linguists, and sociologists coincided with the development of the Frankfurt School and those who extended their work in the following decades. Thomas Kuhn famously suggested that scientific revolution depends on the right combination of social factors existing to produce an environment for radically new ways of "seeing" to be possible, and the schools of both Postmodernism and Critical Theory benefited immensely from the cumulative "accidents of history" present when they both came alive. They disagreed with each other on much, but one could argue they also fed off and depended on one another for their mutual existence. Postmodernity and its analysts created an environment in which Critical Theory could flourish, and Critical Theory returned the favor.[11]

The literature on an alleged transition to Postmodernism is vast, complex, and often contradictory, but for our purposes here let's recognize that "Postmodernism, if it is about anything, is about the prospect that the promises of the modern age are no longer believable because there is evidence that for the vast majority of people worldwide there is no realistic reason to vest hope in any version of the idea that the world is good and getting better."[12] Remember, this is life under the sun apart from God. If modernity offered us optimistic beliefs about human progress and what could be produced through reason and science alone, postmodernity blew them to bits and challenged anything considered normal by modern standards.

At their surface, both Critical and Postmodern theorists share and develop similar ideas while considering the effects of ideology, society, and history on every aspect of culture:

- word games and redefinitions of terms
- erasure of conservative moral lines
- blurring the distinction between "real" and "unreal"
- celebration of the absurd and ironic
- reimagining history from "below"
- hyperconcern for subjectivity and personal experience
- assumption of no big-*T* truth to discover
- replacing the taken-for-granted with new normals
- socially constructed nature of everything
- shape-shifting nature of identity
- appreciating chaos over stasis

The list goes on, but in short, Postmodernity endorses the kinds of social disruptions valued by Marxists, and Critical theorists spill lots of ink trying to make sense of how Capitalism and Conservatism work to shape us as humans in a postmodern world. They help each other to coexist, and much reading in CT has to do with the consequences of living in the kind of world Postmodernism creates. While postmodernity recognizes that "the center cannot hold," CT spends its time both celebrating and grieving the anarchy now loosed upon the world, wondering how to truly be human amid the destruction.[13]

WHY WE NEED TO DIG DEEPER WHEN IT COMES TO CRITICAL THEORY

I'm only briefly introducing these four themes, but I'm doing so to illustrate why blanket condemnations of Critical Theory sound offensive in the ears of people who've grown to value what Critical theorizing brings to the table. When we immediately dismiss CT as an oppressor/oppressed framework without considering what oppression for people might actually look like in the context of how profit, power, politics, and postmodern effects impact human lives, we miss the positive role CT can play in seeing these realities.

More than anything, Critical Theory challenges us to think deeply about the harmful social effects of being trained to live as a constant consumer and the ideological controls needed for its maintenance. I understand why this is problematic for people. We're taught in a thousand ways that only Marxists or Leftists or Communists criticize the implications of Capitalism, and you don't want any association with them. Maybe, like me, you've been conditioned not to criticize it because you know the alternative is worse. We're like fish who never question water because it's all we really know and any alternative equals certain death. I get it.[14]

But Capitalism, even if it produces a long list of positives, is still a godless ideology, unashamedly fueled by greed and the will to dominate. Conservatism, while in many ways overlapping with and preserving Christian ideals, protects the interests of elites at the expense of everyone else. This is simply history, not a radical reinterpretation. Recognizing how evil plays its way out through Capitalism and Conservatism, even if they're my preferred worldly ideologies, doesn't mean I become a Communist or am compromising my faith. It just means I'm detached enough from the current world order to see and acknowledge depravity in my own camp. It means I'm genuinely embracing my "alien and stranger" identity as a Christian.

When I raise these concerns with Christian friends, too often I'm met with a defensive, "What system would you rather have then?" But what if instead we started asking, "What responsibility do I have to address the problems the current system creates for people not living in my house?" What if we defended less as apologists and cared more like Christians?

Too many Christian critics of CT see nothing positive whatsoever in what CT does, while others will nod to a tepid, almost apologetic affirmation before launching into their comprehensive condemnation of it. I'm well aware of where it diverges from a Christian worldview, but even so, I came to realize that many CT writers were able to peel back layers of social reality I'd either chosen to ignore or simply couldn't see while looking through my particular theological and political lenses. They were often right; I just didn't want to admit it, and I came to realize it's easier to focus on what's obviously wrong or anti-Christian in their conclusions than to consider what might be convicting in their observations. Indeed, just because a person agrees with Marx or Critical theorists about something doesn't make them an apostate for sharing his view, especially if the Bible says nothing about it or, in some cases, overlaps with it.

If we're going to have an informed opinion about Critical Theory and what it's trying to do, we might be helped by investing more energy in considering what can be embraced instead of only reading or listening to those majoring in what needs to be rejected.

4

CAN A CHRISTIAN GAIN ANYTHING FROM CRITICAL THEORY?

Theories are like glasses. Some of them make your historical subjects and sources clearer while others distort them. Try some on and see how things look. And never feel like you're stuck with any of them.

WILLIAM MURRELL, "CRITICAL THEORY AS METHOD, METANARRATIVE, AND MOOD"

ONE OF MY CHRISTIAN CLASSMATES ONCE ASKED, "How are you reconciling all this Critical Theory with your Christian faith?" That's a fair question, and one behind many podcasts, videos, and articles that have been sent my way, all exploring the incompatibility of Christianity with both CT and CRT, many of which mistakenly use the terms interchangeably.

My answer was the same then as it is now: I'm not trying to reconcile them. They're not asking to be reconciled. A body of belief that starts by asserting that there is no God is fundamentally at odds with one that believes God exists and has literally spoken in time. I have never felt a need to merge them together.

But many Christians get so focused on CT's incompatibility with Christianity that they fail to see how it can be redemptive despite itself. Critical Theory is much more interesting and potentially useful in Christian discussion than how it's usually portrayed by Christian critics. We don't need to be afraid of or reject Critical Theory as though interacting with its ideas will infect us with a disease whose end necessitates turning from Christ. Handled properly, it can help expose some of our own theological perception gaps that might be hindering our gospel witness in the world. But if we want to understand the conceptual playing field of Critical Race Theory, it will help to first understand Critical Theory as something more than just an overblown oppressor/oppressed lens through which to view the world.

MAKING SENSE OF LIFE UNDER THE SUN WITHOUT GOD

So many of the questions Critical theorists raised struck me as a more hopeless and cynical extension of the philosophical monologue in my favorite book of the Bible: Ecclesiastes. The author of Ecclesiastes and Critical theorists come at their observations from the same starting point: If you remove the intervention of a transcendent supernatural being, what are you left with? How do we make sense of life under the sun apart from God, and how do humans work with and against each other in the midst of it? Why do we have problems? Where is the good life found?

They lament broken social life, wondering if it's beyond repair, and try to assess not only where brokenness comes from but also how to find fulfillment in the middle of it. They both recognize that the human experiment consistently teaches us that people never feel fully satisfied and expertly mistreat one another as a result. No wonder then that oppression is a recurring theme in both Critical Theory and Ecclesiastes.

The writer of Ecclesiastes still fundamentally believes God exists, but he considers life without him across his twelve chapters. Ecclesiastes works as a form of Critical analysis, pulling back the curtain on life to show what's really going on, asking questions of human existence that the rest of the Bible answers. But for Critical theorists, since there's no spiritual reality beyond what can be seen, since there's no individual sin or accountability to a holy God, they have to create an explanation for evil in their material world, and they name it Capitalism and Conservatism.

At their core, Critical Theories are an analysis of how sin works through the logic and processes of Capitalism and Conservatism, and how they combine to negatively affect the way humans relate to themselves and others. Critical theorists would never use the language of "sin" to describe what they are observing, but that's what they're studying. In their world, the basic human problem isn't separation from God—it's a conservative commitment to Capitalism that creates class division and convinces people to embrace their own domination. Capitalism and the conservative mentality controlling its levers effectively suck the soul out of people.

The evangelical world I live in recognizes the evil produced by their opposites—Communism and Progressivism—but struggles to see how Capitalism and Conservatism are just the other side of the same demonic coin. No human economic or political system will save us, regardless of our rational preference for one or the other, but we can thank Critical Theory for waking us from believing one side of the coin actually can.

The writer of Ecclesiastes fears God in the end, while writers looking through critical lenses tend toward the hopeless, bitter, and nihilistically cynical. That's a significant difference, but their starting point and the kinds of questions they ask come from the same existential problems faced by humans since Genesis 3.

MANY INDIVIDUAL THEORIES THAT EMPHASIZE "CRITICAL"

A social theory is an idea or hypothesis about how the world works, a lens we look through to interpret human experience. Every graduate student understands that theories develop because humans want to know why things happen the way they do, and the job description of an academic includes generating answers and proposing solutions. That's why the moment a theory is born it goes in search of application. In fact, the entire academic establishment depends on scholars coming up with intriguing theories so that others can generate studies and write papers on ways to apply them.

Theories aren't necessarily worldviews in themselves, though they may be subsets of a worldview. Theories are methods, singular lenses that produce and answer questions about specific social realities. So it's inaccurate to speak of "Critical Theory" as though it's just a singular all-encompassing idea. Instead, it's more accurate to talk about it as many different theories applied to different aspects of social life, all taking their cues from the school of Critical thought.

We could say that all Critical Theories live under the umbrella paradigm of oppressor/oppressed and are always sniffing out ways that one group of people is exploited by another. But each social context requires a different theory to explain what's happening and why, and the details often take us far beyond oppressor/oppressed. A Critical Theory says, "Let's look at the negative of the social photo and raise questions not being asked due to ignorance or intentional effort to maintain status quo. Let's generate ideas that explain specific human dynamics within people's actual social reality."

It considers the ways a belief comes to be seen as rational and normal, then seeks to challenge and change it. How does dark skin become inferior to white? Or women to men? Why do magazines set the bar for what counts as beautiful and the ideal body shape? Who fixes the social meaning and status associated with having a particular make and model of car, and how does that happen? What determines the qualifications for "gifted" in the school system, and who creates the standards for entrance? How would our educational journey look different if it weren't driven by capitalist necessity? Who gets to decide what counts as "history"? How does the mapping of a city and the choices made about streets and store placement affect our collective psyche and directly affect those in poverty?

So Critical Theory is properly a methodology rather than a singular worldview, and as a methodology it gets used within many academic fields. By nature, it's interdisciplinary and generates ideas that stretch across the academic horizon. It's not one theory, but many theories.

THE METHOD OF CHOICE FOR CULTURE STUDIES

It's important to recognize a distinction between the arrival of culture studies as an interdisciplinary academic field in the mid-twentieth century and the slice of it focusing on gender and sexuality that ushered in the sexual revolution of the 1960s and '70s. Much of the negative energy expended toward "wokeism" today stems from the consequences of that segment, and we mistakenly condemn the entire discipline primarily because of it.

Culture studies emerged in the 1950s when British literary scholars, building on the concerns of Adorno and Horkheimer's work on the culture industry, began studying the texts of cultural production like television, film, music, novels, marketing, the news media, fashion, food production, exercise and health, and other popular expressions of social life.[1] Bringing a Critical approach to the raw material of everyday living, culture studies began analyzing how these texts shape our identities and construct our perceptions of the world around us. Theorists argued that because of its meaning-making power, popular culture is never just entertainment. Instead, "it is the software program of human life."[2] They exposed how pop culture producers can shape and even control how people think, feel, and act in the world by making certain understandings of the world dominant. They literally create reality for people. So theorists analyzed the constructed nature of that reality and its effects on different populations.[3]

In doing so, culture studies became the sandbox where different Critical Theories and pop cultural texts came to play together.[4] For example, Why is a drug like alcohol portrayed so often as a harmless social prop even though it kills and destroys lives, while heroine, crack, and methamphetamines are illegal and portrayed as signs of moral deviancy? What difference does it make that one is the drug of choice for a wealthier demographic while the other usually shows up among more impoverished populations?[5] What should we make of the racial implications surrounding the protection of one drug and criminalization of the others? Those perceptions don't happen randomly; they are intentionally produced by people with a vested interest in a particular interpretation of reality becoming dominant.

I found culture studies endlessly fascinating and dizzyingly diverse in its topics and questions: What happens when a society becomes addicted to spectacle? What role does architecture play in the maintenance of Capitalism? What happens when mass-produced art exists for profit and entertainment and no longer challenges what "is"? We dug deep into the consequences of mass communication product being monopolized by a handful of conglomerates. We discussed the "real" verses the "unreal" and how mass production and marketing dull our ability to discern the difference. We talked fashion and trends and subcultures, and why sometimes resistance gets snuffed out and other times it becomes monetized. How do pop cultural entertainment vehicles and products shape our identities, our values, and our definitions of "normal"? I loved studying the implications of profit, power, politics, and Postmodernism on culture studies topics, even if it was always one-sidedly against Capitalism and Conservatism.

But things got complicated when looking at cultural texts through the windows of gender and sexuality. That's where the problems started and what many people aligned with a Christian view of the world find offensive. It's the main venue where embracing CT conclusions can become toxic to a biblical worldview, leaning heavily on the work of a French theorist whose name you might not know but whose ideas you most certainly do.

Michel Foucault wrote prodigiously on different subjects, but his writing on the history of the social construction of the body fanned the sparks of moral revolution already flickering in the 1960s and 1970s. He argued that how we think about our bodies and what we desire to do with them are never independent of powerful social forces exerting their will on us. Media, education, government, and church all conspire to influence (i.e., control) our bodies, our behavior, and our minds when it comes to sexuality.

Through meticulous historical analysis, Foucault taught that power normalizes sexual behavior. In other words, at various points in history, groups of people—usually men—decided what sexual behavior would be considered normal, what would be considered perverse, and what would be considered pathological or criminal. Appeals to the Bible or other "holy" books played a significant role in this game, but because there's no real God to hear from or reckon with for Foucault, appeals to religion are just another instrument of power used to place moral norms where one group wants them. Freedom lies in breaking from those "oppressive" norms, so Foucault encouraged people to experiment outside the lines, giving validity to all forms of sexual expression.

Later, in 1990, Judith Butler would do this same kind of work around gender, popularizing the idea that gender identities are constructed "performances" we learn to act out through modeling and the force of cultural dynamics rather than essentialized aspects of our being.[6] Gender became another contested site where others control how we perceive ourselves and put limits on our expression. Freedom means performing the identity you prefer, not the one your genitals or others tell you to perform.

My point in unpacking this is simply to show again that most of what happens in culture studies—the venue where Critical Theory has manifested itself most prominently—goes well beyond gender and sexuality and doesn't pose a threat to theological fidelity. Analyzing the texts of culture and their myriad subcategories challenges us more politically than theologically, but these are the parts of Critical Theory we never seem to hear about.

It's possible to read the words *critical* and *theory* and imagine nothing but leftist expressions of moral revolution. I think most Christians today hear "Critical Theory" and immediately imagine the erasing of a biblical vision for gender and sexuality and the Progressive expressions of identity politics. These topics speak most loudly in the media and often pose a genuine threat to what the Bible teaches, but Critical Theory manifested through culture studies serves a much broader slate of topics than gender and sexuality, and it's a mistake to ignore them. The entire world—and certainly American culture—has been altered by the work of theoreticians like Foucault and Butler, and while their contribution is staggeringly significant, they represent a singular floor in the culture studies skyscraper.

THE PROBLEM WITH COMBINING CRITICAL THEORIES INTO A WORLDVIEW
Though Critical Theories represent an approach to interpreting social data, because they exist as an extension of Marxism, they can also be combined to form a worldview. Many ideas and applications under the umbrella of what gets called Critical Theory conflict with Christian teaching, especially since the entire enterprise is founded on a belief that God doesn't exist. In this sense, it's doomed to be demonic when acting as one's predominant lens for viewing the world, making it easy for biblically grounded Christians to tear apart. While arguing for the observatory value of individual theories, absorbing the collective ethos of Critical Theory as a way of life is ultimately destructive.

Endless deconstruction and cynicism produce bitterness. Endless resistance and radicalism produce nihilism. Bitter nihilism makes a person dark and shrinks the soul. Jesus, the cornerstone of Christianity, offers restoration, healing, and hope, an abundant life aligning with what God intended for human flourishing, even in the midst of human brokenness.

Critical theory starts with no God, blames Capitalism and its subsequent Conservatism for the human condition, hangs its hope on gaining freedom from dominant-class "normals," and ties change to the acquisition of political power and individual acts of resistance. Christianity starts with a good and loving God, blames sin for the human condition, hangs its hope on Jesus, and ties change to the resistance of satanic power in individual lives.

Critical theorists believe that transformation begins with the deconstruction and renewal of political and economic society. Christians believe that transformation begins with the deconstruction and renewal of the heart and mind. Critical Theory expects that a revolutionized society will lead to an experience of justice through equality and freedom. Christian discipleship expects that a revolutionized heart will lead to a concern for kingdom justice in society.

Critical Theory puts humans at the center and demands we adjust to Progressive ideas. Christian theology puts God at the center and demands we adjust to his revealed truth. CT wants to erase dominant culture's moral boundaries to set people free. Christianity wants to resist secular culture's moral relativism, or people can never be free. CT seeks to subdue others' power for the sake of themselves. Christianity says submit and leverage your own power for the sake of others.

It's not difficult to see where Christianity and Critical Theory conflict. I suspect that's why Christian folks have developed a cottage industry decrying CT's incongruity with Christianity. When CT is addressed as a comprehensive worldview, this response makes sense. But Marxism and Critical Theory attract people not primarily for their radical activist strategies but for what they draw attention to in the first place, which is their greatest value to us as Christians.

TAKING CRITICAL THEORY AND MARXISM SERIOUSLY

I don't believe most people are attracted to Marxist and Critical ideas because they care about economic theory. While some are fully committed to the philosophy and its implications, I don't believe most want Capitalism to go away or are convinced their ideas about how to run a society would actually work. They're pulled at a more emotional level. They subscribe because Marxian thought taps into resentment felt toward authority. They like it because people resent others telling them what to do and how to live, because everyone not longing for the return of Christ needs an explanation for living life under the sun. It is the promise of peaceful coexistence, prosperity for all, no hoarding of resources, no central figure to dominate the others. It's John Lennon's "Imagine," a world without border wars, without greed or the hunger produced by it, without ideological or religious conflict. Failures aside, Marxian logic accounts for an entirely secular view of human history, and people need this to keep their senses.

The world is broken. People create ways to fix it apart from Christ and make things worse. This is human history. Christians, who have access to a revelation that simultaneously explains, condemns, and transcends human history, should appreciate why someone without hope in God might be attracted to the prospect of what Marx offers. More importantly, Christians should take note of the handful of core ideas elevated by Marx and the Critical theorists that resonate even with non-Marxists around the globe.

Marxism and CT provide a rationale for human angst and alienation. French philosopher Blaise Pascal elevated boredom and anxiety as defining traits of the human condition and famously described people's helpless craving to fill the "infinite abyss" with God's presence.[7] Marx provided an alternative explanation for our restlessness. He rightly named alienation as a problem but traced the cause of our inner alienation to the structure of our economic life, explaining it as a byproduct of capitalist logic. People resonate with his explanation because on one level it's true. The conditions surrounding industrial Capitalism create an alienation from the work of one's hands, a competitive alienation among one's coworkers, and when trapped in an unfulfilling, monotonous job, a subjective alienation from oneself.

Critical Theory redirects our attention toward various forms of conservative social oppression and injustice as the main cause of the problem, but the result is still alienation. Christians don't believe changing those circumstances will remove the angst; only restoring our relationship with God through an encounter with the living Christ begins addressing the inner hole. C. S. Lewis said, "Reality—when looked at intently—is unbearable," and Marxists aren't afraid to stare it down.[8]

They take power seriously. People intuitively know injustice occurs when power is misused. If human history has demonstrated anything, it's that people with power need a motivation outside themselves to use it generously on behalf of others, especially when it comes to economic power. Speaking purely from a human vantage point, power may be the most important form of capital to possess because it often determines the difference between freedom and slavery, justice and injustice. If you hold power, you control the terms of your own life under the sun apart from God. From a Critical perspective, if others have power over you, you cannot be truly free while they are drawing lines to contain you. Conservative folks love the idea of deregulation, but it's naive to assume all people will use their advantages and freedom to look out for one another. Put another way, it's naive to assume people without those advantages won't get trampled. Power is a commodity to be taken seriously.

In a properly Christian vision of the world, power is a sovereignly dispersed commodity to be stewarded on behalf of others. But within a materialist vision of the world, power is a contested, up-for-grabs commodity to be fought over and used to serve oneself. Therefore, the identification and pursuit of different forms of power is crucial to living a free life. This teaching will always resonate the most with people being mistreated and those who see it as their responsibility to stand against abusers.

They expose legitimate problems with Capitalism. Marxian theory examines the many ways capitalist logic works against human flourishing and damages us as people. Despite its advantages, Capitalism commodifies people and forms them into insatiable consumers. It alienates them from their work and each other. It depends on creating and marketing false needs. It chases profit at the expense of communities, generates enormous wealth disparities and social inequalities, and controls educational and financial systems to the detriment of vulnerable populations. It produces unpredictable boom and bust cycles, encourages monopolistic consolidation, and motivates international conflict and war. Like any world system, it practically encourages the exploitation of labor and other forms of corruption. Communism as a way of economic life isn't a better option, but I wonder if Marxism would be as attractive to people if more robust and honest criticism of capitalist arrangements existed, especially among Christians. Ironically, Marx and Critical theorists shine a light on the ways a secularly driven, self-interested approach to economics harms people. But they want to replace it with another secularly driven, socially interested option, which solves some problems by creating many more to take their place. Plenty of people who would never align with Communism still appreciate anyone who has the courage to speak honestly about shortcomings and pains with Capitalism, especially if they're challenging those with power who benefit from its excesses.

They take structural sin seriously. In my experience, people from a Marxist background tend to take structural sin more seriously than white evangelical Christians. Unless you *feel* the effects of structural sin, it probably won't come up in conversation in your friend circles. But should we be surprised that an economic system endorsing greed as a virtue hides sin in its structural arrangements and methods of business?

Marx and his disciples got people to start asking how unequal structural arrangements within the economic system created poverty for some populations while enriching others. What do justice and injustice mean within a capitalist network when it comes to healthcare or housing loans or education? How does capitalist logic maintain the status quo of the elite at the expense of the people? Sin creates real class divisions with real disparity not dependent on choice. Individual and familial choices play a role in outcomes, but so do nefarious policies, patterns, and structures hardwired into the overall system. Marxists devote themselves to digging out these imbalances.

They speak on behalf of the mistreated, vulnerable, and oppressed. If we removed every other reason listed above, this one alone would justify why people remain attracted to Marxist thought worldwide. Marxist thinkers stand with and represent the socially powerless. Like prophets of old, they call out those neglecting the vulnerable in a society. The world is full of genuine, treacherous oppression, and vulnerable people, by virtue of being "vulnerable," suffer the most harm. Marx saw real suffering created by factory life in the mid-1800s. Early Critical theorists developed their scholarship in response to the suffering created by fascism. Even if it's skewed, Marxism gives voice to people's longing for a better, more just, more equitable world.

The world suffers when Christians remain indifferent to these problems. Non-Christians become attracted to Marxist thought because he gives language to people's experience of living in a broken world with real oppression and no God coming to save them. Christians wind up attracted to Marxist thought because their denominational or educational background underplays, excuses itself of responsibility, or ignores altogether important spiritual themes like the ones listed above, usually for political reasons. Christians should pay more attention to the categories Marxists talk about and why people are drawn to them. Marx and his Critical Theory–wielding ancestors aren't the greatest problem facing the church, but failing to address the problems they see in social life with gospel answers could be.

WHAT SHOULD A CHRISTIAN DO WITH CRITICAL THEORY?

Paul said if the resurrection of Jesus didn't happen, "'Let us eat and drink, for tomorrow we die'" (1 Corinthians 15:32). CT paints a darker picture. Not only is there no resurrection—there's no God at all. Everyone fends for themselves in an absurdist postmodern world of power and profit and politics. We're left to make meaning for ourselves, live our own truth, and prevent others from getting the best of us. It's honest, but not pretty.

Among my graduate school takeaways, I learned if you're brilliant yet deny both a Creator and human beings created in his image, if the will to power becomes your endgame, all your answers to social problems eventually produce something dehumanizing, even if you're trying to make things better. Godless worldviews always make things worse to the extent that their analysis and proposed solutions deviate from biblical truth. Embrace a "Critical" worldview comprehensively and you're left with absurdity, anxiety, and meaninglessness.

However, suggesting it's exclusively a worldview whose individual theories can't be productively used by Christians as lenses through which to view society baffles me. We'll unpack this more in chapter seven, but for those who place their faith in its starting points and are fully committed to its solutions, Critical Theory may act as an all-encompassing worldview. But that's not the only option. Remember, Critical Theory is a loosely bound collection of individual hypotheses addressing many different social realities. To varying degrees, these hypotheses raise important questions about specific aspects of social life that can benefit Christians, not in terms of their *solutions* but in their *provocations*. When our theological or political precommitments create blind spots, theory can help us see again.

Libraries are full of atheists who make incisive observations about the way sinful society orders itself and the effects of that arrangement on human relationships. Should I dismiss these insights simply because they may contribute to a total Progressive package I'm inclined to reject? People *are* exploited for capitalist profit, deceived by political agendas, and manipulated by power games leading to inequalities. Unrestrained Capitalism and fascist versions of Conservatism create unjust disparities and unhealthy social relations, and the faces behind those realities are usually white, male, and espousing their alignment with Christianity. There's nothing inherently antithetical to the Christian worldview in these observations. They are concerns the evangelical world should care about but instead tends to ignore.

My own theology convinces me power and privilege will never be distributed fairly in a culture made up of sin-filled humans, at least not for any substantive length of time, and human history is the war zone where people battle for control of both. The best we can hope for is that Christians, who have theological motive to think differently, will demonstrate how kingdom people steward power, privilege, and oppression. But that won't happen unless we first take these subjects seriously.

Christian critics of CT condemn it as an ideology and warn of its danger to the faith, but they never follow up to address the problems it illuminates. We can do better. We should know our Bible well enough to see where CT insights overlap with biblical points of concern.[9] Consider these questions:

Are you able to discern when sin has become systemic?

Can you point to more than "bad choices" as an explanation for poverty?

Can you talk intelligently about how power gets used to oppress groups of people?

You may scoff at "oppression" everywhere, but in a broken world do you see it anywhere?

Why do you so easily accept and ignore the disparities and effects of capitalist excess?

Have you embraced an economic "normal" that's destructive to other neighborhoods?

How have you contributed to the gender wars beyond anything the Bible could affirm?

If you're not asking questions like these, why not? In a world where you believe there's a God, why are you not already asking these real questions about broken social life and seeking biblical answers? Generated by CT, these questions don't offend my Christian mind; if anything, they convict it. And they won't get answered by pointing to a verse or two declaring what "should be." They're complicated and take some serious thinking and spiritual discernment. This is why I disagree with the notion circulating in some Christian circles that "our human condition, and the frailty that marks us, can never be illuminated by the darkness of tattered theories."[10] Our human condition can't be solved or resolved by deifying "tattered theories," but it *can* be illuminated by them.

I think CT draws some bizarre conclusions about how to fix the world, especially when it comes to gender and sexuality. But we need to stop assuming that a Christian referencing CT in a positive light must be selling out Jesus in some heretical way. When I encounter someone declaring that "the whole purpose of Critical Theory is to divide and to splinter and to destroy," I grow angry because the point of CT is to question power, domination, and the status quo when it comes to Capitalism and Conservatism, both of which have done significant damage while skirting criticism in most corners of evangelicalism. Christians condemning CT as fundamentally divisive need to ask themselves, What is being divided and why? Why do those living in a godless world see Capitalism and political Conservatism as enemies to human flourishing? What parts need to be destroyed if we're taking everyone's life seriously? We'll never ask these

kinds of questions if we invest all our energy in demonizing CT ideology instead of grappling with its concerns.

UNTANGLING OURSELVES FROM UNNECESSARY BINARY TRAPS

Authors like Neil Shenvi and Pat Sawyer suggest, "Invariably we will
be forced to choose between critical theory and Christianity in terms
of our values, ethics, and priorities."[11] I'd argue Christians are only
"forced to choose" when they are in the market for a new worldview
or shopping for a new totality. Anchored by a Christian theological
tradition, a person can embrace the Christian interpretation of history
while gaining insight from CT observations about human interactions
and the ways power, profit, politics, and postmodern realities affect
our lives. Their concern is only valid if we accept the binary trap
created by their framing of the discussion.

Consider how they position these questions: "Is our fundamental
problem *sin*, in which case we all equally stand condemned before a
holy God? Or is our fundamental problem *oppression*, in which case
members of dominant groups are tainted by guilt in a way that
members of subordinate groups are not?"[12] A Christian should be
quick to answer "sin," but our faith clearly teaches that sin often manifests itself as oppression. We can take both seriously without compromising Christian convictions. It's the Critical theorist who must
undergo a worldview upheaval to properly appreciate Christianity, not
the other way around. Furthermore, saying dominant groups are
"tainted by guilt" for their sinful action toward subordinate groups
isn't saying anything about the capacity of subordinates to sin. That's
a different conversation.

Shenvi and Sawyer ask, "Is our identity primarily defined in terms
of our vertical relationship to God? Or primarily in terms of horizontal
power dynamics between groups of people?"[13] Again, Christians
should be quick to answer that our identity is primarily *defined* in
terms of our vertical relationship to God, but it is *affected* and *worked*

out by horizontal power dynamics between groups of people, and too often Christians don't think critically enough about those dynamics. Critical Theory doesn't recognize a personal God, so it only analyzes and interprets the horizontal. But Christians can recognize both vertical and horizontal dimensions of life without compromising their priority order.

That's the difference. When embraced as a worldview, Critical Theory must be traded in to benefit from Christianity, but a Christian can benefit from a Critical worldview without forfeiting their faith.

With all this as a backdrop, we can now begin to explore where race enters in and why so many black intellectuals are drawn to the Critical method while working to create something different.

CODA: WHY ARE SO MANY BLACK SOCIAL MOVEMENTS SHAPED BY MARXIST THOUGHT?

Most black folks I've spent life with would be considered socially and biblically conservative in the way they think about society, their conception of morality, their approach to responsible living, and their interpretation of the Bible. But in many of those friends, I sense a sympathy toward Marxian social critique regardless of their political or denominational background. Why is this?

Perhaps they're partial to Marx because he was a champion of fighting against the status quo, of speaking truth to those who hold power. Maybe it's because he assumed those with economic power would never give it up without a confrontation, and despite centuries of words and politicking and pleading at every level of society, many finally conclude that the hold of racial separation won't be released without force. In a world where genuine oppression exists, Marxists aren't afraid to name it and blame it, while those opposed to Marxism often ignore or remain silent regarding real mistreatment of people— usually people in the lower social classes who lack a voice. It's hardly a stretch to suggest minorities struggle to find voices within what gets labeled "conservative" Christianity that take seriously the racial dimensions of experiential angst. They rarely find people in more conservative spaces—whether religious or purely political—willing to be critical of power dynamics or systemic sin or the racist history and complications of Capitalism. When I ask, I get the sense that "the enemy of my enemy is my friend," and therefore they'll welcome allies from wherever they can be found—regardless of where they fall on the political or Christian orthodoxy scale.

Given the cumulative black American experience across four centuries, I'm not surprised that many might find themselves seeking more radical approaches to changing society. It shouldn't be a shock that people who understand racialization often gravitate toward others who are open to confronting oppressive power, toward people who acknowledge structural sin, who give voice to the marginalized, who aren't afraid to criticize the negative and exploitative effects of Capitalism on underresourced populations.

Heroes of the black intellectual tradition like W. E. B. DuBois, Richard Wright, and C. L. R. James were sympathetic toward Marxism and aligned with Communists in the early part of the twentieth century because Marxists took a more radical stance toward civil rights than any other political party at the time. The prospect of patient, incremental racial change didn't interest them any longer. They wanted action, not promises or platitudes. They didn't want to be slowly "integrated"—they wanted to be treated as humans *now*.

But they also recognized that Marxists, even with all their talk of a classless utopia, weren't immune from the cultural racism enveloping the Western world. White Marxists, whether purebred or descended from the Critical Theory tradition, tended to see their revolutionary future through white eyes and white concerns. This remained true even after "Father of the New Left" Herbert Marcuse suggested Marxists should quit waiting on workers who'd settled into middle-class comfort to recognize themselves as "oppressed," and instead partner with groups who literally experienced the feeling of being outcasts and outsiders every day.[14] In his 1964 book *One-Dimensional Man*, he encouraged Leftists to pay closer attention to "the exploited and persecuted of other races and other colors"—organic radicals whose everyday existence in a society that rejected them was already a form of resistance.[15] Activists should embrace the cause of social outliers: women, blacks, sexual minorities, social outcasts. In doing so, Marcuse laid the groundwork for the coalescing of race/ethnicity, gender, and sexuality as a cord of three strands in universities around the world. But he also exposed how difficult it would be for even white radicals to overcome deeply entrenched prejudices and apathy toward social patterns directly affecting black Americans.

In both academia and the broader culture, the white progressive agenda was helped considerably more by enlisting the cause of blacks than blacks were helped by white progressives. Scholars like Cedric Robinson in *Black Marxism* pointed out the inability or unwillingness of white Marxists to view the world through specifically black eyes or to appreciate the black radical tradition.[16] Black people were either minimized within the national Progressive narrative or often still blamed for their negative circumstances, and they had to wonder whether even Marxian utopia could tolerate having POC on equal ground with whites.[17]

Through the middle decades of the twentieth century, it became clear that neither European Marxists nor American Leftists would consistently represent the causes and concerns affecting black folks, paving the way for BIPOC legal scholars to center the black and non-white experience in a way not previously attempted in the world of scholarship.

If Marx built the house, and Critical Theory modernized and refurbished the rooms, then Critical Race Theory added a new wing with its own uniquely stylized decor.

5

WHAT IS CRITICAL RACE THEORY, REALLY?

The name Critical Race Theory . . .
is now used as interchangeably for race
scholarship as Kleenex is used for tissue.

KIMBERLÉ CRENSHAW, CROSSROADS,
DIRECTIONS, AND A NEW CRITICAL RACE THEORY

Critical Race Theory's ultimate vision
is redemptive, not deconstructive.

ANGELA HARRIS,
"THE JURISPRUDENCE OF RECONSTRUCTION"

RECENTLY, I WAS TALKING with a longtime friend regarding his concerns about Critical Race Theory. He was exasperated with my attempts at distinguishing between what's happening in secular culture and the conversation in the church. Finally he blurted out, "Your problem is you don't understand the difference between animals in the zoo and animals in the jungle. You are acting like CRT is caged in a classroom and don't realize it's running in the wild." It was a clever reply, but it was incorrect.

I recognize the difference between an abstract idea within the confines of a classroom and its extreme expression in the world. The "problem" he was trying to target is that I don't believe most people understand the difference between CRT as an academic discipline with many strands and multiple applications and CRT as a weaponized (Conservative) or radicalized (Progressive) political saber. When it comes to CRT, most people have a caricature in mind, a straw man, something they heard on conservative news or were fed by one of the handful of anti-CRT Christian commentators they assume are experts. They don't understand the social conditions that prompted its rise in the 1970s, how it applies today, or why after almost four decades they are just now hearing about it. They haven't tried to understand what those who created CRT believed, so they aren't able to discern true CRT from distorted applications of the original ideas. Simply put, most of the people ranting about CRT don't know what they're talking about, and they will remain in that state as long as they excuse themselves from thinking about the complicated issues it forces us to consider.

For a long stretch of time, I had daily encounters with people wanting to talk about CRT, and they all meant something different by it. More recently, it's become most fashionable to weaponize it in school curriculum debates and anything that has to do with racial history, especially Nikole Hannah-Jones's "The 1619 Project." Others have Robin DiAngelo in mind and what they've heard about *White Fragility* or workplace diversity, equity, and inclusion (DEI) trainings.[1]

I'm not unaware of the politically motivated uses of race in broader society, but I primarily care about what this conversation means for the church. Christians don't need CRT to live biblically regarding race because a kingdom-shaped worldview already supports most of what CRT seeks to rectify. Genuine CRT concepts aren't antithetical to a Christian worldview. You might disagree with them politically, but that's a different issue. That's not "woke" Christianity speaking; it's a reading of what its original authors wrote instead of the spin others put on them. That may sound shocking if you've already concluded that CRT amounts to teaching fourth graders to hate themselves if they're white or be perpetual victims if they're BIPOC. Many argue that CRT has come to include ideas outside the reach of the original tenets, and this may indeed be true, especially as the ideas get taken to radical extremes. But before trying to blame CRT for every progressive ill under the sun, we first need to understand what real CRT seeks and why it's not the boogeyman it's made out to be.

WHERE DID CRITICAL RACE THEORY COME FROM?

It's 1971, and Derrick Bell has just become Harvard's first black tenured law professor. Though now wildly popular among students as a teacher, Bell cut his legal teeth working over three hundred school desegregation cases for the NAACP Legal Defense and Educational Fund across the previous decade. Throughout the 1960s, despite tremendous resistance, federal laws produced immediate changes across society. Martin Luther King Jr. said federal law couldn't change the heart, but it could restrain the heartless, and since the passing of the first civil rights legislation in 1964, the heartless are indeed losing when it comes to formalized, socially visible racism.

Bell had been successful in many cases, and no one could question his work ethic or commitment, but his transition into academia came amid an unsettling self-realization: his efforts to desegregate schools fueled more race-driven maneuvering, and every advance seemed to be countered by groups of white folks working to reestablish racial hierarchy and segregation. White flight, the creation of separate "academies" whose requirements implicitly fostered segregation, complete disregard for the educational distinctives of black students, racially inspired nationwide conflicts over affirmative action and busing—the occasional step forward seemed to produce several steps back.

Bell's integration work wasn't helping black students the way he'd hoped. In the name of equality, he worried he was contributing to a more durable system of segregation, which led him to troubling questions: Could racism be so deeply rooted in the American psyche that it would always find a way to reassert itself despite waves of reform aimed at eliminating it? What if racism and racial disdain were simply permanent features of American life? He began exploring how a commitment to racial hierarchy had soaked into the fibers of the American psyche and concluded that a few legal pronouncements scattered around the country would never completely wash it out. So he turned away from desegregation work and began considering how race and power work together in the context of law to maintain the status quo.

In 1973 he published a casebook titled *Race, Racism, and American Law,* and for the next decade he taught at Harvard developing his own theories. Bell published articles with provocative ideas like "interest convergence," which raised the possibility that the civil rights political initiatives of the 1950s and 1960s were not primarily the result of a white moral awakening, but a response to international pressure and worldwide accusations of hypocrisy. His convergence theory suggested many white folks only made racial concessions when it benefited them. If anything, they were politically coerced, not morally compelled. By challenging the assumed efficacy of liberal and conservative approaches to civil rights, his writing confronted a particular narrative regarding American racial history and the "colorblind" neutrality of policymaking.

Bell left Harvard in 1980 to teach law at the University of Oregon. In his wake, a group of students and minority law professors from different universities continued to develop his ideas. Back at Harvard, a young protégé of Bell named Kimberlé Crenshaw organized a class and invited visiting professors to teach through *Race, Racism and American Law* chapter by chapter, filling the void created by Bell's transfer.

Fast forward to 1989. Now we're twenty-five years beyond the passing of the first civil rights legislation making racial terrorism toward black Americans illegal in public schools, places of employment, voting booths, retail establishments, and all other public accommodations across the country. Both white and black people desperately want to believe we've moved beyond race as a problem. Many want to believe that examples of racism or racial discrimination are just isolated instances of ignorant behavior and not reflective of cultural patterns or systemic sickness.

But something is still deeply wrong. Even with federal laws in place, even with a strong social liberalism backing the civil rights movement and popularizing its ideas, the experience of far too many BIPOC suggests discrimination is still mysteriously thriving. Many law scholars influenced by Bell wonder, *Why do our schools and banks and criminal justice system and housing markets and entertainment industry and professional sports still function operationally segregated in so many ways?* Intuitively, they already know the answer, one Bell popularized in their circles a decade earlier.

White America had been trying to ghost the race topic since the 1960s, and the irony wasn't lost on these scholars. Across four hundred years, white folks not only created the concept of different races and gave them meaning, but they also made racial difference the centerpiece of society, leaving black folks pleading to be treated as part of the human race. Then, just when black folks began effectively mainstreaming ideas like "black is beautiful" and "black power" and "black nationalism," white folks decided Americans should be done seeing race. But these scholars argued that we couldn't treat centuries of policy-fueled racism as though its existence and effects had miraculously evaporated. America had underestimated what it would take for lasting, effectual social change to occur and "wanted to believe that the exercise of racial power was rare and aberrational rather than systemic and engrained."[2] A handful of federal laws banning overt bigotry couldn't extinguish nearly four hundred years of racially infected state and local laws, individual belief systems, and discriminatory patterns.

So they start meeting with other minority scholars to ask how current law maintains racial hierarchy and begin thinking about how to change it. They ask, "How does law help sustain a particular racial order with whites at or near the top and nonwhites somewhere below—even after the breakthroughs of the post–civil rights decades we just experienced? How does the law continue to shield and maintain racist thought and produce—even if unintentionally—harmful racial outcomes? How does the history of American slavery, segregation, and discrimination continue to produce inequality through our legal system—and by extension, in all our social systems? If black skin has been given particular meanings in America, what is the meaning of white skin, and why don't we talk about it?"[3]

They want to legitimize race as a focus area within law curriculums and among their mostly white peers and expose how racism and racial power hide within institutions. In the late 1980s, suggesting the law should be viewed specifically through the minority experience in America was still considered a radical move. Critical legal studies, an academic branch many of them sat upon, took seriously how law could codify biases and protect elite privilege by maintaining the status quo, but it didn't emphasize race as a lens. The liberalism of traditional civil rights discourse took race and racism seriously but tended to ignore or downplay less-than-visible systemic and structural bias, and it certainly didn't publicize the historical, social, economic, or psychological results of legal decisions supposedly "won." They needed a Critical theory intentionally thinking about race, and a racial theory not afraid to be Critical.

So in 1989, when a group of these scholars (led by, among several others, Kimberlé Crenshaw) gathered at the University of Wisconsin-Madison to participate in workshop discussions, they did so around "new developments in Critical Race Theory." It was the first time this phrase was used to formally describe an approach to racial theorization Derrick Bell began teaching at Harvard almost twenty years earlier.[4]

A MASH-UP OF INTEGRATION *AND* NATIONALISM?

Take a class in post–Civil War black American history, and you'll encounter a central point of disagreement among black intellectuals. In striving for freedom, dignity, and both a stable and celebrated identity as Americans, should African Americans pursue integration or separation with "white" culture? Should they integrate into the current system, or must they separate and create their own? Booker T. Washington sought to influence white America from within the political system as it existed. W. E. B. DuBois formed the NAACP to function separately. Martin Luther King Jr. fought for policy change in Washington, while Malcolm X preached a black-is-beautiful-and-stay-out-of-our-way independence. They all wanted the same things for black folks, but they had different beliefs about how to confront the problem of race and employed different strategies along the integration-versus-separation continuum.

Integrationists tend to minimize the place and power of institutionalized racial bigotry in America. They focus on self-actualization and the ability to overcome obstacles. Conversely, separatists, or nationalists, believe racial hostility lives at the core of our national identity, and the only real option for black folks to experience full equality is to mobilize culturally and politically into a functionally separate nation run by and for blacks.

Those who coined the original CRT concepts sought a mash-up of both perspectives in their work. Their thinking went something like this: "We're not okay with the way race and racism continue to impact our daily lived experience in post–civil rights America, and we're going to talk loudly about it. Our self-actualization includes unapologetically forcing white folks to become *more* aware of race, not less. We can and will work on ourselves, but balance equals justice, and that comes through changes to both ideology and policy. We're tired of the 'race problem' only being *our* problem. We're going to dismantle and destabilize anything that continues to promote or maintain racially infected history, attitudes, and behavior. We're not setting up a separate nation for ourselves. Instead, we're going to change the systems of this one because every bit of it is already as much ours as it is yours. You just don't live like that's the case, and for too long neither have we. We're going to integrate on our terms, not yours, and that means promoting the black voice and narrative. Indeed, we're the manifestation of both integration and nationalism, only now you're going to integrate with us and start appreciating the world as we see it."

WHAT IS CRT TRYING TO DO?

What original CRT asks us to think about is complicated and multi-layered. It's not the type of content easily grasped after a quick article read on the way to a school board meeting. Early CRT requires some difficult study in law and understanding the contextual implications of laws on everyday lives, often regarding people in settings facing circumstances very different from our own. While its basic tenets are pretty straightforward, they produce cross-disciplinary implications and contextual nuances that beg for discussion, not flippant dismissals. Indeed, it's practically impossible for a single article or book chapter to capture CRT's range of topics, theories, genres, or camps.[5]

Further complicating the discussion, today both conservatives and progressives politically co-opt the letters *CRT*, stretching and weaponizing the original ideas toward extremes that go beyond what many of the original authors had in mind. But whether applied radically or in more moderate ways, the tenets of CRT can't help but seem revolutionary given their desire to confront liberal assumptions about race.

That said, it *is* possible to construct some working parameters based on the ideas most associated with CRT as a method.[6] The tenets of CRT flow out of a line of reasoning that goes something like this:

1. The racialization of American society put in place across four hundred years didn't evaporate after the passing of civil rights laws in the 1960s.

2. Race-based disparity and inequality live on, unevenly dispersed throughout our social structures, systems, and institutions for many different reasons.

3. Law helped create those imbalances and, in some cases, now maintains, supports, and covers them.

4. A Critical Race theorist seeks to reveal, confront, and reverse how dominant-culture racial power works through laws, policies, and patterns to maintain status quo racial hierarchy in the everyday lives of minority, nonwhite peoples.[7]

5. CRT precepts find application in other academic disciplines and social arenas beyond law, stripping away surfaces to expose racially skewed patterns, policies, and structural realities.

At ground zero, CRT wants to disrupt the idea that racism and racial discrimination are relics of an awful past rather than relevant categories for reflection today. It asks, "What embedded consequences can you expect after fueling a society with racism for hundreds of years, even after making it illegal to do so?"[8] CRT also disrupts the idea that race no longer plays a significant role in personal experiences, organizational dynamics, or social outcomes by intentionally provoking those who've already decided such investigation isn't necessary.

Kimberlé Crenshaw, credited with coining the phrase "Critical Race Theory," called it a "series of contestations and convergences pertaining to the ways that racial power is understood and articulated in the post–Civil Rights era."[9] It contests conclusions about how race plays out in America that fail to reflect the reality of minorities and offers an alternative explanation, and it's the convergence of anecdotes, stories, histories, departmental and national politics, and reflections on real-time results all coming together to change the way racial power is thought and talked about.

Crenshaw says CRT operates as a method more like a verb than a noun. It's not just a static body of knowledge but an active mode of questioning, seeking to uncover and expose the way laws, policies, or default patterns perpetuate race-based inequalities in different social contexts. CRT theorists expose situations where race is present but typically ignored or overlooked, or where common assumptions about race act to camouflage its presence. As law professors they asked, "How does law actually create, perpetrate, even protect racialized distinctions and racist outcomes?"[10]

In CRT, racism goes beyond the individual acts of ill-willed people. Both Derrick Bell and the scholars who followed him took individual racism for granted, concluding it would never go away no matter how many laws were passed or reconfigured. Instead, they focused their attention on how law and policy create and reinforce systemic problems related to race, where racist outcomes become an "operation of established and respected forces in (the) society," not simply the bigoted choices of random, wayward individuals.[11] When it comes to racial differences, people assume law exists to prevent racism, not to make it worse. But how might law and its applications work to maintain racial hierarchy and imbalance throughout society, whether intentional or not?

THE PROBLEM OF RACIAL RETRENCHMENT IN POST-CIVIL RIGHTS AMERICA

There's obviously been great progress, but progress shouldn't blind us to what Devon Carbado calls the "reform/retrenchment dialectic" that marks America's legal and political history. That is, every time there's a positive move forward in racial healing, a corresponding resistance arises to counter it.[12] CRT pays close attention to those "retrenchments," confronting them, interrogating them, and laying them bare so people can see the effect they have on real lives. It counters a particular take on post–civil rights America that says the playing field is completely leveled and differences exist because of choice alone, not race. CRT counters by arguing there's always a racial component at work and we need to make sure we take it seriously.

When segments of post–civil rights America rise up to say, "We don't have a racism problem anymore," CRT says, "We do, and worse, we've all been 'racialized.' We've absorbed racist ideas into the way we think and operate without even realizing they're present—or racist."

When portions of post–civil rights America say, "Racism is confined to the individual actions of people behaving badly toward one another because of latent bigotry," CRT says, "We should always call out individual racism, but racist policy and patterns reside in our social structures—schools, churches, banks, police departments, local governments, retail, etc.—to differing degrees, and we need to talk about how they work."

Post–civil rights America says, "Lady Liberty wears a blindfold. The scales of justice are unaffected by race or racial considerations." CRT says, "That's ridiculous, and it's never been true. Law is written and practiced by people influenced by all sorts of nonlegal pressures: their cultural moment, individual bias, peer pressure, political pressure, financial implications, gender, and a litany of other prejudices—including racial prejudice."

Post–civil rights America says, "Everyone's voice counts equally." CRT says, "BIPOC voices, perspectives, and experiences rarely get taken seriously against the backdrop of white norms and assumptions about how the world works."

Post–civil rights America says, "Since the civil rights laws were passed, society is set up to provide equal opportunities for everyone who participates responsibly." CRT says, "Civil rights laws confronted great overt evil, but society maintains racial roadblocks and speed bumps experienced by nonwhite people that create friction no matter how responsible they may be."

AN EARLY EXAMPLE

CRT confronts the sort of conversation law professor and early Critical Race theorist Alan David Freeman imagined in his provocative 1978 law review article, "Legitimizing Racial Discrimination Through Antidiscrimination Law."

> THE LAW: *"Black Americans, rejoice! Racial discrimination has now become illegal."*

> BLACK AMERICANS: *"Great, we who have no jobs want them. We who have lousy jobs want better ones. We whose kids go to black schools want to choose integrated schools if we think that would be better for our kids, or want enough money to make our own schools work. We want political power roughly proportionate to our population. And many of us want houses in the suburbs."*

> THE LAW: *"You can't have any of those things. You can't assert your claim against society in general, but only against a named discriminator, and you've got to show that you are an individual victim of that discrimination and that you were intentionally discriminated against. And be sure to demonstrate how that discrimination caused your problem, for any remedy must be coextensive with the violation. Be careful your claim does not impinge on some other cherished American value, like local autonomy of the suburbs, or previously distributed vested rights, or selection on the basis of merit. Most important, do not demand any remedy involving racial balance or proportionality; to recognize such claims would be racist."*[13]

Freeman built his satirical-sounding dialogue using actual reasoning and rulings from several civil cases that took place in the early 1970s. Undeterred by the presence of antidiscrimination laws established in the 1960s, other laws and accepted "norms" worked to keep discrimination in place long after the celebrations died down. He and his colleagues were interested in exposing how law not only helped construct ideas about race but also how racial power works in real time.[14]

Crenshaw said, "Rather than engaging in a broad-scale inquiry into why jobs, wealth, education, and power are distributed as they are, mainstream civil rights discourse suggests that once the irrational biases of race consciousness are eradicated, everyone will be treated fairly, as equal competitors in a regime of equal opportunity."[15] But that's simply not true if race-infused habits and patterns remain in place. In response, exposing the consequences of an unwilling stubbornness toward consideration of the ongoing effects of racial power became a central task of CRT. The profound reach of racialization could not take place without the law and legal institutions, and theorists try to expose and comprehend how they work with each other at different points in history.

TWO DIFFERENT PATHS BUILT FROM THE SAME TENETS

Exploring that power journeys down two different paths for Critical Race theorists. The earliest writers focused on the kinds of problems Freeman depicts, those having to do with material conditions faced by minority cultures because of racism: economics, criminal justice, housing, and education. Another branch grew in the 1990s, one more concerned with "matters of concern to middle-class minorities—microaggressions, racial insults, unconscious discrimination, and affirmative action in higher education."[16] These divergent paths reflect two strategic philosophies always present within CRT.

One school believes the most effective path toward realizing equality involves changing the way people think and talk about race. Like Cultural Theorists, they focus on words and power and the way meaning gets attached to cultural texts. When lever pullers controlling institutions change, material conditions will change. The other school believes just the opposite—that changing consciousness doesn't affect social structures or the policies keeping them afloat. Only more direct political aggression will bring change. Minds can follow later.

In both cases, however, their arguments flow out of a handful of concepts that emerged before the end of the century. There's been a wildly diverse range in the way they've been applied, but the basic ideas have remained largely the same.

With this foundation in place, let's turn our attention toward eight examples of specific conceptual lenses CRT requires us to look through and consider what they want us to see when we do.

6

WHAT ARE SOME TENETS OF CRITICAL RACE THEORY?

I would especially think that when charging other believers with whom we disagree with teaching "deadly ideas," "dangerous ideas and corrupted moral values," and "an onslaught of dangerous and false teachings that threaten the gospel, misrepresent Scripture, and lead people away from the grace of God in Jesus Christ," we might want to be specific about what exactly those ideas actually mean.

JOEL MCDURMON, "A RESPONSE TO THE STATEMENT ON SOCIAL JUSTICE AND THE GOSPEL"

What is lacking here is balance, nuance, and a weighing of competing interests and accounts, not to mention the principle of charity whereby one criticizes an argument by first placing it in its best light.

DOUGLAS E. LITOWITZ, "SOME CRITICAL THOUGHTS ON CRITICAL RACE THEORY"

WHILE CRT RESISTS BEING CONTAINED in a single definition, certain foundational concepts are regularly referenced as the bedrock of CRT teaching. Each of these tenets represents an idea that arose in response to prevalent beliefs working against racial progress in the last decades of the twentieth century.[1]

Thinking well about any of these ideas requires considering both the context that produced them and the contexts in which they appear today. Jazz musicians rely on "fake books" with only the basic melody and chord progression of a song. They're then expected to improvise the rest, letting their feel of the moment dictate where a song goes based on the basic structure offered. In the same way, the basic tenets of Critical Race Theory act as a sort of fake book, a starting point, an entry portal into a social situation that requires the theorist to improvise different applications.

There's no universally agreed-upon list, but here are eight of the more commonly argued ideas, defining elements, or basic tenets. For each one, we'll consider what it means, the racial assumption it questions, why it's important in real-life situations, and how it can be misused when taken to dehumanizing extremes.

RACE IS SOCIALLY CONSTRUCTED

What it means. Race is a made-up idea developed by humans to control, separate from, and feel superior to one another. Race is a human creation, labeling a group with qualities and characteristics assumed true because of appearance. It's pieced together over time, as each part of society plays its role in solidifying and spreading beliefs attached to skin color and physical characteristics. As a society we develop cultural rules about race, then "psychologically categorize" them.[2] Racial construction leads to racial hierarchy, which necessarily leads to racial superiority and racial inferiority.

What it counters. The belief that race is essential, fixed, determinant, and can legitimately be used to make distinctions between people. "Social construction" language works to invalidate assertions of essentialized superiority or inferiority based on race.

Why it's important. If race can be constructed, it can also be deconstructed. People need help dissecting why they think the way they do about different races and identifying racial falsehoods they've entertained and absorbed.

Misuse. Denying that any generally shared and observable characteristics are present among a subset of people of a particular color or racial heritage. Also, when extended to gender and sexuality, moving beyond legitimate critiques of social influence to erase divinely established boundaries and essential differences altogether.

People might be surprised to learn that in the early decades of the American experiment, social separation between white- and black-skinned people wasn't an issue. Discriminatory hierarchies had to be *created*—they didn't just naturally arise out of interpersonal encounters.[3] Perceived inferiority or superiority tied to skin color isn't a function of something innately true about humans. It's the product of man-made divisions between people, motivated by a desire to promote one group at the expense of others and usually beginning almost exclusively for economic reasons. Creating and attaching meaning to something called "race" not only helps a group justify mistreating another group but also establishes a social hierarchy to measure folks against. Race, therefore, is socially real but not biologically real. We make it up. Then we reward and punish people based on it.[4]

For example, Count Joseph Arthur de Gobineau (1816–1882) is sometimes referred to as the "father of modern racism." Gobineau proposed the existence of three races: white (Caucasian), black (Negroid), and yellow (Mongoloid). He argued that the white race possessed superior intelligence, strove for virtuous morality, and displayed admirable willpower, while the black race possessed lower intelligence, an animal nature, and a lack of morality. Based on racial "science" like Gobineau's, Americans went on to develop meanings, social rules, and laws—then judged and divided accordingly.[5]

Race and ethnicity are not the same thing, though they are often mistakenly paired or used interchangeably. Ethnicity has to do with tradition, language, and aspects of shared cultural heritage, while race ties to skin color, bodily characteristics, and the meaning ascribed to them. Understanding race as a social construct doesn't contradict the idea of God-created ethnicity whatsoever. God intentionally created people different but equal. Sinful humans exploit the differences to create social inequality. We give meaning to skin color and physical characteristics for nonessentialist reasons, and thus, race is socially constructed.

RACISM IS "ORDINARY" AND EMBEDDED IN THE FABRIC OF AMERICAN SOCIETY

What it means. Every American institution has been "racialized." That means whether we're aware of it or not, if we peel back the layers of any institution's history we'll find racist ideas, behaviors, and systemic hurdles, many of which continue to have power and consequence today. Racism was "built into the constitutional architecture of American society," and its vestiges continue to exert power throughout society.[6] This is where we get the idea that racism and racialization are systemic issues and not solely dependent on the behavior of individuals. Largely invisible patterns developed along racial lines in school systems, housing markets, hiring practices, criminal justice, and the church that all enable and contribute to the maintenance of social division.

What it counters. It exposes how focusing on the dual refrains of "I am not a racist" combined with "Racism is confined to individual acts done by individual people" creates blindness to systemic and structural racial realities. It confronts a starting point that assumes racism is a problem of the past.

Why it's important. It takes energy from constantly having to prove racism exists and redirects it toward exposing the ways it does. Then it can be confronted and corrected as necessary.

Misuse. When you start looking for racism everywhere in response to people who by default never see it anywhere, you start finding it in some places it doesn't really exist. You label things "racist" that aren't, and in trying to counter one error you wind up making another.

People get skittish at the notion that racism is "embedded" or "permanent," implying that nothing has changed or can change in the future. Nobody likes to hear they are predetermined, forever stuck in some evil they can never get free from, especially when they don't experience it directly as part of their own daily life. I share that concern at the extremes. But any deep dive into the history of social institutions reveals dark secrets about the role race played in its formation, maintenance, and sustenance.

In 1992, Derrick Bell declared, "Racist structures are permanently embedded in the psychology, economy, society and culture of the modern world." He went on to call them "integral" and "indestructible" components of American society, unavoidably normal, ordinary, and a regular part of everyday life.[7] Since most white folks had already determined that the problems associated with racism had been fading from the public square since the 1960s, imagine the response to someone suggesting we should reflect on its permanence. Which is more outrageous: Suggesting that after four hundred years of racial evil, the country healed with the passing of a few laws? Or that racism seeped so deeply into the social pores of the nation it couldn't help but remain active in its institutions?

When CRT suggests that racism is "ordinary," it means that we all live upon a centuries-old foundation laid by those who created and emphasized racial differences, attached meaning to those differences, then developed every social institution with those differences hardwired into their core. No one can claim total immunity from the racialization already baked into our social lives as Americans. White people may remain oblivious to this reality, but that ignorance only serves to prove the point that racial hierarchy became normal, justified, unavoidable, and unnoticed for those who most benefited from it. It doesn't mean it should be that way or that every square inch of social life is dripping in racism, but it confronts the notion that racism, or even racial discrimination, are outlier attitudes reserved for the less cultured or less virtuous.

If we have a systemic problem, we don't have to be *intentionally* racist to be *functionally* racist. Functional racism can play out in our hiring patterns, how we vet for leadership roles, how we choose organizational priorities, how we pay people, how we decide who gets to speak into issues and how often, where our headquarters exist, who does our employee training and development, and so on. Functional racism is a result of patterns. When those patterns produce a discriminatory effect or when they exclude minority voices and concerns, minorities are left out because of the structures in place.

When theorists say, "Racism has contributed to all contemporary manifestations of group advantage and disadvantage along racial lines," they aren't saying racism is to blame for *every* manifestation of group advantage or disadvantage.[8] Choices play a role. Class discrimination plays a role. Family structure plays a role. And race plays a role.

LEGITIMIZING THE VOICE AND EXPERIENCE OF MINORITIES

What it means. It validates the centrality of experiential knowledge, taking seriously black perspectives on what they experience instead of simply explaining them away. BIPOC voices provide knowledge gained from critical reflection on the lived experience of racism. It only makes sense that black folks would have unique insight compared to white folks regarding feelings of subordination in a white-dominant culture. If you haven't experienced it, you'll be at a deficit in your ability to understand compared to someone who has experienced it.

What it counters. Marginalization of BIPOC experience; not taking seriously black accounts of mistreatment; always finding ways to discredit or diminish the value of BIPOC experience, especially as it compares to white accounts of the same reality; and interpreting the black experience through the white experience instead of considering the white experience through the black experience

Why it's important. Black Lives Matter resonated with people not primarily because of the politics behind the words but because of the history behind them. People cry "black lives matter" because for so long they haven't.

Misuse. Drawing the conclusion that BIPOC voices are always more important than white voices. Assuming a nonwhite recounting of an experience always reflects an accurate rendering of what happened. This tenet easily devolves into "black is always right and white is always wrong." It's being misused when its user implies white voices should never be centered or should always take a back seat to BIPOC voices or that white voices should be canceled in retaliation for the many decades in which black voices were aggressively and violently snuffed out. It shouldn't mean BIPOC people can use their perspective of an experience to excuse wrong behavior, though it sometimes may come out that way.

Legitimizing the experience of minorities represents calling for a change of perspective, a demand that racial problems be viewed from the perspective of BIPOC folks instead of always through white eyes. We talk about cancel culture as though it's a new phenomenon, but until recently the minority voice being canceled has been the norm across American history.

Put in action, this tenet brings counternarratives to the table, offers different interpretations of policy, challenges assumptions made about POC, and strives to empower traditionally excluded views while believing that all-inclusiveness leads to collective wisdom.[9] It's not about BIPOC having secret access to some kind of gnostic truth. Rather, as Mikhail Bakhtin suggests, outsiders in a story may often have a fuller perception of what's happening than insiders because their "outsidedness" puts them in a better position to see what's going on.[10] If your voice is already legitimated in society, it might be difficult to appreciate the cry of those who feel constantly dismissed, to sympathize with people who sense that you consider their well-being optional.

All ethnic groups bring different eyes to social interactions. They bring different ways of communicating and understanding, and this tenet takes seriously the context and personal experience of non-dominant folks living in dominant culture. How people perceive and think about social reality gets constructed through language, and centering black voices counters the white-is-normal interpretation of daily life.

EXPRESSING SKEPTICISM TOWARD MERITOCRACY

What it means. In a racialized cultural environment, racist policies, attitudes, and patterns often make hard work and determination irrelevant.

What it counters. If you find yourself at the lower end of the social ladder, it must be because you didn't work hard enough or failed to apply yourself. It's entirely your fault. The competitive playing field is equal, whether in the job market, classroom, or financial world, and you just have to outperform or at least keep up with others and you'll be rewarded for it. In this case, skepticism suggests there may be racial complications that keep a person from succeeding, regardless of how hard they work.

Why it's important. It takes seriously the racial dimension involved in moving up the social scale and complicates why some struggle to succeed.

Misuse. Skepticism toward meritocracy can devolve into rejecting the importance of hard work altogether. We shouldn't scoff at the reality of success being tied to performance across time. Racial factors may play a role in both opening doors and shutting them, regardless of one's level of responsible living or of hard work.

I grew up with a strong sense of meritocracy. Clevelanders practically invented the blue-collar industrial vibe for this country. When I read the Marine recruiting slogan, "Never given, always earned," I assume a Clevelander penned it. Whether in the classroom or the weight room, the McDonald's kitchen, or the steel plant boardroom, you get what you earn. Hard work overcomes a host of limitations. I still believe in that principle, generally. Some get away with putting in less extra work through natural talent, but anyone who succeeds must put in *some* work. It's unavoidable.

But race complicates the sufficiency of hard work. Sometimes hard work doesn't matter because racist attitudes or racial discrimination woven into institutions negate it. CRT draws a circle around racial potholes that undermine the natural effect of hard work or that force a person to work even harder than necessary to succeed. America makes a big deal about the importance of hard work, but it also makes a big deal about the color of your skin. Critical race theorists aren't against the importance of hard work. They just take seriously how race hinders its efficacy.

American mythology encourages the notion that hard work overcomes a multitude of social sins. Critical race theorists suggest that for many, rungs on the ladder of educational or vocational or financial success are broken because of racial discrimination. Climbing a broken ladder is a slower journey, regardless of one's work ethic.

EXPRESSING SKEPTICISM TOWARD OBJECTIVITY

What it means. Law is neither objective nor separate from human frailty. In the world of jurisprudence, claims of objectivity get challenged as "a way of smuggling the privileged choice of the privileged, to depersonify their claims and then pass them off as the universal authority and the universal good."[11] Objectivity is a worthy pursuit, but when it comes to race, powerful perpetrators use it as a cover for injustice.

What it counters. Belief in the purity of jurisprudence, or that decisions are made simply by letting the law, unhindered by the vagaries of human intervention, speak to a situation. It disagrees that the law can be written from a neutral perspective since we all speak from a positioned perspective. Even if written law could manage to be objective, it's still being activated and applied by biased humans.

Why it's important. Because the application of law hasn't favored African Americans historically, often as a result of racially biased interference. This tenet changes the starting point. Instead of assuming purity of application, it assumes human bias, the cultural moment, economic pressure, power plays, class interest, and so on all influence how law gets talked about, developed, and practiced in a particular situation. When it comes to confidence in "objectivity," people always get in the way.

Misuse. Distortions may conclude objective facts don't exist at all or that we shouldn't attempt to recreate events as they actually took place. Skepticism toward objectivity can devolve into extreme forms of relativism that don't conform to reality and can rely too heavily on "disagreement discourse" rather than trying to understand what really happened.[12] In this case, we move beyond asserting every "truth" is mediated and distorted by human agency to suggest even small-t truth doesn't exist. It leaves us with "my truth" and "your truth" but without belief in the possibility of discovering "the truth" about anything.

Across American history, white folks produced evil laws and discriminatory social norms while appealing to objectivity. So CRT scholars became suspicious of all claims to objectivity, pointing out ways they were used to veil subjective discrimination and a desire to maintain status quo racial relations. They became highly sensitized to the smuggling of the privileged into proceedings, abstractions passed off as universal authority and universal good.[13] Theorists expose a long history of white people in courtrooms tending to trust their version of objectivity and their version of facts compared to dissenting nonwhite interpretations of the same incident.

Bell argues that challenging objectivity stems not from a postmodern disdain for truth but from a history of intentionally suppressing nonwhite voices.

> The problem is that not all positioned perspectives are equally valued, equally heard, or equally included. From the perspective of CRT, some positions have historically been oppressed, distorted, ignored, silenced, destroyed, appropriated, commodified, and marginalized—and all of this, not accidentally. Conversely, the law simultaneously and systematically privileges subjects who are white.[14]

If this is the case, no wonder talk of objectivity would be the target of theoretical backlash.

Some counter, "Judges, juries, lawyers and legal scholars are charged, among other things, with being objective; and if objectivity is unattainable, then so is the rule of law itself."[15] The world of jurisprudence takes pride in objectivity and reason manifested in rational argument and the linear recounting of events. But everyone knows subjectivity plays a significant role in the way a jury works, the way a judge sentences, the way lawyers make their case. Emotions interfere with reason and affect outcomes, as does the ability or failure to tell a compelling story. CRT claims that the idolatrous assumption of objectivity downplays nonrational influences on outcomes, and when it comes to cases with racial implications, this usually works against nonwhite people.

EXPRESSING SKEPTICISM TOWARD
COLORBLINDNESS AND RACE NEUTRALITY

What it means. Besides the simple fact that nobody is completely colorblind in a highly racialized culture, claims to skin-color neutrality often obscure the preservation of an already existing racial hierarchy that we shouldn't ignore. Intentional blindness isn't a virtue when justice demands we see racial imbalance caused by unjust behavior and precorrupted social arrangements.

What it counters. Both the assumption that colorblindness produces neutrality and the fear that color consciousness produces a new form of discrimination or preferential treatment. "I don't see color" often maintains status quo arrangements within existing racial inequalities.

Why it's important. Challenging colorblindness calls into question those inequalities that already exist because of racial history. It also helps people appreciate that differences should not only be recognized as something positive but also be intentionally noticed and embraced.

Misuse. The quest to not judge one another based on skin color is a good one, and recklessly confronting or shaming people who assert their innocence about race isn't helpful. Most people who aspire to race neutrality haven't thought about the racialization that's already taken place and need patient education, not shaming.

What's wrong with being colorblind? Shouldn't we all strive to judge one another by the content of our character and not the color of our skin? On one hand, of course. When colorblind means not judging people or making assumptions based on the color of their skin, we should all applaud while recognizing the impossibility of that ever being entirely true. But when colorblind prohibits us from seeing the role color already plays in a particular context at a particular time, that's a problem.

Colorblind sounds virtuous until it's exposed as a covering for status quo racial indifference, as a way of ignoring important ethnic or racial differences while privileging one's own. Colorblind often presents as a double-edged sword in the lives of POC: "You don't see or appreciate the deep cultural significance that my ethnic heritage produces. You don't see or appreciate the deep cultural damage and benefit that your attachment to 'whiteness' produces." Colorblindness can disable us from discerning injustice, masquerading as a virtue while perpetuating racial ignorance. It's a card too often played by the person who feels their preferences are at risk.

BLACK FOLKS ONLY EXPERIENCE SOCIAL CHANGE WHEN THERE'S "INTEREST CONVERGENCE"

What it means. Dominant culture will only do right by minorities when they stand to gain something from it. Black people achieve civil rights victories only when white and black interests converge, not based on the good will of those in charge. Whites will eventually promote racial advances for blacks, but only when those advances also promote white self-interest.

What it counters. Belief that liberal values withheld for centuries will suddenly be given generously and without reservation by those who control them because of suddenly awakened moral virtue. Classical liberals believe that political, economic, and social benefits will be experienced by everyone as their philosophy produces moral awakening in people. CRT cries foul at this assumption.

Why it's important. In a world where evolutionary theory becomes the predominant origin story for human beings, where survival of the fittest remains the unspoken ethos guiding our social interactions, why should anyone have confidence in the moral motivations of anyone with power, regardless of their political position? Interest convergence recognizes human hearts are evil and won't give up power or reduce the benefits they receive while hoarding power from others without intervention.[16]

Misuse. Soaked in cynicism, interest convergence is a hunch based on intentionally selective history. Taken to an extreme, it can convince a person that white people are evil all the time and never to be trusted under any circumstances. The reality is people always do things for a mixed bag of reasons. No one is really in position to judge the heart but God alone. Taken to an extreme, it leaves no room for any acts of selfless benevolence by anyone in dominant culture, ignoring the possibility of spiritual or philosophical transformation.

Perhaps Derrick Bell's first significant contribution to the canon of Critical Race Theory, the interest convergence principle recognizes that when one group of people historically benefits at the expense of another, the dominant group has no inherent incentive to change. Justice on behalf of others doesn't become a priority until there's something to be gained in return. It's morbidly pessimistic, but Bell is simply recognizing a fact of human nature. When Jeremiah 17:9 says, "The heart is deceitful and desperately wicked: who can know it?" Derrick Bell says, "Exactly."

Bell didn't come up with interest convergence in a fit of imagination. He developed it in the wake of the *Brown v. Board of Education* legislation outlawing school segregation in 1954. He maintained for the rest of his life that the circumstances of black education didn't improve after *Brown* because it wasn't decided for their benefit. So why would the government enact *Brown* when they did?

He reasoned that both World War II and the Korean War featured black men fighting alongside white men, making them unlikely to willingly return to a position of inferiority in American society, which forced lawmakers to consider at least some form of public concession. But more importantly, evidence revealed many US officials worried that the domestic evil of Jim Crow would make it more difficult to get world support in their fight against Communism at the height of the Cold War.[17] So the political needs of white people aligned with the equality needs of black people, and action was taken.

Of course, people are offended by this tenet. It undermines black agency. It minimizes the courageous actions of judges and other white authorities who use their platform for racial justice at great cost to themselves. It doesn't recognize the complexities of racial justice or the inability to represent a singular black or white interest. But while offering an honest appraisal of the human heart, it also presents an apologetic to strive for win-win compromises between different people groups despite its skeptical starting point.

INTERSECTIONALITY

What it means. A person can experience different forms of discrimination depending on the various social identities they wear in a specific context. For example, an elderly BIPOC woman in a room full of young white men may internalize different treatment by virtue of being a woman, by being BIPOC, and by being older.

What it counters. The assumption that generic antidiscrimination laws will account for the different ways a person might experience mistreatment. Also, it counters ignoring the interplay between different identities and their effect on how a person experiences the world. For example, the experience of being a black woman cannot be understood by studying only being black or being a woman, but instead must account for interactions between the identities.

Why it's important. Intersectionality takes seriously the various hats a person wears in the presence of others and the identity markers that make up personhood. It helps us recognize how dominant cultural behaviors may, intentionally or unintentionally, create stresses for a person embodying different nondominant identities.

Misuse. A hyperfocus on identity can easily devolve into a quest for victimhood, moving beyond simple awareness and instead becoming an obsession. If the quest to label oneself with more identity markers becomes more important than striving for more egalitarian relationships with the people in our lives, it results in absurdity.

Kimberlé Crenshaw first used the term *intersectionality* in a pair of essays published in 1989 and 1991, though the idea could be found as early as 1851.[18] Reading Crenshaw at the turn of the century, I remember thinking nothing could be more obvious. Drawing attention to the interaction of different forms of inequality when nondominant identities find themselves among dominant identities and calling it "intersectionality" struck me as academia taking a simple observation and making it sound more complicated. I wasn't being snarky or disrespectful to the idea—just the opposite. I'd heard enough examples of both black folks and white women feeling the weight of inequality in rooms full of white men for years. A black woman experiencing the same negative quality on two levels, each producing different relational implications for her when engaging the men in the room, makes sense.

Certainly, a hyperfocus on intersectional identities can act as an accelerant for outrage attitude, causing a person to be on constant alert for offenses. It can lock a person behind a wall of their own creation. Our current cultural moment certainly validates this concern, as it seems people are prone to play the victim in every conceivable situation.

But long before intersectionality became popularized as a concept, I'd been in plenty of ministry gatherings with BIPOC women present who would later tell me when they felt invisible, ignored, or patronized by the men leading the meeting. Can people misread or misinterpret behaviors? Of course. But the fact remains that unless the dominant group becomes sensitized to interpersonal dynamics in a setting with diverse identities represented, those bearing nondominant identities will always be at a disadvantage.

CRT ON ITS OWN TERMS

One of my chief aims in writing this book is to help people slow down and deal with the basics of CRT concepts on their own terms. I want to carefully think about the types of situations the tenets have in mind instead of reading them outside specific contexts or relying on critics who are doing the same. Conservative activist Christopher Rufo has said that in confronting CRT, he wants a "central point of attack," a way for conservatives to "push back on anti-racist programs without getting into the details."[19] But getting into the details is exactly what CRT wants to do, and it's precisely what's missing in most of the verbal chaos taking place, even within the church.

The law professors who developed CRT in the last decades of the twentieth century were responding to personal situations, perceptions of experience, and real details embedded in real contexts. They weren't a group that randomly generated some radical-sounding ideas in their leisure time just to stir people up. They were personally agitated by the unwillingness of majority culture to see what they collectively saw through their own lived experience and wanted to confront that gap in the majority vision. They meshed their own stories with the narratives of others, motivating them to speak out. The details matter.

Critical Race Theory intentionally disrupts a person's inability or unwillingness to take the truths of racial history seriously. It forces race into your field of vision and asks you to slow down long enough to allow uncomfortable questions to be asked. That's when it can be useful, even if you disapprove of its proposed solutions.

What if we invested less energy in assumptions and dismissals and instead gave more energy toward understanding why people think the tenets ring true in the first place? There's still plenty of room to disagree and reject what we disagree with, but we need a more honest understanding of what we're dismissing, and that's impossible without understanding before declaring guilt.

That said, CRT can still function in different ways for different people depending on their relationship to it. So now we will turn our attention to examining these various manifestations and how they occur.

7

WHY CRT MEANS DIFFERENT THINGS TO DIFFERENT PEOPLE

We must do better. We must repent of our shoddy, unjust presentations of CRT. We must labor to understand and evaluate CRT in light of history, political philosophy, sociology, and theology and the movement's internal diversity. This is what neighborly love demands.

NATHAN CARTAGENA,
"WHAT CHRISTIANS GET WRONG ABOUT CRT"

LIKE MY EXPERIENCE WITH CRITICAL THEORISTS, when I started PhD work, I didn't remember reading Derrick Bell or Kimberlé Williams Crenshaw or Alan Freeman, though I recognized some of their ideas. They were cynical and skeptical about how power works in favor of one race at the expense of others, but they never struck me as a threat to my Christian faith. If anything, they gave language to the way sin manifests itself in society through racism and made me think more deeply about how demonic spiritual powers attack the image of God in the world. Anchored by an understanding of Christian theology, CRT presented itself as an analytical tool for understanding how the law creates and maintains racial sin, and then it moved beyond law asking the same questions of every social institution. I always measured its observations against biblical notions of righteousness and justice. CRT didn't replace my Christianity—it served it.

The ways my classmates responded to the tenets of CRT depended on the political commitments they brought to the discussion. Real CRT confronts legal practice and the way law works to functionally maintain racist policies and patterns. But CRT is fundamentally political, concerned with practical change on behalf of people significantly influenced by those policies and patterns. That political tension created great conversations, and we moved back and forth between abstract ideas versus lived experience, political idealism versus real-life effects.

I loved the thoughtful interaction, but I started to realize what my classmates did with CRT depended first on their relationship to the mother ship of CT and its role in their identity formation. For Christians trying to understand why people have such different responses to CRT both in general society and within the church, appreciating these differences is crucial.

IS CRITICAL THEORY A FRAMEWORK OR A FAITH?

Once Critical Theory became the ground of the much broader discipline of culture studies, it quickly exploded into many subdisciplines, bringing a "Critical" edge to the study of women, sexuality, history, media, law, colonialism, and art. CRT, though initially a subset of Critical Legal Theory, moved beyond law to seek application across society.

But I noticed a person's faith in relation to Critical Theory determined both their posture and the way they'd frame ideas in class discussions regarding CRT. Their subjective relationship to theory mattered, and it affected the way they talked about CRT readings.

Traditionally religious people who remained anchored in their beliefs but gained insights while looking through "Critical" lenses.

Those already committed to a religious faith tradition engaged Critical concepts as a lens for examining social interactions, a method to interrogate how people think about themselves in relation to others, and a way to critique the negative consequences of American and global Capitalism. What can we learn from looking at specific social moments through these lenses? What conclusions might we draw if we asked questions about how different forms of power are being used and to what ends? Who does power serve in this instance, and how is it being leveraged to maintain the status quo? How could power be stewarded to help those who need it most? What does history look like "from below" among common folk instead of "from above" with the elites?

Rather than threatening their religious worldview, these concepts enhanced it by forcing them to consider how their faith tradition responds to Critical concerns. Anchored by theological commitments, a person could glean from many Critical Theory insights and observations while still rejecting Progressive conclusions or solutions.

Nonreligious people who embraced CT and all its offspring as data points comprising a comprehensive Progressive worldview. This group used Critical Theory concepts as an interpretation of history, a metanarrative explaining the beginning and end of material life. Anything having to do with "Critical" identities—race, gender, class, sexuality—functioned as a denomination whose language, topics, and debates they depended on to make sense of their life. For them, Critical Theory offered conscience-shaping, identity-forming, mission-producing meta stories, with each "Critical" lane contributing something toward their comprehensive worldview. All their thoughts about the world were processed through a Critical lens and nothing more.

Nonreligious people who maintained a conservative political bent and therefore rejected the leftist interpretation of historical events CT relied on. They went along for the ride but remained suspicious of conclusions drawn by anyone associated with Marx or his theoretical offspring. These people consistently played the role of antagonist. They scoffed at every idea associated with "Critical," always voicing a critique for our readings and class discussions. They were certainly a minority voice in this space, sounding like Fox News analysts in every discussion, and obviously at odds with CT perspectives, though they would grudgingly concede points on occasion. They weren't representing any religious faith system, just a political one.

Undecided people bouncing between traditional religious ideas and Critical secular ideologies. They were figuring it out as they went along, and CT gave them an interesting way of seeing and critiquing the world toward that end. They resonated with the general attitude and mood of Critical Theory—resisting the powerful, embracing the language of justice and care for marginalized and vulnerable populations, disdaining human oppression in all its forms, maintaining a negative posture toward capitalist excess. They *felt* their way through Critical Theories and aligned with both the language and spirit represented by reform-minded activism but wouldn't identify themselves as a Marxist or a Christian or even an atheist.

These responses taught me the difference between using Critical Theory as an empirical method and relying on it as a foundational metanarrative to explain and interpret all aspects of life. For those already anchored in another tradition, Critical Theories functioned like lenses in a frame you could wear at will. For others, Critical Theories shaped the ceiling of their universe, becoming stars whose light helped them understand their place in the world. The difference mattered.[1]

Critical Race Theory, as a prodigal offspring of Critical Theory, followed a similar reactionary path in our class. Thus, what people did with CRT depended on prior commitments. It could contribute insights to a preexisting religious worldview without taking it over. It could be another arrow in the quiver of the Progressive worldview. It could be rejected and dismissed for political reasons. It could be a curiosity for those trying to figure out what they believed about the world. It could simply be a voice representing all ignored voices among POC in a white-dominant culture. But what it *was* depended on what people did with it and where it fit into their preexisting catalog of thinking.

SO HOW DOES IT GO WRONG?

CRT concepts grew out of both the Marxist and Critical Theory traditions, but they can live independently of them.[2] Accepting the tenets doesn't make someone a Marxist or even a proponent of all Critical Theories, nor is a commitment to Marxist thought a prerequisite for appreciating what real CRT proposed.

But that doesn't mean the tenets of CRT aren't co-opted and weaponized as components serving those and other worldviews.[3] Only when the tenets are distorted or applied in an extreme way do they become problematic to me. I don't think most of my white classmates really cared all that much about the black experience in America, but they loved to talk about destabilizing the conservative political and economic systems, and if they could utilize a CRT concept to do it, they would. Black Nationalists brought their own extremism, but CRT was just one arrow in their quiver, and Black Power as a movement existed long before CRT ever came on the scene. CRT helped, but it didn't make people radicals. They already *were* radicals.

Theory doesn't prescribe solutions. Theory analyzes. People motivated by political ideology recommend solutions. Politics tries to fix what theory exposes, and different philosophies will fix what gets revealed in different ways. I learned that most people's problem isn't really with theories themselves but with the ways people try to solve the problems they reveal.

Because I believed in what the tenets critiqued regarding the application of law, the ignored racial dimensions of social life, and what they sought on behalf of marginalized people, I often found myself in the peculiar position of defending them against radical application. That may sound strange, but it's true. By their own admission, radical secular progressives want to destabilize the current order so they can replace it with their own version of how things ought to be.[4]

When CRT concepts become co-opted by people leaning progressively hard left, they are often weaponized and used to slay, especially when packaged with personal anger, pain, and nihilism. In my interactions with people, I have noticed a difference between being *Progressive* and *progressive*. Small-*p* progressives want to see social wrongs made right. They see those in power hurting others and desire justice for both parties. They want racial and gender minorities to have equal rights and protection from evil. They're not trying to do away with white people; they're genuinely trying to level the playing field in a just way.

But capital-*P* Progressive is a philosophy of life, a political movement with a particular vision whose values run contrary to most of the Christian worldview. These folks tend to be titillated by the idea of revolution, questioning everything ever produced by white, male, capitalist heterosexuals. They are better at deconstructing and destroying than building something inclusive and new. Of course, I'd say the same now about radical conservatives, who question anything attempting to disrupt the status quo that maintains the story they tell themselves about themselves. Both extremes distort real CRT, often without caring about the people real CRT serves. They end up doing their own damage with mischaracterization and partial truth.

I'm disturbed not by the tenets of CRT but by people who repackage and exploit the tenets for extreme political positions through radical application. They take statements meant to correct injustices and use them to create new ones. When they venture away from race into "race-plus" coalitions, they seek solidarity with other "outsider groups," like feminist, radical LGBTQ, or any other identities derivative of white

Progressive politics, just as Marcuse encouraged his Marxist acolytes decades before.[5] Especially in university settings, advocates of CRT are practically forced into building coalitions with other groups that share a common enemy, even if disagreement toward one another's specific agendas exists within the different camps.[6]

They partner because of peer pressure to stand together against common oppressors under the assumption that when it comes to oppression, you can't cry foul for yourself and then remain silent on behalf of others. But coupling the study of racial evil with other forms of discrimination is merely a disciplinary convenience and an effort to be at least superficially consistent, not a necessity. It's not necessary to combine the quest for racial justice with the quest to destabilize Judeo-Christian norms regarding gender and sexuality. I understand their logical alignment, but I've never felt compelled to receive them as a package. The racial corrections being sought are usually biblically aligned, while the gender and sexual revisions often are not.

This is why we find Christians who say they can use CRT as an analytical tool and others who find that impossible. One is looking at CRT tenets as corrective declarations about the way race and power work together at various points in American history, while the other is looking at CRT tenets as extensions of a Marxist political agenda striving to destroy Western culture by blowing everything up. Both can be true, depending on what role the tenets play in the life of the handler or user.

So when someone asks me what I think of CRT, I find it a complicated question. For the most part, when I read real Critical Race theorists, especially those writing in the first few decades of the discipline, I largely agree with their observations and analysis. I don't experience a threat to my Christian beliefs. My political perspectives are challenged perhaps, but not my Christian beliefs. Yet today, CRT means something far more in the ears of people than what the original tenets intended.

So if we ask whether CRT is a method or a metanarrative, an analytical framework or an all-encompassing worldview, the answer must be that it depends. CRT presents itself as a framework but can conspire in the work of worldview formation if people choose to use it that way. If you define your world by a compilation of "Critical" theories, CRT can certainly play a role in that effort.

But to accuse CRT of being an all-encompassing worldview on its own doesn't even make sense. CRT analyzes very specific aspects of social life through a focused lens. Its primary concern is limited to how racism and the law work together to produce negative realities for people or, more broadly, how race and power conspire to create structures and patterns that affect real lives. That's it. Anything more is an extension of the user's motive, not a necessary function of the ideas or their insights.[7]

HOW DID CRT BECOME SUCH A LIGHTNING ROD IN THE LAST DECADE?

Some of the uproar about what's getting called CRT is justified and some is not in both the greater culture and in the church. Like most theories, the actual tenets of CRT have always been contested among scholars whose political and philosophical commitments cause them to view the significance of race differently. Conservatives, Liberals, and Progressives share many overlapping social concerns but have wildly divergent beliefs about how to address them, what needs to change, and who is to blame for current circumstances. So we shouldn't be surprised that an emotionally charged topic like race would generate wildly different responses. But the confusion and negativity generated toward the letters *CRT* in broader culture isn't an accident of history. It's been created on purpose and has origin stories in both political and church spaces.

If you've heard about Critical Race Theory in the last few years, it's probably thanks to the work of Christopher Rufo.[8] Rufo, a senior fellow at the Manhattan Institute, became an activist celebrity overnight after sounding an alarm on *Tucker Carlson Tonight* in September 2020. Rufo discovered CRT after hearing from frustrated employees across the country who felt forced into diversity training seminars. Researching the training materials and their footnotes, Rufo discovered scholarship referencing CRT. As a result, he concluded CRT was a "distinct ideology" with "radical roots," labeling it an "existential threat to the United States" and "America's new institutional orthodoxy."[9]

While on Fox News, Rufo challenged then-president Trump to issue an executive order abolishing diversity or inclusion trainings from the federal government, seeing them as conduits for CRT. Three days later Trump obliged, saying, "Critical race theory is being forced into our children's schools, it's being imposed into workplace trainings, and it's being deployed to rip apart friends, neighbors, and families."[10] That month it was mentioned more than seventy times on Fox News, an astronomical increase from the few times it had been mentioned the previous year, and the outrage fuse was lit.

In short order, Rufo saw how CRT could be leveraged as a political saber. In a now legendary tweet, Rufo explained his strategy: "The goal is to have the public read something crazy in the newspaper and immediately think 'critical race theory.' We have decodified the term and will recodify it to annex the entire range of cultural constructions that are unpopular with Americans." Keep repeating "CRT" alongside every nontraditional idea, and you can demonize both the letters and the ideas they now represent.

In a short time span, Rufo realized his goal. "We have successfully frozen their brand—'critical race theory'—into the public conversation and are steadily driving up negative perceptions. We will eventually turn it toxic, as we put all of the various cultural inanities under that brand category."[11] Rufo wanted CRT to become a stand-in for any politically progressive idea deemed a social threat by conservatives—and he pulled it off.

By repeating that CRT is an "existential threat to the United States" or citing examples of it being "weaponized against core American values," moderate-to-conservative Americans' righteous desire to "stamp out this destructive, divisive, pseudoscientific ideology" were fully aroused.[12] Suggesting "this ideology won't stop until it has devoured all of our institutions" and "CRT prescribes a revolutionary program that would overturn the principles of the Declaration and destroy the remaining structure of the Constitution," he created Pavlovian hysteria with little effort. The Critical Race Theory brand Rufo helped create now includes—and condemns—practically anything resembling an examination of America's racial history or its consequences.[13] Ironically, CRT came into existence *to encourage* those examinations, and now they're being condemned for their association with the letters.

Part of me finds Rufo simply disingenuous. I don't like his motives as a political operative. I don't like how he hijacked the term *CRT* from those who created it, how he extended its definition and now uses it for his own purposes. I've read curriculum materials he cites in which he pulls statements out of context and makes them seem more ominous than is justified. But I have also sat through cringey diversity trainings and understand how it can leave people feeling worse.[14] I believe many of the examples he cites reflect a progressive attempt to bring their definition of equity to workplaces. I don't know how effective DEI programs are in bringing about racial and ethnic understanding in secular workplaces, but I'm guessing they don't have a good track record.[15] I'm in favor of crosscultural education, but people don't like having education forced on them, especially when it involves a topic they're invested in avoiding.

For Christians, what Rufo did is problematic on two levels. First, he demonized the term *CRT* and all the language that comes with it so that now people won't explore what any of it means for themselves. Second, he demonized all forms of diversity training, including missionally driven approaches to cultural competency. I don't get the sense there's much effort invested in separating bad DEI from good, nor even discussion on how to tell the difference. It's easier just to reject it all and remain unchallenged in our cultural literacy.

If a distortion travels halfway around the world before the truth puts its boots on, then we shouldn't be surprised at either the hysteria or the confusion surrounding a discipline most people had never heard of until the politicians—and Christians influenced by the worldview of those politicians—got ahold of it. However, the framing of Critical Race Theory as an unbiblical threat to the church was already circulating several years before Rufo sounded his alarm.

EVANGELICAL CONCERN OVER CRT

At the start of the 2010s, several cultural events led to more denominations and parachurch organizations focusing on race and racial justice. I remember sitting in a YMCA parking lot in February 2012 as my car radio broadcast the senseless murder of seventeen-year-old Trayvon Martin at the hands of George Zimmerman and being dismayed learning of Zimmerman's acquittal. Then came the highly publicized, one-after-another black-skinned deaths at the hands of police officers, beginning with Eric Garner pleading, "I can't breathe" on a sidewalk in New York City in 2014 and culminating in the viral murder of George Floyd outside a corner store in Minneapolis in 2020.[16] After the murder of Martin, the Black Lives Matter (BLM) movement gathered steam. It was a loosely connected group of activists who formed demonstrations protesting racially motivated violence against black people. Politically motivated themselves, BLM both provoked and contrasted with the "law and order" rhetoric undergirding the election of Donald Trump in 2016 and the evangelical support of his presidency.

I remember being both surprised and encouraged that several influential Christian conferences with significant attendance and social media followings foregrounded the topic of racial justice through key-notes and panels in response to these and other racially charged cultural events.[17] At least one keynote at each of these conferences addressed the need for white evangelical Christians to take the topic of race more seriously, and I either attended or heard sessions from all these conferences.

Some speakers explored the systemic dimensions of racism and racialization and suggested the ongoing need for reconciliation between races, the possibility of personal or pastoral complicity in racial trauma, or the local church's role in speaking against injustice in their corners of the world. Speakers challenged listeners to consider what it feels like to be a minority ministering or attending church in majority culture and how aligning with the politically motivated conservative right causes people to miss important biblical themes concerning vulnerable populations. Nonwhite evangelicals had discussed these topics for years, often within the same organizations now foregrounding them at their conferences, but for most conferees they were relatively new concerns addressed with language they'd never heard before and applying Bible passages to contexts they'd not considered. The backlash was swift and aggressive.

In talking about justice, racism, and social responsibility, often using language and assumptions of CRT alongside Bible passages to reinforce their points, these speakers produced a swelling fear that "ideologies currently stylish in the left-leaning secular academy" were now taking over the church, presenting "a more ominous threat to evangelical unity and gospel clarity" than anything else in recent history. They were charged with "trying to get evangelicals on board with doctrines borrowed from black liberation theology, Critical Race Theory, Intersectional Feminism," generating concern that previously orthodox institutions, pastors, and teachers were catering to a progressive agenda by smuggling unbiblical teaching into the minds of their followers.[18] All of them were variously accused of coddling CRT, of trying to be "woke," of catering to younger progressive-leaning church members, of allowing a great heresy to compete with the gospel, of smuggling Marxism and Critical Theory into their congregations, and of introducing a new "canon" through both non- and Christian-authored books.

The result is that "large numbers of Christians who now hear unfamiliar or unpopular arguments about race not only think those ideas are 'CRT' but also that they're positively unchristian and poisonous to their souls."[19] My goal in writing this and the previous chapter is to show that if we slow down and pay attention to what CRT tenets ask us to think about and the contexts they're addressing, they aren't a direct threat to Christian doctrine. Similarly, I want you to see how one's relationship to "Critical" determines the ways a person uses and applies CRT. On inspection, the tenets of CRT are not "unchristian," and they are only "poisonous to souls" if the soul is already poisoned.

Some fear we're suddenly focusing too much on race in the church. I get that. I believe some probably *are* emphasizing it too much by overcorrecting for historical neglect. But I'm more fearful that the demonization of CRT and subsequent labeling and rejection of anything addressing racial injustice will leave us even less capable of thinking biblically about the complications of American racism and ongoing racialization. Most of the talks from those conferences are available online, and in re-listening to them I struggle to understand why there's such a Christian backlash, unless the concern is less about Bible and theology and more about politics.

For example, speaking at Together for the Gospel (T4G), Pastor David Platt asked his mostly white audience, "Have we been, or are we now, slow to speak and work against racial injustice around us?"[20] He answered his own question with a "resounding yes" and asserted that white evangelical pastors and church leaders in the United States have collectively been hesitant in this area within their sphere of influence. Because of their relative silence, pastors have historically widened and, where silence is still the norm, are currently widening the racial divide in our country.

He then proposed six corrective action steps in response to the gospel:

1. Look into the reality of racism.
2. Live in true multiethnic community.
3. Listen to and learn from one another.
4. Love and lay aside our preferences for one another.
5. Let's leverage our influence for justice in the present.
6. Long for the day when justice will be perfect.[21]

Platt was crushed on social media for this message, and many in his own church took issue with it. Why? Some believed his message implied that all white pastors are guilty of racist attitudes. Others didn't like him defining racism as "a system in which race profoundly affects people's economic, political and social experiences" instead of sinful individual actions toward those who are different from us. Still others simply heard "race" in the context of a message and immediately assumed "woke."

In *Divided by Faith: Evangelical Religion and the Problem of Race in America*, Michael O. Emerson and Christian Smith long ago provided substantial evidence for what was already hidden in plain sight: across white evangelicalism, it's difficult to find congregations acting like Christians when it comes to thinking about or addressing race.[22] Unless a pastor has intentionally countered this trend within his own congregation, guilt by association deserves consideration. In a different context, Platt's six points could have been part of dozens of messages that wouldn't have caught anyone's attention. But attaching them to race caused an uproar.

In another case, Ligon Duncan wrote the foreword to Eric Mason's *Woke Church*. In it he confessed that as a young seminary professor teaching ethics, he entirely skipped racism. He admitted, "It did not even occur to me that this was a pastoral issue that I needed to prepare future ministers to address biblically in the church, much less in the communities where they would serve." From his own upbringing he saw the damage of racism firsthand, but now he didn't address it with men who were going to minister "in places where overt racism in the church (e.g., majority white churches denying membership to black Christians) was still an ongoing reality."[23] For his efforts, he was called "compromised," an "enabler of the social justice movement," and not to be trusted.[24]

Max Lucado received similar treatment when, just months after George Floyd was killed, he got on his knees in front of three thousand people at a multichurch event in San Antonio and prayed, "I am sorry that I have been silent. I am sorry that my head has been buried in the sand. My brothers and sisters are hurting, and I am sorry. I made them to feel less than. I did not help. I did not hear. I did not see. I did not understand." Dorian Williams, a black pastor and organizer of the event, said, "Never in my life have I ever seen a white person say to me . . . that I'm sorry."[25] Williams continued by extending forgiveness and exhorting the crowd to do the same with people in their lives. "Max Lucado bows to the woke mob" and "Max Lucado just bowed like a coward to the outrage mob of this day" were responses waiting for him, and he had to defend his gesture on podcasts and in interviews afterward.[26]

These are men who haven't changed their theological moorings. They haven't deconstructed their faith. As men of God, they've simply realized their passivity in the face of real injustice and are trying to address it.

When it comes to race in the church, CRT isn't the problem. It wasn't before people heard about it and won't be long after we stop talking about it. The problem lies somewhere deeper, and it's worth digging for it.

8

HOW CHRISTIANS GET RACE WRONG: WHY CRT ISN'T THE PROBLEM

Although the ways in which we will live out the gospel mandate of becoming one new humanity may take somewhat different shapes in different subcultures . . . certainly we must not be perceived to be knee-jerk reactionaries who are dragged into racial reconciliation kicking and screaming, bringing up the end of the pack, the last to be persuaded."

D. A. CARSON, LOVE IN HARD PLACES

You can't address a problem you won't admit exists.

EMMANUEL ACHO, "UNCOMFORTABLE
CONVERSATIONS WITH A BLACK MAN"

I'M IN REGULAR CONVERSATION with two different groups of people. There's the mostly white crowd with a smattering of non-whites that despises what's happening to American culture because of progressive politics. They're concerned about leftist political policies, the cultural decay wrought by the educational system and the entertainment industry, and the retooling of American thought through the media and legal professions. Forced diversity training. False notions of justice. Cancel culture. Erasing of moral lines, especially relative to gender and sex. Group condemnation through identity politics. All of that *is* happening, and it feels like a threat to conservative, upper-middle-class American life. There's concern that the gospel message is being changed to accommodate Democratic values and talking points.

When it comes to race, this group fears that Christians dabbling in CRT-as-an-extension-of-CT-as-an-extension-of-Marxism are enabling a satanic worldview to seduce the church. They proudly strive to be anti-antiracists, viewing Ibram Kendi and others as either creating a problem that doesn't exist or exacerbating a problem that's trying to go away.

The other group, mostly POC with a smattering of whites, has been appealing to the Bible for years to focus white evangelical attention on issues surrounding race and ethnicity. They're exasperated by Christian brothers and sisters' inability to see the effects of living in a racialized world. They perceive an unhealthy commitment to Republican political values that ignore biblical teaching on immigration, real oppression, prejudice, restorative justice, and the misappropriation of power. This ignoring occurs at best because of those themes' association with the increasingly radicalized Democratic Party, and at worst to maintain a cover for old-school supremacist power structures.

These folks are lighthouse workers who say CRT illuminates areas of neglect that white Christians have avoided since the first slave ships landed on American shores in the 1600s. Though they have a high view of Scripture and submit to its authority in their lives, they might use language borrowed from Marxist or Black Power or even liberation theology to talk about relational conditions in the church where they see biblical overlap. Paranoia surrounding CRT becomes the latest excuse for ignoring biblical themes that don't align with

Republican or white evangelical politics or theology, another way for white Christians to avoid talking points that matter to POC.[1]

CRT language has been circulating since the early 1970s (and arguably long before that), but most people in Christian circles never heard of it until Fox News and social media feeds started attaching it to almost anything in the news regarding race. Now it's considered the greatest threat to the church since the Reformation in some corners of evangelicalism. That's quite a statement, and whether you agree with it or not, it needs to be taken seriously.

In my ministry world, I've heard people secretly complain, "Race is all we ever talk about anymore." At times, I've felt that myself. The extremes pull at us, either never talking about it at all or making it the centerpiece of every ministry event. The question is, are we actually *changing* because of all that talking?

Complicating matters, most Christians don't arrive to the current conversation with a history of substantive preaching or teaching on the topics associated with CRT like racism, ethnicity, power, oppression, social and economic inequality, and immigration, leaving us vulnerable to the loudest voices from both sides. Frankly, it's easy to align ourselves with whoever seems to represent most credibly what we already believe.

HATING AND SLANDERING IN THE NAME OF JESUS (OR ON BEHALF OF JESUS)

One article describing the above breach concludes that for Christians caught in the divide, "Unity is fundamentally no longer tenable."[2] That should be a ridiculous statement to Christ followers. I understand the tensions, but unity only seems impossible if we've allowed ourselves to operate like the world—being overly reductionist, creating and attacking straw men, assuming truth resides on a "side," and convinced of the other's heresy. It's become too easy for Christians discipled by our political climate to see enemies wherever there's initial disagreement instead of realizing that what our experience most needs might be represented by that other side.

I can tell you for sure what will not produce unity. Sometimes I get the sense that people on both sides of the race debate meditate on verses from versions of unauthorized Tribal Bibles:

- Be kind to one another, tenderhearted, forgiving one another as God in Christ forgave you—unless people talk about race in a way you think is unbiblical, then you can be mean as snot in the name of protecting the gospel.

- Share one another's burdens—unless you don't think they'll minister to you exactly the way you want, in which case you can just keep to your own.

- When you cared for the least of these you cared for me, unless you voted Democrat—then you're a deluded Marxist bound for hell.

- But I say unto you, forgive one another seventy times seven— excepting for microaggressions, after a handful of which you can cuss them out and keep receipts.

- Do justice, love mercy, and walk humbly with your God as long as it involves abortion or human trafficking but not race or poverty—and never challenge Capitalism or the United States government.

Caricatures. Assuming the worst. Excusing vengeance in the name of righteous anger. Sticking to a narrative about people even after it's been shown false. Using quotes to hear what one wants to hear instead of seeking the meaning of the speaker. None of this helps bring healing. It only aids the forces of darkness. This negative posture comes from both directions, but it seems especially virulent toward people initiating conversations about race.

I once wrote a paper on a slice of Marxism called "commodity fetishism." I chose the topic after we briefly discussed it in class because

I wanted to argue that by rejecting belief in the supernatural, Marx fell short in his analysis of the longings of the human heart. I thought this "fetishism" idea would be a great prop to smuggle Christian theology into the mind of my atheist professor. I was pretty proud of it.

It came back to me with "UNACCEPTED" scrawled across the top. I arranged a time to meet with him, convinced his rejection came from his own anti-supernatural worldview. I showed up braced for a fight, armed with my best apologetics for the existence of God, but it turned out my Christianity wasn't the problem. The paper was unacceptable because I misrepresented Marx. He said I was entitled to my supernatural worldview, but I wasn't allowed to use Marx as a straw man for my own purposes without first making a good faith effort to understand his point about "fetishism." He was right. I couldn't have cared less about understanding his point. I was consumed with making mine.

I know there are exceptions, but most of the Christian voices being maligned as woke heretics are trying to have different conversations with their people than what they're being accused of. Calling people Marxists or racists without context, conversation, or appreciation for complexity is simply wrong. To read that someone with an impeccably orthodox history is suddenly an "unashamed Marxist" because they talked about race using secular language is not only absurd but treacherous slander. Conversely, an isolated comment or incident that smells racist doesn't mean the perpetrator behind it is actually racist. Giving ourselves permission to assume the worst without real conversation needs to stop.

THE GREATER THREAT: CHRISTIANS WITH AN "UNCRITICAL RACE THEORY"

Despite the claim that CRT is the greatest threat to the church, I expect this Christian storyline to fade away as quickly as it arrived. Like the secular news cycle, modern church controversies tend to have a short shelf life before being replaced by something else. My concern is that after people stop fretting about CRT in the church, we'll still be left with the real problems it seeks to address in the first place.

CRT strikes me as the very kind of Marxist-inspired ideology Carl Henry warned us would become attractive to people who weren't receiving compelling Bible solutions—not because the Bible doesn't address issues like race, but because those with platforms weren't using them to teach what the Bible says about it. When I hear Christians using language borrowed from sociology, Critical ideology, or radical progressive social justice, I don't immediately assume heresy. If anything, I assume they have legitimate concerns about legitimate issues the Bible speaks plainly about, but they either don't know their Bible well enough to answer with theology or they've been taught a truncated, personalized theology devoid of confrontation with social sin.

For the sake of the gospel, we should be more concerned about the consequences of identifying as a Christian while maintaining what Rasool Berry calls an *"uncritical* race theory." Anti-antiracism rhetoric from some leaders within evangelicalism convinces us to focus on distortions of CRT as the critical problem while excusing our negligence toward more longstanding ones. By devoting all our energy toward crushing every aspect of the secular antiracist agenda, we allow legitimate interpersonal and theological racial concerns to remain unaddressed, effectively throwing the baby out with the bathwater.

Race is one of those subjects that Christians should have the best answers for, but far too often we're more resistant and less able to engage it meaningfully than people outside the church. Christians should be running with theological vigor toward words like *racism*, *justice*, and *oppression*. Failing to think substantively about Christian witness in a racialized culture reminds us of Carl Henry's concern. Unless we're intentional to fix it, we'll still face that catastrophe long after the CRT crisis fades away.

If you are part of the tribe genuinely trying to understand where blind spots exist in the churches' engagement with race and ethnicity, consider the following as an example of how the race conversation gets distorted and thrown off-track before we're even given a chance to think about the real issues causing concern for POC.

HOW TO CREATE A STRAW MAN

I'm listening to a panel of men who helped construct the *Statement on Social Justice*.[3] Nearing the end, the moderator asks the panel to collaborate in a mental exercise. He offers a Christian or evangelical term and wants the "postmodern, intersectional equivalent" from his colleagues.[4] Obviously, he's framing them off against each other as competing philosophies of life. He says the words on the left, and they answer with the words listed on the right.

Original sin / white privilege/racism/patriarchy

Gospel/born again / woke

Sanctification / activism/saying the right thing

Orthodoxy / political correctness/expanded canon

Indwelling of Holy Spirit / unification around oppression

Church discipline / public shaming

Reformer Martin Luther / Martin Luther King Jr.

Redemption / perpetual penance

Canon of Scripture / the new canon of sociology

I participated in years of classroom discussions over Critical readings in a secular institution. It's not an exaggeration to say something like the right column has congealed into a sort of worldview, but it's more a reflection of Progressive political influences, a bricolage of Critical ideas contributing to a radical mood and posture. Further, having embraced this worldview, the people I know who use those words the way the panel referenced them have nothing to do with the gospel of Jesus Christ. They've already rejected the authority of Scripture and harbor disdain toward those who claim the name of Christ. They use those words for fundamentally political motives and are seeking to destroy what they see as Conservative strongholds in their world. These men are correct in pointing out a cultural development coinciding with and loosely labeled secular "wokeness."

But I've been in this discussion around Christian people since the late 1980s, and "the perpetual penance of white people" has never been a goal of my BIPOC Christian friends—or white friends who've been influenced by them. This panel acts as though "penance" has characterized the historic posture of their denominations and congregations regarding both racial history and current racial realities, but I think my BIPOC friends would be overjoyed if this were actually so. They aren't replacing the Bible with a "new canon of sociology." If anything, they're using sociology to describe racial sin and point out issues the Bible already speaks about but many of its readers seem to miss. They're resorting to sociology because those most committed to the "sufficiency of Scripture" seem insufficient in their ability to interpret it when it comes to race, the powerless, and the politically vulnerable.

I've never experienced anyone in my Christian circles attempting to replace the indwelling of the Holy Spirit with an apparently more powerful "unification around oppression." I *have* heard hundreds of stories (usually accompanied by great emotion) reflecting the feeling of "otherness" ministering in predominantly white spaces and the comfort derived from being with other BIPOC who understand—or with white folks who at least try to understand. They're definitely unified around having shared painful experiences and unified with others who will grieve with them in the ache, frustration, and exasperation—but they're not trying to replace the Holy Spirit in their lives.

White privilege, racism, and *patriarchy* have wildly different connotations depending on who is using the words and how they are being used, but in my conversations with Christians trying to wrestle with their lived experience, those words aren't taking the place of original sin—they expose its manifestations in real time. The ideas themselves are worth exploring within and through a Christian worldview.

The anti-CRT crowd is right that Christianity is under attack in the culture at large. We're trying to be salt and light in the midst of non-Christian, Jesus-rejecting worldviews that would love nothing more than to see Christianity wiped from the face of the earth. And to be clear, I'm against any spirit that denies Christ or attempts to make sense of life under the sun without the cross of Christ. I'm against the imposition of any worldview seeking to erase biblically rooted moral boundary lines. I'm against a worldview that believes life's problems get solved through the acquisition of power or that political power or coercion of any kind will effectively eradicate racism, inequality, or mistreatment of people. In any age, we can name ideologies that have declared war against Christianity, and that battle is real.

But it's a vicious misrepresentation to depict every pastor trying to talk about the racial climate of their congregations and the church at large as a Marxist or woke social justice warrior or heretical sellout—even if they're using Marxist-inspired terms to do so. It's a distortion to constantly conflate Christian terms with leftist equivalents every time someone wants to talk about "privilege" or "oppression" or "lament" in the church.

Christians constantly warning each other to beware of signs that their church is "going woke" when they use certain language isn't helping the racial discussion—it's empowering those who already avoid it to feel justified in ignoring it more.[5] We can't educate ourselves or personally decide whether terms like *white privilege* offer helpful insights when they've already been demonized without discussion.

Far more people are questioning (and in many cases leaving) the faith because of negative evangelical response to conservative media-constructed caricatures of CRT than because they've dabbled in legitimate CRT categories and now view Marxian or Materialist or academic sociology or any number of ungodly isms a more attractive faith home.[6]

Consider the impression left on BIPOC men and women in the church when (mostly white) folks with a social platform suddenly see the need to write huge documents and organize conferences and sound alarms because of what they perceive to be an unbiblical approach to social issues—Critical Race Theory in particular—but don't see any current social oppression or racialized structural patterns or mistreatment of particular groups or a need to confront any of it (since for them it doesn't exist) with a gospel response. For many nonwhite folks, that selective application of energy regarding race by white leaders inside the parameters of evangelicalism has been the consistent experience across the decades of their lives. It's real. And it's been a problem affecting the spread of the gospel in minority communities much longer than the onset of Progressive ideologies supposedly making their way into local congregations.

Anti-antiracists suggest we should be primarily concerned with the *effects* of CRT and not its intentions, and I find myself offering the same warning to them. Their intentions may be to protect the church and biblical authority, but their rhetorical strategy enables people holding an unbiblical approach regarding power, justice, and concern for marginalized people groups to remain unreflective about these issues from a biblical perspective. Too many Christian minds are shaped more by their politics, not their prophets, creating seismic problems that predate CRT.

STOP ASSUMING "WOKEISM" EVERY TIME SOMETHING SOUNDS "WOKE"

Some folks overreact to hearing Marxist themes, as though learning a term was used by Karl Marx negates the possibility that it might be true or have a biblical corollary. Marx hated Christianity, but that didn't stop him from addressing biblical topics. Many in the evangelical world hear the word *oppressive* used in reference to a POC's experience and immediately conclude the topic should be forbidden in church without even asking why that person feels oppressed or what they mean by the word. We coexist without asking what it feels like to be one of a small number of nonwhite people serving among mostly white folks or what they wish we knew about their experience in our community. Too many squash discussions in Christian circles because they also are talked about in an unbiblical way in secular circles, but Solomon made observations through an oppressor/oppressed lens long before Karl Marx, as did most of the minor prophets.

It's a problem when we hear certain words and immediately think in terms of politics instead of recognizing an issue of biblical concern. It's a problem if, for whatever reason, we hear the word *oppressive* and think Karl Marx and not King Solomon (Ecclesiastes 4:1); if someone concerned for the poor brings to mind Al Sharpton instead of the prophet Amos (Amos 8:1-12); when we're confronted with a failure of justice on our watch and we think BLM instead of Micah (Micah 6:6-8); when we hear racism described as "a founding pillar in America and the church" and think Nikole Hannah-Jones, founder of the 1619 Project, instead of Absalom Jones, founder of the AME Church; when the word *immigrant* recalls ICE raids and Trump's border walls keeping out illegals instead of Jeremiah, who warned his listeners to bring about justice and righteousness, to rescue the disadvantaged, and to not tolerate oppression or violence against the immigrant, the orphan, or the widow (Jeremiah 22:3).

Ibram Kendi doesn't have the answers we need for the problems of race in the church, though he deserves respect for having thought about them more than most Bible believers I know.[7] Replacing the Bible with regular readings from a CRT handbook is not the way forward, though they can be helpful as supplements. But being reactionary and chasing red herrings every time race gets mentioned won't produce the righteousness God requires, either. I'm not sure which is the greater problem—being ill equipped to think biblically about the structural issues CRT exposes or being unable to discern where CRT overlaps with biblical concerns and ethics—but they are both problems.

THE WORK: DETECTING AND DISMANTLING RACIAL "WALLS OF HOSTILITY"

The conversation about race among Christ followers has a different launching point, motive, and end goal. The racial "oneness" idea isn't just a trendy wokeness concept, nor is it a Trojan horse covering for Marxist or socialist radicals sneaking into the body of Christ. It was Jesus' expectation all along for those who counted themselves as followers. But oneness doesn't just happen. Jesus had to pray for it, as though it requires spiritual intervention to disrupt our normal ways of relating.

In Jesus' longest recorded prayer, he asks that his disciples "be one" as he and the Father are one (John 17:11). This must have been startling for everyone who could hear his voice. If you're in the listening crowd, you've been taught to hate Samaritans. It's likely you resent Pharisees or Sadducees or any other religious leader. You loathe and fear the Romans occupying your land. All non-Jews deserve judgment, but you feel almost the same toward compromising Jews working as tax collectors or any others conspiring with the Romans. If you're a man, you've been taught to treat women like second-class citizens. If you're healthy, you avoid lepers and anyone unclean. Even in the crowd around you, folks are getting on your nerves while you're listening to Jesus. Separation and hostility come naturally; oneness does not.

Jesus also prayed "for those who will believe in me through their message, that all of them may be one, Father, just as you are in me and I am in you. May they also be in us so that the world may believe that you have sent me" (John 17:21-22). He was praying for us, implicating his future followers' oneness with evangelistic outreach, another mind-blowing concept his original hearers wouldn't have categories for. Later, as the church grew and worked to understand what it meant to follow Christ together, Paul explained the mystery of Christ's blood creating peace between humans and God, a peace fusing both Jew and Gentile into "one new humanity out of the two" (Ephesians 2:15).

Paul's words would have been even more radical in the ears of first-century Jews and Gentiles than they are for Americans today. They'd invested centuries toward building religious, political, and ethnic walls between one another and took those identity-establishing walls very seriously. Christ's life, death, and resurrection dissolved not only the individual, law-based breach between people and God but also the collective identity behind their cherished and entrenched labels. They were to become something different, "one new humanity," a confounding reality for everybody familiar with their historic disdain for one another. People who once worked to build hostile interpersonal walls based on their differences were exhorted to dismantle those differences forevermore in submission to their shared oneness in Christ. Ethnic and cultural distinctions still matter, but they're secondary to our primary identity as "one" in Christ.

But what does it mean to be "one" with each other? Jesus' work on the cross guaranteed certain things positionally true in heaven, but it takes our intentionality to make them conditionally true on earth. Oneness for Christians is positionally guaranteed, but it cannot be conditionally assumed. Put another way, we are one in Christ in our standing before God as you read this, but in our present condition, experiencing the oneness Jesus prayed for takes work. If we want to enjoy racial and ethnic oneness within the church, it requires acknowledging and addressing what is broken instead of pretending decades of hostile wall building simply disintegrate when we claim Bible verses for ourselves or because we're not experiencing racial tension in our immediate relational circles.

Jesus' blood is sufficient, but for oneness to become a norm in our congregations, we must examine walls of hostility wherever they still exist and commit ourselves to their dismantling. We need to look a little closer at what humans have done—and still do—to disrupt

God's wall-destroying work both inside and outside the church. Whether walls are torn down will depend on real-time choices made within the body of Christ.

It's an evil historical incongruity that across centuries in this country, white Christians invested in and contributed to building walls of hostility between themselves and black folks, Native Americans, Asians, and Latinos. It's our collective heritage as white-skinned people, whether we acknowledge it or not, whether we're currently involved in "wall building" or not. Our level of personal guilt will be relative, and there are certainly differences between us, but if you're white skinned, you share a heritage with those who are set apart from those who are not.

Too many speak as though we were nearing racial harmony when suddenly evil intruders under the guise of CRT started building racial walls sometime in this century or in the waning decades of the last.[8] But walls of hostility that were present fifty years ago are still standing strong in many places. They may have been partially torn down, but they leave behind remnants whose jagged edges affect interpersonal relations today. Examples of racial healing and racial trauma coexist alongside each other across the country. We can't assume either represents the entire story at this moment. It takes discernment, but for too many white Christians, an assumption and posture of positional healing seems easier to assume than engaging ongoing conditional trauma. It's easier to embrace the conditional possibility of dividing walls of hostility being torn down without appreciating the real-time work needed to bring it about. Instead of assuming that if you can't immediately see them they don't exist, ask what role you can play in detecting and dismantling them in your relational spaces. We need to invest more energy in our own stumbling blocks when it comes to thinking biblically about race and less energy toward concern about the boogeyman of CRT, Marxism, or whatever ism we perceive to be currently threatening Christian doctrine.

9

FIVE STUMBLING BLOCKS TO THINKING CHRISTIANLY ABOUT RACE

The churches are wrong not because they haven't obeyed
the politically correct agenda, but because they haven't
obeyed their own foundation charter . . . Rejecting racism
and embracing the diversity of Jesus' family ought to be
as obvious as praying the Lord's Prayer, celebrating the
Eucharist, or reading the four Gospels. It isn't just an extra
'rule' we're supposed to keep. It is constitutive of who we are.

N. T. WRIGHT, "UNDERMINING RACISM"

If I love you, I have to make you conscious
of the things you do not see.

JAMES BALDWIN, "THE CREATIVE PROCESS"

I'M WITH FIVE THOUSAND CRU MINISTERS at our biennial staff training conference. Latasha Morrison finishes her talk on racial injustice and asks us to stand together to engage in a group exercise. She's going to recite sentences, and at the end of each one, she wants us to respond with, "We lament."

Cue the discomfort. I don't like the feelings I'm anticipating, and I sure don't want them forced out of me in a college gymnasium standing with five thousand people, most of whom I don't know. This is my fourteenth staff training since 1992. We're used to celebrating ourselves at these training events, not mourning our failures. I'm already on edge.

Everyone is on their feet. There's palpable stress in the air. Inside the next three minutes reside all the arguments, all the disagreement, all the misunderstanding circulating throughout the evangelical world regarding the ominous CRT and the "race in the church" issue.

Latasha starts by asking us to acknowledge that we don't seek restorative justice that benefits everyone.

"We lament."

We do not defend the oppressed, take up the call of the fatherless, or plead the case of the widow.

"We lament."

We've mocked the poor with our partisanship and apathy.

"We lament."

We've stood by as lies of racism became founding pillars and structures in America and within the church. We've allowed agendas of empire and dominance to infiltrate the church.

"We lament."

We've developed church denominations while excluding the voice of the global church due to racism and racial segregation. We've tolerated racial hierarchies and structures of privilege that some have benefited from and others have been oppressed by. We've ignored the cries of children because they weren't our own. Discounted the pain of mothers because they weren't our own. Turned a blind eye to the affliction of black and brown men and women because they were not our own.

"We lament."

We've replaced God's supremacy with idolization of a nation and racial identity. We have not required justice, we have not loved others well, and we have not walked in humility and in our brokenness.

"We lament."[1]

Latasha is smart. She knows what she's saying will get a reaction out of people. Her statements demand critical reflection on multiple levels. I am forced to consider them as an individual and as a minister in Cru. I think about them as an evangelical and a member of a local congregation, a United States citizen and a white person, and each association creates different feelings relative to my need for lamentation. I don't like any of what I'm feeling, and I find myself looking for a justification to not think about what she's saying at all.

After she finishes, I encounter three different responses among people outside the arena. The first is anger. Rather than feelings of lament, they juggle outrage, insult, and concern for the direction of Cru. They're immediately triggered by hearing the words *oppressed, privilege, racial identity,* and *justice.*

Others come away with questions. What is "restorative justice"? What does it look like for us to seek it? Wouldn't that take us away from spreading the gospel? Who are "the oppressed" she's referencing, and how did they get that way?

Finally, a third group has their Christian consciences pricked. With each line, they feel more aware, more conscious of their lack of concern, convicted of their indifference toward the categories mentioned.

What distinguishes these groups? I'm convinced that what separates them from one another isn't primarily people's relationship to CRT, though it's easy to give that our immediate focus. Instead, the difference has something to do with mental frameworks Latasha's words drop into and the prework done—or lack thereof—around five self-reflective competencies or "awarenesses." How a person responded to Latasha depended on their reckoning and interaction with these categories.

1. SEPARATE THE SECULAR CULTURE CONFLICT
FROM THE CHURCH CULTURE CONFLICT

I'm leading a multiweek seminar with campus ministers on the history of black cults on campus, which eventually leads to a discussion on how the black church started. We read portions of Jemar Tisby's *The Color of Compromise*, a historical overview of blatantly racist moments in American church history, along with other writings on Absalom Jones, Richard Allen, and the start of "black" denominations.

One of the participants seems annoyed but isn't saying much, and after our online meeting I call him. He's hesitant but finally admits he was disturbed by the conversation. He doesn't think all white people should be considered guilty for others' historic evil. He transitions to disgust with "cancel culture" and CRT being taught in schools. I ask him what happened in today's call that caused him to feel I was decreeing all white people guilty for the past sins of the church. He thinks for a moment, then says none of that came up directly in our meeting. I ask him about the connection between CRT being taught in schools and our examination of black church history. He finally concedes that there isn't one. As we talk, we both realize most of what he's feeling comes from news and social media, and he's projecting political concern onto our discussion about church life.

When I hear anti-CRT rhetoric from a Christian, I first want to know whether they're reacting to an incident in secular media or political culture or something specific from church culture. Overlaps certainly exist, but these are two very different discussions on two radically different playing fields. Much confusion exists simply because engaging in a culture war against progressive politics and seeking to understand and remove anything creating a dividing wall of hostility between Christ followers are two different missions. It takes discernment to separate what we hear while watching national news networks from the discussions that should be happening among church folk.

Is the culture war real, playing out on the social stage with anti-Christian worldviews competing for the attention and souls of people? Absolutely. I understand some people's concern that a moral revolution is being ushered in by radical leftists. But are you really experiencing it among your church friends or just reading about it on social media? You may be concerned that the 1619 Project is erroneously affecting high school curriculums, but whether true or not, that's a different conversation from critically examining racist moments in the history of your denomination and trying to extricate their intracongregational relational consequences today.

A university professor clumsily suggesting "all white people are irredeemably racist" has different motives than a campus minister helping a mixed group explore how racial privilege factors into their life narratives.

A politician suggesting "the system needs to be stripped to the studs" has different motives than a pastor becoming self-critical of the racial implications of his patterns of leadership.

A POC person saying that it often feels oppressive being part of a mostly white parachurch organization isn't the same as a Harvard transgender advocate saying it feels oppressive living in a gender-fixed culture.

Media outlets might treat them equally, but these are different conversations with different motives and different appeals to different authorities with different endgames in mind. Treating them all as part of the same "woke" heresy is a mistake. Political heresy and theological heresy are completely different problems, and what CRT asks church people to consider within their congregation, denomination, or parachurch or mission organization isn't necessarily contrary to Scripture. We need to differentiate between the political/social and the ecclesial/social.

I don't expect the world to ever solve its racism, injustice, and oppression problems. The prince of the power of the air empowers these behaviors and will do so until Christ returns. I do, however, expect Jesus followers to embrace a radically subversive approach to racism, injustice, and oppression, and to be conversant in biblical texts that confront these issues. At the very least we should be making sure our own racial environment in the church resembles a different kingdom by confounding this one.

2. EDUCATE YOURSELF OUT OF CROSSCULTURAL SHALLOWNESS

A few months after George Floyd's murder, a pastor in Michigan hosted a series of interviews with black pastors from churches in his region. Afterward, responding to the onslaught of angry and condemning emails he received, he posted a letter to his congregation. One of his explanations for why he did the interviews included the following confession:

> Here is my honest admission. Six weeks ago, I would have scored zero on a quiz with the following questions: Explain the Jim Crow era. What is redlining? Who was Frederick Douglass? What was Dr. Martin Luther King, Jr.'s, Selma march about? . . . Name one current system in our society that continues to make life difficult for blacks. I really knew very little about the past or present of black life in our country. I am ashamed to say that it has taken me this long to learn something . . . but that is my reality.[2]

The pastor admitted he didn't know these crosscultural historical moments, so he couldn't know their effect on the crosscultural interactions he has with black folks who *do* know what those incidents signify. He cited an influential preaching text which says, "The more diverse people's backgrounds, the more we have to learn. It is important for us to listen to representatives of different generations as well as of different cultures, especially younger generations. . . . Humble listening is indispensable to relevant preaching," before concluding his letter, "Yes, I know my Bible. No, I did not know my world."[3]

It's rare to encounter pastoral humility when it comes to race, but it shouldn't be. I don't meet many white Christians who've thought meaningfully about race in either their broader cultural or specific church context. So it's not a stretch to suggest most white Christians live with an underdeveloped racial consciousness. It's not acceptable, but it is understandable. With limited meaningful interaction with nonwhite people, a lack of crosscultural *relationship*, and little education regarding the black or any other POC experience in America, it makes sense that this aspect of my mental world might be operating at a deficit.

Why do we so easily take for granted that white audiences operate in a righteously Christian way regarding race and their interactions with POC? Where does that assumption come from? I would guess most white people haven't thought meaningfully about race. I don't need a statistical analysis to draw this conclusion. I can arrive at it simply from over fifty years of conversations. They haven't thought about the ongoing implications of a racist and racialized national history, a racist ecclesial history, and the racism in their own family tree. They don't think about power or social capital or how it works out in relationships. They don't think of their church environment as being part of a system developed in a cultural setting over time, or what the implications of that development might be for different ethnicities. Nor are they aware of key social and historical moments that shape the interpretive consciousness of POC. Frankly, unless our social context is sprinkled with diversity, too many of us have the convenience of living with crosscultural shallowness.

Most evangelicals haven't received much direct Christian teaching on how the embodied gospel counters social ills. A sermon here or there. Perhaps an outlier message in response to a highly publicized racial blowup. But recurring, substantive teaching regarding our engagement with social sin? People might take a class hoping to make that connection, but they don't expect to learn it in church—and that's a problem. I'm struck by the irony that the people claiming to be most concerned about the effect of CRT on the church might be the ones who most need the type of corrective that real CRT provides.

And that shallowness extends to our understanding of the black Christian tradition and their own application of the gospel to evil social conditions. In *Reading While Black*, Esau McCaulley explains how the history of theological reflection among black folks in the church produces strong scriptural confrontation with both racism and injustice, coupled with a history of belief in traditional theological terms and traditional meanings, and all of this happens without the least dependence on Karl Marx or any of the resulting "Critical Theories" his followers produced.[4] But how many white Christians know anything about the black Christian tradition? How many know about the race-shattering message Tom Skinner gave at the 1970 Urbana conference, the prolific history of the Impact Movement in Cru, the bold racial reconciliation message of Promise Keepers, or anything of significance produced by black church leaders in the last couple decades, let alone the last century?[5]

Crosscultural depth requires paying attention to someone else's history. It forces me to lay aside my own lenses and filters at least long enough to try experiencing someone else's. A desire to understand people who are different from us coupled with imagination to walk in their shoes creates empathy. We don't seek crosscultural competence to satisfy a human resources department. We do it to satisfy our calling as missionaries charged with the Great Commission.

3. TAKE SERIOUSLY YOUR THEOLOGICAL MYOPIA

Our theological history determines what we'll emphasize, what we're afraid or suspicious of, what we will tolerate, who constitutes our tribe, who we'll work with, what political party represents the longest list of our concerns, even who we separate from inside the church. Dozens of church buildings scattered across our community testify to denominational choices emphasizing certain parts of the Bible while neglecting others. We need to consider how our theological commitments can get in the way of thinking Christianly about specific issues. We tend to be selectively countercultural depending on our theological background.

Though I didn't understand the implications at the time, as a new Christian at Kent State in the late 1980s, I spent time in two radically different theological camps. One group held firmly to a dispensational, premillennial view of eschatology, was enthralled by Dave Hunt's bestselling book, *The Seduction of Christianity*, and their "Every bit of culture is going to hell in a handbasket until Christ returns to make all things new" take on society caused them to virtually ignore all social ills. They weren't interested in strategies to confront or transform culture—they wanted individuals to accept Christ in this life and be discipled in preparation for the next.

The other group lived with a postmillennial view of the end, circulated Gary DeMar's less popular response to Hunt, *The Reduction of Christianity*, and their "Let's strive for the transformation of society, including churches, businesses, education, economics, journalism, the media, and civil government" view of the world caused them to spend less time talking about heaven and more time strategizing for cultural engagement.[6] They expected individual discipleship to confront social systems, and they expected social change.

They shared the same faith. They loved Jesus, the church, and the Great Commission, and both promoted a historically orthodox view of the Bible. But they had completely different expectations for what it meant to be a Christian in the world, which greatly confused me as a new Christian. They had different theological conversations, different verses they used to develop their theology (or different readings of the same verses), and different emphases for what it meant to be a disciple of Jesus in this life. Both groups assumed "the other side" was not only reading their Bible wrong but doing so borderline heretically.

One group thought it a Christian responsibility to confront racism and racialization with the gospel, while the other thought it a Christian responsibility to teach about Jesus and let him work out the rest. Could both coexist at the same time? Overemphasizing one biblical truth at the expense of another becomes idolatrous when we set it against other parts of the Bible. Were they unnecessarily creating a dichotomy between their positions that left both sides lacking? I thought so then and still believe many of our problems regarding race today stem from allowing theological myopia to cloud our biblical vision.

I have a pastor friend who used to say, "We're all going to get a major theological adjustment in heaven." He recognized that even the most comprehensive theological minds on earth will fall short of the truth, as it will be revealed on the other side of death. In the meantime, a measure of humility and recognizing that blind spots exist in our understanding and application of the Bible should characterize our lives. When it comes to race, it's beneficial to reflect on how your theological background has shaped your ability, approach, and even willingness to address it as a topic.[7]

4. EXAMINE YOURSELF FOR BIBLICAL SELECTIVITY

Theological myopia and biblical selectivity are similar, but sufficiently different to justify separation. Theological myopia has to do with entire systems of thinking, while biblical selectivity concerns itself with which Bible passages stick to us and what life experiences draw them out.

Many church people are acquainted with their Bible, but there's a danger in assuming people have equally robust understandings of what the Bible teaches about specific topics like oppression, the poor, social disadvantage, racism, ethnicity, and power. Some congregations are from theological backgrounds that leave them woefully unprepared to think in gospel-constructive ways when it comes to social issues, especially those issues that tend to wind up on Democratic political tickets. What if we've mistakenly assumed that the people making up conservative-leaning, evangelical church congregations are well-grounded in a biblical vision for ethnicity, justice, and oppression? What if we really do have significant cultural blind spots that weekly preaching hasn't illuminated?

We can make a case that biblical literacy is down significantly, and therefore we should be careful not to assume everyone has been exposed to important verses and themes connected to race or any other significant cultural topic. But what do we make of people who *do* know their Bible? Many of the most vocal opponents of CRT and anything having to do with race are Bible teachers. They obviously know their Bible, but could it be that they know it selectively?

I was in a church recently when a pastor announced that for the first time in twenty-seven years of preaching, he was giving a full sermon on mercy. He self-reflectively spoke of his surprise that he'd never done it before. This man is conservative in his view of Scripture, loves the Bible, takes seriously teaching its principles, and somehow, in nearly three decades of preaching, he never devoted an entire message to a concept appearing over three hundred times in the Bible. How can this happen, especially to a Bible-loving preacher? Easy. I don't think he's an outlier. I would guess he's the norm, because even Bible-loving pastors selectively camp on certain passages and themes and unintentionally ignore or gloss over others. That's not a condemnation. It's just what naturally happens unless we're hyperintentional.

I was talking with a longtime ministry colleague of mine. He was exasperated by, as he put it, "the incessant talk about 'justice' for vulnerable populations" happening in his parachurch organization. He said, "Where in the Bible does it say we should give special attention to vulnerable or poor and marginalized populations?" His question shocked me, and Jesus' words to Nicodemus floated through my mind: "Are you the teacher of Israel (or college students) and don't know these things?" So I cited the Minor Prophets and their scathing rebuke of God's people for not protecting the vulnerable. I cited how the Law had statutes imploring the Israelites to watch out for immigrants and poor and indentured servants and people who could be exploited. I went to more common places in the New Testament where Jesus talked about care for prisoners and orphans and widows (all vulnerable populations) and equated concern for those groups as concern for him. In both the Old Testament and the church age, it's always been the responsibility of God's people to look out for vulnerable others, to have special awareness and sensitivity for those being taken advantage of.[8] It doesn't detail exactly what that will look like in every case. It just constantly charges our heart posture to be tilted in their direction. My colleague let me speak uninterrupted for a while, then said something like, "Well, I just don't think we should support what the Democrats are trying to do."

Wait . . . what? I encounter this mentality enough among mature Christian folks that I think it's a problem we should take seriously. It wasn't that he didn't know the verses I shared were in the Bible. He just didn't pay much attention to them. At best, he simply failed to make connections from their context to ours; at worst, he ignored them because they sounded "Democratic."

I'm not worried about trying to discern relative levels of racism existing within individual believers, nor am I much concerned about CRT categories smothering Bible teaching in the church. I don't think either of those are the magnitude of problems some would have us believe they are. But I am concerned that we've absorbed a particular version of Christianity that minimizes certain biblical themes at the expense of others, and those themes matter to nonwhite people in a way that needs to be taken more seriously by white Christians. What if your rigid alignment with Republicans—or simply against Democrats—renders you unable to read your Bible properly? What if your theological tradition emphasizes certain themes at the expense of equally important others?

5. CONFRONT YOUR ETHNIC INDIFFERENCE

Racism has been a problem in the church since the first century. We shouldn't be surprised. People are endlessly wicked toward each other, and Satan recognizes racism's strategic effectiveness to mar the image of God in humans. The American version, while heinously cruel and intentionally systematized across centuries, is simply one version of racial evil among many since the beginning of recorded time.

While confronting people in the church about racist behaviors and racism as a cultural disorder certainly has its place, I'm not convinced it's the best strategy to bring reformation. Accusations of racism breed hostility and defensiveness. Further, we can call legitimate "racism" racism, but there's a much more pervasive problem lying at the root of so many of our racial tensions that lives and grows undetected.

I remember the day video surfaced of the Ahmaud Arbery murder. Within the first few hours, a black friend who was emotionally shaken called. I saw other black friends grieving on social media, outraged at both the visual violence and the initial cover-up by law enforcement, now concerned about what it meant for them as a POC.

Three days later, I spoke with a white minister friend who still didn't know it had happened. I went to lunch with another friend, and we talked about ten different things before I asked him what he thought about the case. He'd seen it on the news but had no thoughts about it, except that he'd heard that Arbery was engaged in criminal behavior before he was shot. He hadn't watched the video yet. He had exactly zero emotional reaction when he finally did.

I know this is just one social moment, but it's an example of a pattern I've experienced repeatedly. What should we attribute the different responses to? Racism? Have my white friends mastered hiding a socially polished but ongoing disdain for dark-skinned people? Possibly, but I think it's more likely something arguably worse than racism.

It's ethnic indifference.

Racism hates, but indifference feels, well, nothing. It just doesn't care. It doesn't bother itself with the concerns of others, especially others outside our ethnic circle. Holocaust survivor Elie Wiesel took it further when he famously said, "Indifference, to me, is the epitome of evil. The opposite of love is not hate, it's indifference." *The epitome of evil.* It's an apathy that allows me to not see you, to ignore your pain, to assume if all is well for me then it must be for you too. Indifference doesn't care about injustice or negligence or your invisibility. Indifference walls itself off from any responsibility regarding others' lived experience.

But for Christians, a posture of indifference doesn't correspond with being "in Christ." Churches used to be full of people who were not only blatantly and openly racist but also completely inattentive to the lived experience of African Americans. We may have removed the blatantly racist, but our disinterest remains a problem.

A person doesn't have to sympathize with a Marxist worldview to call out the white evangelical world for racial and ethnic indifference. I know there are pockets of believers who've done great work in this arena long before the recent decade of legitimate moral and not-so-legitimate virtue-signaled outrage, but I've been running in predominantly white church circles long enough to know where teaching on race and racism fit in the discipleship curriculum for most believers and congregations.

CRT is useful to the extent that it helps expose pockets of racial and ethnic indifference. The Christian who assumes racial tension is simply a byproduct of race baiters and radical academics needs to consider that threads of racism are woven throughout the fabric of our social lives, whether we're conscious of them or not. (This doesn't mean *everyone is a racist*; it means *everyone has been racialized.* Understanding the difference matters.) The Christian who rarely hears POC voices articulating their own experience will benefit from the intentional centering of POC stories. The Christian who believes in the idea that "you get what you earn" will benefit from exposure to people who work hard but still lose because of systemic realities. Christians who embrace a righteous colorblindness need an appreciation for how much meaning and value and assumption get ascribed to skin color, including white skin.

The goal isn't to sniff out racism; it's to understand the ongoing effects of living among the weeds of a racialized culture and the historically racist root system that produces them. Empathy always precedes action, and without it, there's little hope of real change among people experiencing the same cultural data in different ways. But it's impossible to empathize with a story you don't know.

TAKE A LOOK IN THE MIRROR AND START AGAIN

The idea that we should be in the world but not of it has a long history in Christian discipleship. We're challenged to be engaged socially and politically like any other citizen while recognizing not only the limits of all that goes on in this kingdom but also that another is soon coming to replace it. That's a form of "double consciousness" that all Christians from all nationalities and ethnicities are burdened to live out, and it involves both mental and behavioral intentionality.

In but not of demands a lifestyle of countercultural engagement, being the aroma of Christ while walking among people who are, as Walker Percy poetically described them, "lost in the cosmos." I need to remember that if I'm thinking like everyone else in the world about race, alarms should be going off. If we find ourselves struggling between two extremes offered by a lost world, our first move should be one of separation, of reflectively starting the process over again and painting with a brush offered by Scripture and theological reflection, not movement toward the secular or denominational worlds that dominate our headspace. We need to think differently to live differently, and to think differently we need to consider both how and what we're thinking in the first place.

BACK TO LATASHA

Months after that uncomfortable training conference, I heard one much-circulated podcast host reference Latasha's session as a "weird civic ceremony," saying, "This is a new religion. You're not apologizing for things that you've done against God, you're lamenting structural injustice supposedly that's been there that you're complicit in and you're not even really going to God and having it done with, you're just lamenting it. It's just an endless lamentation."[9]

He must not have listened to the entire session because at the end, Latasha prays, "We cry out to you, oh Lord, our redeemer, as the only one who can save us from ourselves. Show us our blind spots; don't let us hide from you in our shame and guilt. Restore us to your perfect union that can only be found in Jesus Christ. Lord, show us how to do justice, love kindness, and walk humbly with you. In the powerful name of Jesus let it be so."[10] Biblical, Christ-centered prayer. No mention of a Marxist overhaul of society. No appeal to CT or CRT. No secular solutions. Instead, a nod to Micah 6:8 and a pleading with Jesus Christ to reveal, to heal, to help us grow. Those who got tripped up when she used the word *oppressed* never made it to her appeal to the man of sorrows. Their mental scaffolding wouldn't allow it.

Among Christians, it's futile to ask whether CRT can be of use without first considering the difference between secular goals and church goals, addressing crosscultural shallowness, taking seriously the limits theological commitments and biblical selectivity place on our conceptual receptivity, and assessing the level of our ethnic indifference. People may still disagree about CRT concepts, but doing the work above creates a much different environment for dialogue.

10

CAN CRT BE OF USE?

We should totally reject CRT and Intersectionality in the same way that we reject the Book of Mormon, the mission of Planned Parenthood, and the use of the Ouija Board. We do not say of these things, "Use the good and reject the bad." We simply and clearly warn folks to stay away.

RICK PATRICK,
"WHAT'S YOUR PROBLEM WITH RESOLUTION 9?"

I do not write about Gandhi because he had the answers for our planet. To the contrary, I write merely because he asked the questions most eloquently. We may reject his answers, surely, but can we do so before first considering his questions?

PHILIP YANCEY, OPEN WINDOWS

AT THE 2019 SOUTHERN Baptist Convention, a firestorm began during the report by the Committee on Resolutions, a group put together by the president to receive, write, and recommend resolutions to the convention for adoption. A pastor submitted a resolution condemning what he called "CRT and Intersectionality ideology" in an effort to both denounce their ideas and hold accountable those teaching them in Southern Baptist Convention (SBC) institutions. However, before being brought to the convention for a vote, his resolution was edited into something significantly more nuanced, a document suggesting CRT had use as a sociological lens within the boundaries of a Christian worldview.[1]

The revised Resolution 9 said that evangelical scholars have "employed selective insights from critical race theory and intersectionality to understand multifaceted social dynamics" and that it was possible to gain "truthful insights found in human ideas that do not explicitly emerge from Scripture." It went on to suggest that CRT offered value as an "analytical tool" and an aide to understand interpersonal social dynamics but remained "subordinate to Scripture" and only "the gospel of Jesus Christ alone has the power to change people and society."[2]

Negative reaction to the passing of the resolution was swift and fierce. Not long after, six presidents of SBC colleges and universities made a collective statement distancing themselves from CRT, declaring, "Affirmation of Critical Race Theory, Intersectionality, and any version of Critical Theory is incompatible with the Baptist Faith and Message."[3] Several prominent black pastors rescinded their membership in the SBC.[4] Many articles, podcasts, and short videos were produced, positioning CRT as an insidious threat to the gospel. CRT became a battle line, a gauntlet dropped between actors on both sides, with each side viewing themselves as either protectors of biblical orthodoxy or purveyors of biblical justice.

So why do we need CRT if we've got our Bibles? What do people mean when they suggest CRT can be useful as an observatory lens without compromising their commitment to Scripture, and what are the practical implications for the church? What are the most common objections among those opposed to its real precepts and the questions it forces us to ask? We'll turn now to answer these questions.

WHY DO WE NEED CRT IF WE HAVE OUR BIBLE?

The Bible talks about race and ethnicity, but it doesn't directly address the nuances of American racism or its effect on the church. CRT concepts force us to reckon with *why* particular racial patterns remain entrenched in society as well as in our local churches, denominations, and parachurch organizations.

We shouldn't need CRT, but for too long the white American church hasn't paid careful attention to what the Bible says about racial or ethnic division, our responsibility regarding various social injustices, or how we protect marginalized and vulnerable populations. What do we do when the Bible could be enough but hasn't been for many cultural and political reasons?

Black Christians pleaded with white Christians to be unified for decades before Derrick Bell concluded racism is endemic to the American experience. They asked for Christian help in standing against racial injustice in their communities. They asked to sit at the leadership table in Christian organizations. They tried to get their white brothers and sisters to appreciate what it was like to be black in both their congregation and their broader communities. They asked for help changing policies that made it difficult to get good jobs, buy affordable homes, and attend good schools. They tried to get them to recognize patterns that maintained a racial hierarchy. Too often, they were met with active resistance. Or passive silence.

We shouldn't need CRT, but in 1970, were white Christians known for giving dignity to the subjective black experience in their congregations? Did Christians who knew their Bible understand the depths of racialization as experienced by both white and black Americans? Their Bible acknowledged the spiritual dividing wall had been torn down both between God and humanity and between humans, but were they acting like it when it came to black- and brown-skinned people? Were they taking seriously resisting cultural prejudice to be a united people of God? The answer to all these questions is a resounding no. Since before the Civil War, there've always been abolitionist-minded outliers, so "no" doesn't mean it *never* happened. But our collective reputation in these matters isn't positive.

Recently, I received a classic video message made by Campus Crusade for Christ founder Bill Bright. I don't think it's an exaggeration to say that in the twentieth century, what Steve Jobs was to personal computing, Bill Bright was to personal evangelism. His leadership impacted millions around the globe. The video was sent from the Cru headquarters as an encouragement that we're still living in a world that needs Jesus, the same world Bright described in his video five decades earlier:

> Today we live in a world of rapid and radical change. Men's hearts are filled with fear and dread, frustration and despair. Mankind has proven incapable of coping with the pressing problems of our time: the population explosion, the pollution of the environment, the rising tide of crime and violence, sexual revolution, alcoholism, drug addiction, abortion, pornography, urban sprawl, widespread political, social, and moral decay.[5]

Conspicuously absent is any mention of racial injustice. The video was made with the smell of Jim Crow still in the air, with race riots appearing on the nightly news, and "population explosion" beat out racial injustice as a priority concern.

I love Bill Bright and what he did in the world. I've spent my entire vocational life working for the organization he founded, and I know the good reasons he had for avoiding politics. But today we're still experiencing the consequences of significant evangelical leaders like him minimizing the intersection of the gospel and race from fifty years ago. Forget 1970. Research and experience suggest that even at the turn of the century, white evangelicals as a collective were still oblivious to how their "culture, values, norms, and organizational features that are quintessentially evangelical and quintessentially

American, despite having many positive qualities, paradoxically have negative effects on race relations," perpetuating the very racial divisions they mentally opposed.[6] Neglecting Carl Henry's warning, they framed gospel redemption as practically opposed to social concern, and the chickens have indeed come home to roost.

If your current reading of the Bible allows you to see how sin can become systematized and woven into social structures in an unrighteous and unjust way, then you don't need CRT. If you trace the history of the biblical kings and understand how their cultural prejudices dominate and oppress people, you can see how centuries of commitment to state-sanctioned racism isn't easily undone with the passing of a law or two. Your biblically formed imagination will recognize how easy it would be for the voices of nonmajority culture to be overlooked and dismissed.

You know how power works, exemplified in the books of Kings and Chronicles—how sinful people abuse it at the expense of vulnerable populations. From the Minor Prophets, you know God's people are prone to ignore cultural injustice while performing worship routines and regularly need to have it pointed out to them. If you've absorbed the Wisdom literature, you aren't surprised when marginalized and vulnerable populations get taken advantage of in your community when power gets used selfishly.

Even a casual reading of the Bible reveals themes now considered controversial to discuss in conservative-leaning church circles. In a different time and place, God speaks through his prophets to condemn abusive treatment of the poor, immigrants, and foreign visitors. He condemns pious religious activity practiced by worshipers who ignore unjust treatment of their neighbors. He expects his people to give particular attention to the vulnerable and needy of a community, checking the uses and abuses of power wielded at their expense. Exploitation and partiality centered around wealth and privilege receive regular rebuke.

He has Solomon record, "I looked and saw all the oppression that was taking place under the sun: I saw the tears of the oppressed—and they have no comforter; power was on the side of their oppressors—and they have no comforter." And again, "If you see the poor oppressed in a district, and justice and rights denied, do not be surprised at such things; for one official is eyed by a higher one, and over them both are others higher still."[7] If a pastor preaches this today in some churches, he'll immediately be dismissed as "woke." This is why Thabiti Anyabwile says we need to stop protecting people from their Bibles.[8] These categories and areas of concern were prophetically biblical long before they were politically and socially weaponized. Why are so many Christians seemingly unaware of this?

From cover to cover, the Bible shines light on the poor and exploited, the misuse of wealth, and the subjugation of others with state power, all hiding behind pious religious activity. It chastises God's people for failing to protect the vulnerable, condemns mistreatment of the powerless, and rebukes those responsible for making the foreigner feel foreign. If you see all that when you read your Bible, and you've thought meaningfully about how the ancient text relates to similar situations and concerns today, you certainly won't be offended by the type of work real CRT is trying to do in secular culture, and you'll be able to discern seeds of grace even among the toxicity produced by secular ideology. You'll also recognize the difference between legitimate biblical concern and progressive secularization and how they sometimes overlap. Marxist-inspired liberation theology arose when people grew desperate from church leaders in South America ignoring or remaining silent regarding these Bible truths in the face of crippling poverty and injustice. Christian people become attracted to Marxism when their Bible teachers stop teaching the whole Bible or fail to bring it to bear on horrible social suffering.

Can they be reconciled and made compatible as coexisting, intertwined worldviews? No, but can they speak to each other? Do they have overlap in anything they affirm or condemn? Can CT or CRT shine a light on sin-stained aspects of social life, especially areas we've grown apathetic about, that the Bible expects us to address? Most certainly. A God who uses a donkey to get the attention of his prophet may use extra-biblical tools of observation and analysis to get the attention of his church.

DISCERNING TRUTH FROM CARICATURES AND UNHELPFUL DISTORTIONS

Context is crucial when we're discussing both the Bible and the complex lives of people. Fueling antagonism within the church by misrepresenting people offends God and does more long-term damage than whatever racial heresy people are accused of promoting. Too much criticism from self-identified Christians flies around social media before landing permanently in articles and web pages as a cocktail of truth mixed with context-free misrepresentation. These distortions create division about race that isn't helpful to the body of Christ.

Consider the following sentences pulled from a chapter titled, "Can White Men Understand Oppression?":

> To understand oppression requires that we accept others' experiences as truthful, even though they may be very different from ours. To live with equality in a diverse, pluralistic society, we have to accept the fact that all groups and individuals have a legitimate claim to what is true and real for them.[9]

I came across this passage in an article saying CRT proposes a view of truth that contradicts the Bible. It argued that CRT depends on a feelings-based, subjective view of truth and goes against the Bible's objective understanding of truth. CRT is unbiblical relativism dressed in racial clothing.[10]

But reading the context from where these sentences came reveals that human relativism is the whole point. The author is saying if you've already decided ahead of time that your perception of events is the objective standard, then you won't accept the possibility that someone else experiences something entirely different through their own lenses. It has nothing to do with objective claims to universal truth, nor is he suggesting "accept" means you can never challenge or push back.

If you've never felt the negative effects of Capitalism on your daily existence, you may reject the reality of anyone who despises it because they have. If you've never experienced racial discrimination, it might be easy to assume it doesn't exist and question anyone who blames racial bias for an outcome. If you always feel comfortable in a group, it might be difficult to appreciate someone saying they always feel like an outsider. Blind folks touching different parts of an elephant will describe it in different ways, and all should be taken seriously even though they sound contradictory.

Christopher Rufo, while critiquing an FBI workshop curriculum, described intersectionality as "a hard left academic theory that reduces people to a network of racial, gender, and sexual orientation identities that intersect in complex ways and determine whether you are an oppressor or oppressed."[11] Intersectionality isn't dependent on being "hard left." It doesn't "reduce" people; it observes one aspect of their experience. It doesn't "determine" anything; it simply exposes potential additional stresses experienced by someone living with multiple minority identities among majority cultures. Word choices matter in these discussions.

Do extreme applications of those precepts exist? Of course. Some will say all white people are irredeemably racist. Some will take the suspicion of objectivity and never trust anything from any white person or submit to an objective truth from Scripture. But those extremes don't represent the essence of CRT any more than angry, condemning preachers represent the Christian gospel even though they're backed by Bible verses. We should expect to find non-Christians spouting those extremes, but even if Christians wind up doing it, the first step should be seeking to understand how the person got there rather than pointing out how CRT ruined them. It helps to slow down, get context, and ask questions before immediately moving to strike, being triggered by words not yet defined, or assuming the worst because you've read an article training you on what "woke" sounds like. People can sound like a Christian and be headed for hell, and people can sound unbiblically woke and be the godliest person in the circle. It takes time to discern the difference.

WHAT DOES IT LOOK LIKE TO USE CRT AS A TOOL OR A LENS IN THE CHURCH?

The most common tenets of CRT can function as a tool by forcing us to ask questions we tend not to ask, hopefully helping us to see the effects of living in a racialized world more clearly. At best, it might help us work biblical muscles that have atrophied due to simple lack of use, intentional neglect, or ignorance.

What does this look like? The most fundamental starting point in every definition of CRT says that racism is "normal" or "endemic" or "ingrained in the fabric and system of American society." This doesn't mean every white person hates POC or is a closet Klansman in their heart. It means as human beings living together on this land, we've got a several-hundred-year history of marking people with conse-quential value labels based on the color of their skin. *That* behavior is a normal part of American life. It's not an outlier attitude—generally, it's how the majority has operated at least since Bacon's Rebellion.[12]

Labeling one another. Attaching value to skin color. Developing prejudices based on skin shade. Absorbing those values as individuals and then taking them with us in the way we operationalize society through our institutions. Even if you're intentional not to live this way today, you live in a world surrounded by many others who still do. Our need to counter or correct that tendency among ourselves only con-firms its pervasiveness. It changes by degree depending on location, exposure, education, and a host of other factors, but these complex variables only make it more necessary to pay attention.

So this tenet that racism is a normal, endemic part of American life becomes a useful tool when Christians use it to ask: What role has racial discrimination played in our history as a congregation? As a denomination? How does race factor into what we value, or ignore, or elevate? What would we learn about our attitudes toward others if our congregation's ethnic demographic suddenly changed? As an individual within a congregation, how have I been affected by my family's racial history? How has coming to Christ fundamentally affected the way I view other races—if at all? These are great questions for both white and BIPOC Christians to ask themselves. Asking them might expose some sin that needs to be addressed, make us more aware, or help us have necessary conversations. Asking them helps us compare the world's response to racial tension with a gospel response. This is one example of how a CRT tenet works as a tool. There's nothing inherently unbiblical about asking those questions.

Christians should be the most prepared to see a tenet like this work. If we understand the nature of sin in general and the depth of sin in our own hearts toward others who are different, if we realize how easy it is even among folks in the church to discriminate against one another cross-denominationally, how Satan despises the *imago Dei* and encourages us to do the same, and the deep wells of racial division within the church still being drawn from today, how could we not conclude that this tenet helps us ask important questions?

How should we approach CRT's suspicion toward claims of objective truth? I assume Christians overreact to this tenet because it sounds like postmodern relativism or because it calls into question whether objective truth exists at all, undermining God's revelation. But "suspicion" toward something is different from denying it outright. CRT theorists aren't making a statement about whether a correspondence view of truth exists. As legal scholars, the originators of this tenet implied that in a court of law, "truth" has a way of changing based on many factors, and historically race played a huge role in determining what constitutes "objective" and "true." It recognizes the limits of human knowledge and forces us to reckon with how racial bias affects our perception of reality.

We can hold a high view of Scripture and biblical authority while still benefiting from this tenet. Why do we emphasize certain social issues but not others in our congregation? Why do we emphasize Paul but not Isaiah? The Gospels but not the Minor Prophets? When it comes to social issues, why do we get behind abortion as a cause but not racism? The assumption of objectivity looks suspicious when certain biblical themes are emphasized while others are conspicuously absent. Why was there such disagreement about what the Bible taught on slavery in the Civil War years if not for a problem with objectivity?[13] While God and his "breathed" Word may be objectively true and unimpeded by culture, history, or bias, those interpreting and wielding the transcribed text are not.

How does the CRT emphasis on valuing the individual subjective black experience help us? It prompts us to ask questions like, Do I know the stories of people who might be marginalized in our context? How is their perspective different from mine, and what do we need to learn from each other? Have I been guilty of explaining away someone's experience because it didn't line up with my unspoken political or theological prejudices? Is there a voice in our congregation that doesn't get heard that needs to be? What possible prejudices do I hold that keep me from hearing some voices compared to others?

It doesn't mean BIPOC experiences are the final arbiter of truth. It means my life as a church member is incomplete without acknowledging and understanding what those experiences mean in our life together as a body. How is it a threat to the gospel to suggest we prioritize minority voices in contexts where the majority culture already has the mic most of the time?

The CRT challenge to a colorblind approach to race asks us to reckon with whether we downplay race to such an extent that we devalue legitimate differences that need to be understood, appreciated, and properly leveraged. Have we allowed our fear of difference to keep us from appreciating the reason God brought our differences together in the first place? Does our assumption of collective "colorblindness" cover over real discriminatory policies or ways of doing body life that we need to address? Does my assumption of personal colorblindness ironically blind me to unintentional racist thought patterns I don't even know I hold? Christian colorblindness comes packaged in appeals to dividing walls that have been torn down in Christ, but what happens when dividing walls still present among us were initially built up in the name of Christ? What happens when the positional reality established by Christ's work on the cross doesn't align with people's conditional reality in certain communities?

I regularly read that intersectionality is a "rebellious, sinful way of thought," or "a nonsense narrative from neo-Marxism expressed in CRT," or "a toxic, evil worldview that undermines Scripture." How does it undermine Scripture when we acknowledge that some in our midst wear social labels that make them more vulnerable than others to mistreatment or being overlooked, even in a church setting?[14] Why is it alarming to consider that a woman in a Baptist church may be fighting an uphill battle to even have her nonteaching gifts affirmed and that a black woman in a majority culture congregation will be aware of two levels of potential stress? Or that different labels create different identities for a person depending on who they are with, and in certain contexts those subdominant identities might leave them feeling doubly marginalized? Why is it so difficult to distinguish between how a radical feminist on campus might use this lens compared to a group of church leaders asking it as a function of their leadership? Or a professor in the context of his or her class? Or a campus minister leading a staff team? Christian hysteria concerning intersectionality seems ridiculous.

Do we know CRT and our Bible well enough to understand where they overlap and where they diverge? If we know our Bible, we shouldn't be concerned about what CRT is trying to do. If we understand what CRT is trying to do, we should be able to see how the Bible wants to fix the problems it points out. What is the extent of the ongoing, experiential damage created by centuries of racial terrorism and the fallout of its absorbed consequences? How should we think about the role race plays in various specific contexts? How do both historic and currently present expressions of racism still work between people? How do our systemic patterns maintain problems along the race line? Christians don't need to fear asking these questions, nor should they be quick to assume they already know the answers.

11

RESPONDING TO CONCERNS ABOUT CRT, PART 1

The problem, of course, is that to write off your opponents as "mad," "bad" or "deranged" means giving up any attempt to understand them. And giving up any attempt to understand people who disagree with you means that you will lose the argument.

MICHAEL LAVER, "THE MADNESS OF CROWDS"

The test of a first-rate intelligence is the ability to hold two opposed ideas in the mind at the same time, and still retain the ability to function.

F. SCOTT FITZGERALD, "THE CRACK-UP"

I'M WITH MY KIDS in the theater watching *The Daily Bugle's* J. Jonah Jameson rant about Spider-Man. He's developed a tribe of haters by creating and doggedly circulating a narrative of Spider-Man as a masked villain, then aggressively filtering every bit of information made available about him through that grid. People love a sensationalist rant unleashed on shared enemies, and Jameson consistently feeds the anti-Spidey group what they want to hear. As viewers we know the truth—Spider-Man is actually *fighting* villains—and it's both laughable and painful how wrongly the surface "facts" get interpreted and retold by Jameson. It's not entirely clear whether he's distorting the truth about Spider-Man on purpose or just because his precommitment blocks his ability to ever see him differently, but if shallow takes get the job done, why change? He's built a celebrity persona around "Spider-Man as villain" and it serves him well.

Much critique aimed at folks talking about race in the church strikes me as being from the J. Jonah Jameson school of villain hunting. They see what they've predetermined they want to see, context and meaning be damned. There's a danger in projecting preconceived prejudices onto an idea before I've really worked to understand it, but I can't do better than that if I'm only hearing perspectives that encourage what I already want to believe. Listening to *understand* is different from listening to *confront*, and it's a woeful condition to become known as "the incurious," the people who never have any questions because they're already rigidly satisfied with all their answers.[1] We need to put some of these ideas in slow motion so we can better understand the issues, to replace reflexive, antagonistic objection with more thoughtful, informed interaction. Here are some common objections worth revisiting.

"CRT FOCUSES TOO MUCH ON RACE."

Of course it does—that's the whole point. It started as an attempt to provoke legal scholars who didn't want to see race anywhere in their discipline to start seeing it everywhere. CRT exists as a reaction to those who conveniently now *never* consider the racial implications of living in a country that for centuries made everything a racial implication. Did it overcorrect? Does it train people to see race problems where they don't exist? In some cases, yes. It's not difficult to find black intellectuals and BIPOC scholars who will say the same thing, either because they think class is a more significant category, they think too much emphasis gets placed on black history, which minimizes other nonwhite histories, or because they disagree with the politics usually backing race-centered rhetoric.

Race gets talked about more now in media and education than at any time in our collective history, and sometimes race gets blamed when other factors are more central, but it's still better to take race too seriously and back off than to never consider it at all. In the end, who gets to decide how much is too much when it comes to centering race in America? I don't know, but in a country whose history is saturated in racialization, perhaps it's wiser to assume a racial component rather than presume none exists.

"CRT SAYS THAT RACISM IS EVERYWHERE ALL THE TIME"

Most white folks I know never get past this point. They reject the idea that racism is a normal, endemic, regular part of social life. They assume it means *they* are racist and, of course, immediately reject that possibility. Or they think about their own experiences and realize they've never actually seen people treated unfairly because of their skin color. Or they simply hold to the belief that the civil rights era washed away the race-based attitudes of our collective past.

But in America, the development and cultivation of race as a legislated category of differentiation extends far beyond individual acts of mean behavior toward those with different skin from us. Building on what Derrick Bell wrote decades earlier, Duke Kwon and Greg Thomson say, "(American) racism is not simply a matter of personal prejudice, relational division, or institutional injustice but rather a fundamental cultural (dis)order that is both the source and sum of all these." They call racism "an entire culture, a comprehensive way of being and doing that is embedded in our structures of meaning, morality, language, and memory, and expressed in terms of individual, social and institutional behavior." In this more technical use of the term, racism as a category includes but extends well beyond your own attitudes toward people.[2] It's a persistent stain, deeply soaked into the fabric of society, and requires careful, thoughtful inspection.

I know of a local, well-known Christian school system that, amid a list of other more noble reasons, was founded out of concern for desegregation. I've spoken with people connected with its founding in the 1970s, and while they're certainly not proud of it, they will admit that racial segregation was a major motivation in creating the school fifty years earlier. These Christians didn't want their kids forced to attend school with black kids from the city. Today none of them are still directly working with the school. There's no evidence of Klan rallies being held on campus. Nothing is explicitly written in school policy that nonwhite students are unwelcome. So how does this institution's racist history continue to spill into today?

These questions are a good place to start: How does race factor into its current student population? How does it affect hiring practices for teachers and other staff? How do ethnicity and race get discussed in its history, sociology, and theology classes? How does scholarship money get distributed? For this school, racism was institutionalized into the fabric of its existence, and unless those who came after have been just as intentional to reverse the normal, endemic, regular nature of this racism as their predecessors were about putting it in place, faculty and students are walking its halls still touched by the trickle-down effect of latent racism.

CRT isn't saying Klan-level, overt racism fuels every social interaction. CRT says every bit of society has been powered, steered, and directionally affected by racism, and unless we're intentional to acknowledge and address it, its lingering aftereffects don't just go away but remain as a form of social inheritance. That's what it means for it to be normal, regular, endemic. It doesn't help to counter this tenet by pointing out every instance we come across where good people of different races get along well. That's not the point. Rather, slow down and ask how others have experienced this tenet in their own journey, and how race has effects we might not notice if we don't open ourselves to the possibility that they exist.

"CRT SAYS THAT ALL WHITE PEOPLE ARE RACISTS WHETHER THEY ACT LIKE IT OR NOT AND THAT BLACK PEOPLE CAN'T BE RACISTS."[3]

This needs to be considered on two different levels, both dependent on our understanding of the word *racism*. As described in the last section, nontechnical understandings of racism involve "prejudice, discrimination, or antagonism directed against a person or people on the basis of their membership in a particular racial or ethnic group, typically one that is a minority or marginalized."[4] I find it strange how adamant so many of my Christian brothers and sisters are regarding their own innocence when it comes to racism defined as such. Biblically speaking, everyone is racist, if by racist we mean someone inclined toward prejudice and bigotry. It's a part of fallen nature that must be continually redeemed.

I'm sure Jesus shocked the self-righteousness out of many of his listeners the day he declared, "Everyone who looks at a woman with lustful intent has already committed adultery with her" (Matthew 5:28 ESV). Is it that much of a stretch to imagine, "If you've had a negative thought toward someone because of their skin color or ethnicity, you're a racist"? As philosopher George Yancy suggests, the best any of us can claim for ourselves is being an "antiracist racist."[5] We've grown so accustomed to defensively asserting our own innocence that we sound almost ridiculous given the reality of our sin nature. You don't have to long for the days of Jim Crow to be a racist—you just have to think less of someone who God made different from you.

But CRT implies something very different when it says that in various ways white people can't help but be racist—or that *only* white people can be racist. Some popular antiracist scholars like Ibram Kendi assert that black people can't be racist because one must also have social power to be racist, a direct extension of the work of CRT scholars from the 1980s.[6] Not just individual moments of social power, but comprehensive social power over specific social systems. The kind of power that can reverse centuries of injustice. Scholars like Kendi argue that a white-as-a-way-of-being normative hierarchy continues to permeate every aspect of society, and that until black people or other POC control the policies maintaining the hierarchy, they cannot be racist.

White people created both race and the systems that support racial division and continue to benefit from that racially inspired and racially developed social system. This doesn't mean all white people benefit equally. It doesn't mean nonwhite people can't benefit at all. It's saying that because of hundreds of years of racial hierarchy and a systemically developed status quo, the problem of race in society runs far deeper than individual choices, and that the definition of racism itself should be rethought given this particularly American reality.

What should we make of this? First, we should recognize that when theorists first made this assertion decades ago, it was in direct reaction to white people's stubborn insistence that systemic racism doesn't exist at all—even in eras when it most obviously did—and their unwillingness to acknowledge how much of a hierarchy they'd absorbed without realizing it. Nonwhite folks' emphasis on redefinition countered the commonly accepted narrative among white people that racism is *only* a function of individual attitudes. If white folks couldn't expand their understanding of racism beyond individual choice, BIPOC scholars would strategically respin the popular understanding of racism to include and require power. Thus, racism got redefined as a countermove, another effort to get people to see the pervasive social consequences of legislated racism soaked into the fabric of society. Even if you disagree with this move, it helps to understand the motive behind its redefinition.

Second, recognize that the sociopolitical landscape of the Bible illustrates racism understood in this way. For example, both the Jews and Samaritans were guilty of prejudice and discrimination toward one another. They invested energy in creating ways to avoid and extend hatred toward one another. But the Samaritans could not control the systemic marginalization of the Israelites, which was exactly what the Jews did to them. The Jews controlled what happened in the synagogue, in their courts, and how Samaritans were viewed in popular imagination. They could turn their discrimination into law, build it into their religious structures, and soak it into the educational system. Thus, understood in this way, the Jews had power to systematize their discrimination while the Samaritans did not. They could be racist while the Samaritans could not.[7] Racism and discrimination do not mean the same thing. Discrimination is prejudicial hatred. Racism requires the power to systematize. It's the ability to weave prejudicial hatred into social structures through legislation.

Third, we shouldn't get stuck simply trying to assess our own relationship to individual prejudice, nor should we invest much energy in arguing that nonwhites can be just as racist as whites. That misses the point. Instead, recognize that white people benefit from a racially inspired and racially developed social system. To what degree depends on the specific system we're discussing, the location, the people involved, the awareness regarding racialization, and other factors like these. Think about the systems you're a part of and the role race played in both their establishment and the way they operate today.

But don't let haggling over definitions become the issue. My job isn't to argue that black people are racists, too, nor is it to constantly assert my own innocence regarding racism. It's to recognize what's in my own heart while examining my microcommunities and the patterns that shape our lives together.

"CRT EMPHASIZES A MARXIST 'OPPRESSOR/OPPRESSED' PARADIGM— MAKING ALL WHITE PEOPLE GUILTY AND BLACK PEOPLE VICTIMS"

I'm trying to understand my Christian colleagues' near-hysterical re-action to any hint of what they call the "oppressor/oppressed" par-adigm. It's almost comical how easily race-themed discussion can be redirected simply by forcefully stating, "They're looking through an oppressor/oppressed lens!" as though sounding that dog whistle si-multaneously resolves and transcends whatever conflict we're facing. Conscientious financial donors and concerned coworkers are trig-gered when they hear suggestions that "elements of the victim-oppressor worldview have permeated our ministry, creating havoc." Missionaries are leaving their organizations and donors are pulling their money, and both question the salvation of those in leadership at the mere suggestion of these words. Accusing a pastor or ministry leader of teaching "oppressor/oppressed" ideas will stain their repu-tation more than a sexual affair in some circles.

Why do people recoil so violently at the word *oppression*? From my conversations, I think many associate the word *oppression* with "op-pressive regimes" and imagine gulags, enforced slavery in Communist labor camps, militancy, starvation, and inhumane poverty. Nobody wants to be associated with slave masters and tyrannical leaders. Put like this, I understand their fear of the association.

It's also because secular versions of "oppression obsession" can be just as reductionistic as race obsession, and neither produces the righ-teousness God expects among his people. Seeing oppression and racism *everywhere*—regardless of what people mean by those terms—gives both realities far more explanatory power than either deserves at this point in American history. There's always far more going on in any social context than just power gone wrong.

But immediately dismissing concerns simply for sounding "Marxist" or because we have a myopic view of what oppression can mean doesn't help much either. Just because Critical Theory–based progressive politics find oppression under every stone doesn't mean there's no real oppression taking place, especially when it comes to racial realities in our local congregations, denominations, and parachurch organizations. What if oppression is tied to something more psychosocial? What if, instead of physical deprivation, it means draining of the spirit or has to do with behaviors working against the flourishing of someone's life? What if oppression has more to do with a person's social and emotional freedom and less to do with brutality seen with the naked eye? If this is what oppression has come to mean, shouldn't we at least ask more questions before asserting our innocence?

Progressive politics may find oppression in places it doesn't really exist, but too many evangelicals have an underdeveloped sensitivity to genuine race-based trauma in their communities. I don't know many white folks who would know it among BIPOC even if they saw it, and they certainly don't realize the many ways BIPOC experience emotional trauma, especially if they've already decided in advance that social/racial oppression doesn't exist except in outlier situations. How could they see the pain oppression produces if they don't believe oppression exists? You may still conclude the specific subcultures you inhabit aren't producing oppression of any kind, but how could you do that before carefully asking difficult questions and listening to others' answers?

What if people *are* experiencing feelings of oppression in your community because of race? And what if constantly reasserting your own innocence keeps you from seeing something you need to see? In that case, isn't it a grace when someone brings it to your attention, even if they might initially do so angrily? Maybe your subjective feelings about the possibility of "oppression" aren't the place to start. It's been said, "If you want to know about water, the last one to ask is a fish," a maxim that too often describes the failure of dominant culture to recognize feelings of oppression among BIPOC in their midst. Can we slow down long enough to ask the questions that most need to be asked instead of responding with hysteria or defiance toward people confessing their feelings?

I'm perplexed when I hear Christians blaming CRT for dividing humanity into groups of oppressors and oppressed. It's ridiculous to suggest CRT created the racial dividing lines as though they didn't already exist. Bradley Mason says:

> Critical theorists, whether past or present, are not attempting to invent divisions, carve people up into groups, nor haphazardly dub one group 'oppressor' and another 'oppressed' based upon theory or ideology. Rather, they are explicitly seeking to find the actual, local, and historical causes of EXISTING, socially constructed groups and group memberships (whatever they may be), identify the imposed hierarchies and resulting inequalities, and craft new discourses, narratives, and social actions to remediate them.[8]

It's too simplistic to suggest CRT labels those with white skin as oppressors and those with nonwhite skin as victims. I'll replace that simplification with one that's more accurate: CRT tries to expose how "groups" came to be labeled in the first place, identifies meaning systems attached to those groups leading to good/bad hierarchies, and then seeks to disrupt whatever needs change in an effort to reestablish *imago Dei* equality.

CRT isn't dividing the world into oppressor/oppressed buckets along color lines. It's saying that those with power in the dominant culture created the buckets in the first place and that the entire system should be checked for how advantage and disadvantage get distributed as a result. Why is it threatening to consider what it means to dismantle habits or patterns that might be working against segments of the community flourishing?

"CRT CREATES A RACE CONSCIOUSNESS THAT DIVIDES"

It's not usually put this crassly, but I often hear complaints from white Christians in my own ministry organization along these lines: "We want the unity we had before all the POC got riled up from CRT." They say we were all fine until some Christians started taking their cues from secular culture and introduced controversial political and social topics into our fellowship. But it's important to recognize that many, if not most, POC never really felt that assumed unity.

The questions produced by CRT operate as a counterpunch to a jab that's been getting thrown by too many white Christians for decades, namely, the assumption of unity coming from those largely unaffected by the longstanding reality of disunity. White folks in an organization may want things the way they used to be, but don't mistake that for unity. Often, what we had before was just selective vision on our part and tolerance on the part of POC. It implied, "We want to be 'unified' with you as long as it's on our terms." We want a unity based on our normal, our concerns, our preferences. A unity that smells like us, sounds like us, and styles like us. What we called unity may have been just a status quo arrangement protecting our own comfort at the expense of nonwhite people in our group, especially if we've never explored the conflicted feelings experienced by minorities in our community who've chosen to assimilate rather than disrupt. But don't mistake consensual toleration for genuine unity. It may just be a benevolent subjugation, an accommodation that maintains our priorities while taking for granted that everyone *not* in the majority agrees with the list.

Race consciousness disrupts by shaking the status quo, but how do you talk about touchy subjects with people whose collective history created the touchiness in the first place? How do you talk about the role white church people played in creating and fostering negative conditions that POC still experience today without white listeners feeling uncomfortable, even if those white listeners had nothing directly to do with the original sin? People insisting a different list of issues and problems be taken seriously by those who for years were content not to discuss them at all will certainly feel divisive. Disruption always feels uncomfortable, but don't mistake that feeling for division.

Talking about race doesn't have to be divisive. Whether it becomes redemptive or divisive depends entirely on those doing the talking and listening and how much they allow the Spirit of God to love others through them. If a racial conversation becomes divisive, it's because those conversing fail to love each other, not because of the topic itself. Stubbornness divides. Self-centered pride divides. Indifference divides. Dominant cultural tone-deafness divides. Conversely, escalated accusation divides. Dumping decades of racial pain onto an unsuspecting individual divides. Assuming white skin means guilt divides. But humility and empathy restrain those fleshly impulses and allow the Spirit of God to bring healing and redemption where necessary.

When it comes to race and whatever ministry you're a part of, there's always been an elephant in the room. If you don't see it, realize that many others do, and when they start pointing it out to you, resist getting angry at them for doing it. It may feel like you're being blamed for the elephant, but don't let defensiveness trigger division. Most of the time, POC aren't accusing you of bringing the elephant in, but they may be frustrated that you don't see it or care that it's there.

If you don't see it, use your energy asking lots of questions of those who do. Folks who don't see the elephant and who get defensive when others point it out remind me of Malcolm X when he complained, "The white man has such a guilt complex of his record of hate toward Black people that as soon as you begin laying out that history, instead of addressing those wrongs, the white man accuses you of hating him."[9] Here's a better option: study the elephant. Find out all you can about it. Don't act like it's not there or become offended when someone lets you know it is.

For many white Christians, the race conversation comes to them as a sort of interruption. It's new and hasn't been a part of their Christian history. Rather than asking why we must start talking about it, some of us need to ask how we've avoided the subject until now. In a country with our racial history, in a church with our racial division, how can we escape having substantive conversations about race and its implications for ministry? We need to consider why it's a new conversation for us, while so many others have been working to bring healing in this area for years. One of the most discouraging things for people who've been embroiled in these discussions for decades is the realization that so many people think it's a new topic in Christian circles, prompted only by liberal media headlines.

Some see POC separating for times of prayer or gathering to discuss moments of cultural trauma, creating what amounts to POC-only spaces and leaving white folks out. "This kind of separation isn't healthy," my white friends say. "The gospel should be bringing us together, not separating us when hard things happen." Of course, they're right, but I always ask frustrated friends to consider what we or others are doing that causes them to not want us with them in vulnerable times like this. What past patterns have so scarred them they believe it will be worse if we're with them in the next crisis? How many times have my POC friends been hurt worse by someone trying to bring perspective or challenging politics or assuming the guilt of a black person shot by police or remaining silent when horrible racial things happen? It's not a long-term solution, and you may not have personally done anything wrong, but these temporary separations are the collective consequence of not doing enough crosscultural work so we can be good friends, ministers, and fellow journeyers when racially traumatic events happen.

My POC friends and acquaintances don't need a challenge toward unity from me in that specific moment. They need confidence that I'm learning how to be with grieving people in racially charged spaces before the next crisis occurs. That starts by understanding why, in the short term, it's sometimes better for them not to have to manage my ignorance or educational growth when they are hurting the most. As I do that work and stay in relationship by listening instead of trying to teach, the trauma circle should, at some point, expand to include me. Sometimes the loving thing to do is to give space, at least temporarily, instead of pouting or confronting with theological truth. Good theology says we should weep with those who weep, but if those who are weeping weep *more* because of what I represent in the short term, or if I'm lousy at weeping with a ministry of presence in crosscultural situations, why should I make things worse for them? Maybe I need to earn the privilege of being trusted instead of just assuming it.

"CRT JUDGES EVERYONE ACCORDING TO 'GROUPS'"

Again, I'm amazed at how easily my Christian friends give Marx all the credit for social group analysis, as though he invented it and anyone who attempts to dissect people as part of an aggregated "group" must be following in his footsteps. I've listened to people within Cru share their deep concern that we've fallen into a Marxist trap by allowing speakers to talk about "white evangelicalism," "white responsibility," or "BIPOC," as though those categories are too broad to be meaningful, or that they're simply offended at the possibility that they could be scrutinized as part of a group called "white," especially if that group is being confronted for some form of negligence.[10]

This defensiveness seems especially ironic within a ministry like Cru, since the organization prides itself on contextualized ministry to specific groups, organizing entire ministry divisions based on socially recognized and understood labels: college students, athletes, city dwellers, high schoolers, college professors, military personnel, politicians, and so on. The labels don't entirely define the people targeted for ministry. They simply help us to know the group "athlete," for example, shares certain physical and emotional characteristics, has been shaped by a particular ethos, and struggles with a common set of identity issues. We don't assume "all athletes are always like this all the time," but we understand from years of interaction with the group category "athlete" that "most athletes struggle with most of this list most of the time."

So what's the issue? I don't think we have a problem with comparing and contrasting using group identities. We have a problem using *racial* group identities. That's when the alarms start going off, as though nothing could be more offensive than being collectively studied based on skin color. But why can't we do with "white evangelicals" what we do with athletes or other understood groupings? Are we really unable to draw any comparisons between "white" and "BIPOC" groups in America?

If you've ever played a team sport, you've probably had an experience where the coach gathers everyone together and lays into the entire team, demanding change in some area critical to the success of the group. She doesn't call out any one specific player but blames everyone for what's happening within the culture of the team. It's highly unlikely that everyone is equally guilty of whatever infraction she's pointing out, but we all understand that, as a team, we must wear it together. What do you do when you hear that blanket call for correction?

When I'm at my best I almost reflexively do two things: first, if it's unclear, I ask myself what role I'm playing in this problem, and second, I consider how I can help fix what's going on with the rest of the team. At my worst, I get defensive, claim innocence, and separate myself from responsibility for the rest of the team. Not my problem.

If I am directly responsible for what's happening, I'll have to resist getting defensive and making excuses to justify myself. I'll have to overcome whatever insecurities I feel, own what I can own, and work to do better. That's it. If I'm indirectly responsible because I've passively tolerated or enabled other teammates to behave in a way that undermines our culture, I'll have to assess what role I can play in correcting my indifference. I'm not directly responsible for their negative behavior, but as a member of the team, I am responsible for playing some role in helping them change it. That's what it means to be part of a team.

There's no reason why we can't take this same approach when a speaker makes observations calling white Christians to task for realities BIPOC experience as part of the body of Christ. There is a white social, political, and ecclesial tradition in America characterized by discrimination and oppression toward certain ethnic groups. Pretending that this treachery has evaporated from our communal Christian life or that identifying and discussing both past and present history according to racial group realities is somehow an affront seems disingenuous.

It's insulting to BIPOC when white Christians declare organizational ethnic division to be effectually obsolete while maintaining a powerful grip on status quo norms and institutional ways of being that still resemble 1970. When BIPOC wanted racial groupings to go away in the twentieth century, white folks worked hard to maintain them through signage, policies, and procedures. Now that BIPOC want to talk about the effect of living as racialized groups, white folks act as though they never existed.

Blaming CRT for putting people in groups is ridiculous if we really understand what CT tries to do. A major thread of both CT and CRT is "troubling and complicating the notion that there are easily identifiable dominant and oppressed 'groups.'" As Bradley A. Levinson continues, while we can't get away entirely from the language of groups, "groups are not permanent or metaphysical categories."[11] In other words, how "white" and "black" groups are formed is a function of historical processes, not simply acknowledging shades of skin color, and they can be reformed as circumstances change. For example, those considered "white" change in different contexts in different historical moments in different places around the world. This explains why Jews or Italians or the Irish can at one moment in American history not be considered "white" while at others they are.[12] It's why lighter-shaded black folks throughout American history have been treated differently than darker-skinned black folks.[13] Group identities change based on historical and cultural circumstances, and while your skin color never changes, what it means and who you can associate with as a result does.

CRT seeks to dismantle ideologies and social mechanisms that produce or help sustain inequality. It pays attention to how racial hierarchy works through embedded patterns and processes. If my skin color or cultural preferences allow me to benefit from certain patterns, processes, and social mechanisms while another person's skin color or cultural preferences cause them to be overlooked or to experience duress because of those same patterns and processes, Christians should have a theologically vested interest in working to break them down. It's not about being in a group. It's recognizing how social dominance works through social structures and assessing my relationship to it all. CRT doesn't have a problem with my skin color. It has a problem with me not recognizing social patterns already in place associated with my skin color and my relationship to those patterns in specific, real-time situations.

12

RESPONDING TO CONCERNS ABOUT CRT, PART 2

Before white churches pursue racial, ethnic, and cultural diversity as the solution to our segregation, we must first address the discipleship that led to our segregation in the first place.

DAVID W. SWANSON,
REDISCIPLING THE WHITE CHURCH

IT'S THREE MONTHS after George Floyd's murder, and we're visiting a high school friend who lives in the South Minneapolis neighborhood where it went down. We walk to the makeshift memorial outside Cup Foods in the middle of Thirty-Seventh and Chicago and stand reflecting on the different ages and ethnicities scattered around the intersection. Walking south on Chicago, dissonant graffiti confronts us—cursing the police, inviting readers to "trust Jesus," encouraging revolution—testimony to the conflicting worldviews competing for allegiance around this tragedy.

We come to a small park transformed into a makeshift cemetery of one hundred tombstones, each with the name of an African American killed by law enforcement. It's a performative art exhibit titled *Say*

Their Names. Like all art, the silent and somber walk among the tomb-stones means different things to different people, but you can't help notice that the specific details of their cases take second place to the permanent tragedy of their lost lives. There's a magnitude created by all the headstones together, lined up like Stormtroopers, a vast collection of lives testifying to death by the sword, whether they lived by it or not. The breeze in the park carries the faint, endless grief of all the mothers and fathers and family and friends behind the names on the stones, and even if only a sampling of the history, I'm wrecked by the cumulative effect of seeing them all together.[1]

It's the same feeling I had decades ago walking out of the Holocaust museum in Washington, DC. Before the visit, I knew Hitler as a per-sonification of evil and *Schindler's List* and Anne Frank and the parts served up for popular imagination. I had what psychologists call the "illusion of explanatory depth," but that was good enough for me.

But then walking through the building, "Holocaust" as a dispas-sionate concept became a holocaust with real faces, real families, real terror. After a couple of hours, I was silenced, distressed, feeling like I needed a shower to clean the experience off my body and out of my mind. I was marked by stories of actual people with names who kept calendars, made plans, made love, then in a day had it all taken away without explanation. In short, I felt something toward actual people, and that changed not just my mind but me. It gave me new eyes and ears and an ability to perceive that transcended arguments and debates.

Frederick Buechner said, "Compassion is the sometimes fatal ca-pacity for feeling what it is like to live inside somebody else's skin." It's the *splagchnizomai* that Jesus had for people, the deep, guttural ache for their condition, regardless of how they got there. Whatever con-cerns people have about CRT, understanding real people begins at the heart level, not the intellectual level. Objections often ignore context and the particulars people face, and I need to remember that as we consider another set.

"CRT BLAMES ME FOR OTHER PEOPLE'S RACIAL SINS"

"Why should I be made responsible for the racial sins of others? I'm not a racist. I have black friends and I think what happened in the past is awful. But I didn't do any of it. Besides, the Bible teaches individual responsibility for sin."

I find it startling how easily Christian people of all races assume their innocence regarding racial sin. Many talk as though they're almost impervious to it, but how can anyone with a Christian theological background claim purity when it comes to racial sin? The Bible offers us plenty of examples of individual repentance for both personal sin *and* collective, representative prayers of repentance for others' sins.[2] I've heard people go through amazing theological gymnastics trying to explain away clear biblical examples of communal repentance for the sins of forefathers and contemporaries. Repenting for personal sin needs no explanation. But what does it mean when people confess the sins of others?

It doesn't mean those repenting are guilty or personally culpable for what others did. They aren't suggesting they should be punished for something that happened in the past. It means their hearts break for the idolatrous rejection of God in their family or community line. It means they recognize sin destroys and has consequences in peoples' lives, and as humans they feel a godly sense of sorrow for it. It means, with great humility, they recognize before God their connection to their ancestors and acknowledge that the consequences of their forefather's sins still hover over the landscape, including their own hearts. Usually, they're confessing some aspect of their forefather's idolatry, fully cognizant of the hereditary nature of idolatrous behavior and their own susceptibility to it. They recognize their people momentarily traded in their spiritual birthright for some form of cultural or religious idolatry and confess their people's mistreatment of outsiders because they know it runs in the family. Acknowledging and owning their forefathers' sins represents a particular perspective, attitude, and posture, the fruits of humble and broken hearts. They not only acknowledge their own sin, but they also cast the net wide enough to account for the current damage of their ancestors' choices.

I'm not sure if it's unique to Americans, but our commitment to individuality undoubtedly hinders our ability to feel this kind of spiritual connection to past and future generations. As Americans, we understand paying our own debts, but we have less appreciation for communal responsibility for others' infractions. Our holiday calendar testifies to our ability to connect with and celebrate what we'd consider past victories, but we don't make room to align with inherited shortcomings. It's just not the way we operate.

But folks in the Bible embrace their genealogies—both for good and bad. So when they pray, we frequently discern an attitude that says, "God, we're connected to past generations. We don't see ourselves as somehow disconnected from their successes or failures. We're an extension of them, a living, visual legacy of both their proper submission to you and the consequences of their sinful rebellion. We're not above aligning with what they did wrong, nor are we unaware of our own susceptibility to the same sins. We represent them today by reacknowledging their wrongdoing, admitting our own, and asking for both your mercy and the courage to live out kingdom justice toward one another as we move forward."

In a country—more importantly, in a church—that's been ravaged by racial sin, why wouldn't it be a recurring part of our spiritual tradition to continue acknowledging it? Not because of woke pressure or social trendiness, but because we recognize the devastation wrought in people's lives because of both past and current racial sin. I don't directly bear the guilt of teachers who fabricated the curse of Ham to justify slavery and the mistreatment of nonwhites. I don't imagine being held directly accountable for those pious people who gathered in crowds for post–church meeting lynchings. I wasn't present when preachers Richard Allen and Absalom Jones were refused seating among the white folks and instead left to start the formal black church. But as a white-skinned Christian, I still exist as an extension of all this behavior, even while soundly condemning it. I live on their shoulders, even if I despise what's under my feet.

Today, reactions to this line of thinking tend to sound something like, "That wasn't me! I condemn what they did. I'm not a racist. I would have done differently!" Conversely, prayers in the Bible seem to say, "That wasn't me, but it could've been. I condemn their behavior but see it in my own heart. I hope I would have done differently but I'm not sure I would have. Have mercy on us for their sins and forgive us for our own. What they did exists in me, and I'm not going to act like it doesn't." See the difference?

We need to think more carefully about the word *responsible*. I'm not required to pay the debt for someone else's sin. The Bible makes it clear that I'll stand alone before God to give an account for the specifics of my life and be dealt with accordingly. In that sense, I'm responsible for my own actions and no one else's. But I remember talking with one older Christian man who told me, "I don't think most white Christians understand just how hurt black folks are because of racial ignorance in the church." He went on to describe the hurt as a constant ache, an ever-present burden he bears not only from wearing our collective history but also from his own personal experiences with racist actions.

Now, I'm not responsible for all the racial hurt he bears as though it's my fault, nor am I directly responsible for current structural conditions—in the church or broader culture—that affect him negatively. But as a Christian, I *am* responsible for carrying that pain with him (Galatians 6:2). I *am* responsible for pursuing the clarity to see what he sees and feel what he feels (Romans 12:15). I *am* responsible for an ongoing recognition of how the sins of the past continue to have consequences in the present (1 Corinthians 12:25-26). And I am responsible for traces of racial prejudice still alive in me (1 John 1:8-10).

As much as it depends on me, I am responsible for living in a racially redemptive way within my sphere of influence (Ephesians 2:14-16). I may not pay for others' sins before God, but I may have to experience consequences for those sins by absorbing others' hurt. It may not directly be my fault, but I represent those who created the hurt. I am called to this work by the Spirit of God, not out of woke pressure or trending psychology or weird conceptions of white guilt.

Some may ask, "Why—just because I've got white skin?" For now, yes. That may be what love requires in this moment. It doesn't mean you're an awful person or deserve to be treated as one, but you can stand in as a proxy for the awful done by others and crack open a door of healing by responding to people with empathy, understanding, and a shared brokenness for the human condition. And, if you'll let yourself, you might even become more aware of your own racial failures in a way that produces growth.[3]

"The (insert denomination or organization) issued a public statement acknowledging the racism of their past and their repentance of it. What more do they all want?" Formal statements of repentance on behalf of denominations are certainly healing gestures, but it helps even more to have a living proxy, a majority culture stand-in who has broad enough shoulders to absorb the hurt a minority culture person carries. Organizations may set the tone, but healing and restoration happen one relationship at a time. In the church, the solution to racial division starts small and local and personal. Then it becomes structural and communal and generational.

"How many times do I have to do this?" I don't know. Probably more than will seem right or fair to you. But how many times do I need to love my brother or sister in ways that don't always align with my personal comfort? I know we'd all like to have one good racial cleansing moment and be done with it. But that's not how it works for people who are on individual journeys with specific and personal hurt. It's messy, because one majority culture person can do a lot of damage without even realizing they're doing it until it's too late. But under the gospel, one majority culture person can also create a ton of healing by shouldering more than they feel responsible for—simply as an act of agape love.

"CRT EMPHASIZES 'WHITE PRIVILEGE,' BUT MANY BLACK PEOPLE HAVE MORE THAN MANY WHITE PEOPLE"

The word *privilege* prompts many to think of a life of ease and material gain. I often see white folks arguing, "How can white privilege exist when I know black people who have way more than I do?" But limiting discussions of white privilege to financial prosperity misses the larger point—the privilege of a way of being. The idea of white privilege isn't that as a white person your life hasn't been circumstantially hard or that no black people can succeed among whites. White privilege is an invisible comfort produced by not having to worry about skin color at all. Indeed, it's a racial privilege to never have to think about racial privilege.

We only talk about privilege that comes with skin color because at significant moments in American history, white folks put values on skin color. If racist inequality didn't go away after the Civil War, why do we believe that a handful of laws put in place in the 1960s would abruptly and effortlessly dismantle both structural and psychological fortresses that took generations to build? It's why, decades after those laws were enacted, CRT began asking how discrimination still felt so palpably present in our nation.

White privilege rejects the view that status quo racial disparities are simply the cause/effect result of individual choices and meritorious behavior. It considers what law professor Devon Carbado calls the "historically accumulated social effects of race." This "racial accumulation" is economic (influencing current income and initial wealth), cultural (influencing the social capital from which a person can withdraw), and ideological (shaping perceived racial worth).

Expanding on the financial market metaphor, Carbado says,

> CRT exposes these intergenerational transfers of racial compensation. Building up over time to create racial shelters (hidden and protected racial privileges) and racial taxes (hidden and unprotected racial costs), racial compensation profoundly shapes and helps to support the contemporary economies of racial hierarchy. CRT intervenes to correct this market failure and the unjust racial allocations it produces.[4]

If we get outside our political tribe and lay aside the phrase *white privilege* itself, people know intuitively that across a lifetime, a person with black skin in America doesn't get treated the same way as a person having white skin in America, even given the current racial reversals being experienced. That doesn't mean there aren't white folks struggling. It means that regardless of what you have or don't have materially, psychologically white folks and black folks move through American society differently relative to one another.[5]

Dark skin comes with social baggage that's regularly being inspected, and until relatively recently, white skin passed through societal customs duty-free. Some white folks like to suggest this baggage either doesn't exist at all or has diminished to the point of irrelevancy. Some black folks despise recognizing the baggage because doing so renews its power. I sympathize with both takes. But the baggage *does* exist. If we lived in a society characterized by hundreds of years of equal treatment for people regardless of how God created them, this conversation wouldn't be relevant. But our heritage as Americans comes to us from exactly the opposite direction—tragically, even in the church.

In most pockets of America, the social world is set up for the convenience of white people. Most people remain oblivious to the invisible, taken-for-granted power that comes with belonging to the group that gets labeled "normal" in culture. In my normal, I'm not forced to think about life as a person of color. I get to contend with race and racism as an optional exercise. Racial discrimination comes to me as secondhand information, not through direct experience. That's not the case for POC.

But my normal gets challenged when I'm sitting alone in the buzzing student union of a historically black college or university at lunchtime, exiting the subway on Lenox/Malcolm X Boulevard in Harlem, introducing myself on a Sunday morning from the fifth row of an African Methodist Episcopal church, or working security at a predominantly BIPOC three-thousand-student conference. In those situations, minority-status insecurity helps me reflect more honestly and accurately on the perks of being in the majority. Fundamentally, white privilege is not having to feel like a minority or contend with the psychological stress that comes with being one. Most white folks don't realize how much security comes from being in the majority until they find themselves in a place where white skin becomes noticed for being white.

As Christians, paying attention to white privilege should be about stewardship and loving people different from us, not the demonization of skin color or all things that come from white society. It does no good to remove one form of injustice only to replace it with another.

Lawrence Blum reminds us that we need to develop an ability "to appreciate moral differences of degree."[6] There's a difference between having access to something everyone should have, like getting a quality high school education, and having access to something everyone should relinquish, like being allowed to develop ethnic indifference. Some advantages come by way of being part of the majority, which isn't a moral issue per se, but it often encourages lack of awareness regarding nonmajority concerns.

The majority doesn't have to apologize for being the majority, but it *does* have to take responsibility for stewarding the social and racial power it holds. The majority may have to feel the discomfort of losing a little control, giving up a few preferences, and centering nonwhite people in spaces they haven't been in before. It always feels uncomfortable to have our normal challenged. Some disequilibrium always accompanies creating new openings in a social fabric that fit snugly before.

"CRT OVERPLAYS SYSTEMIC INJUSTICE AND UNDEREMPHASIZES PERSONAL RESPONSIBILITY"

For the first five years of my Christian life, I attended a Sunday school class taught by Pastor Richard Walker. Still one of the most brilliant minds I've ever encountered, Walker was an enigma to me. He absorbed both testaments of the Bible in their original languages and read walls of theological works coming from all directions. One minute he'd sound like the staunchest conservative, emphasizing personal responsibility and accountability, and the next he'd be sharing stories of his involvement with civil rights protests and decrying structural problems at every level of society.

Among his many provocative statements, none rattled me more than when he said, "Because there is free will on earth, there will be inequality in heaven." Personal choice matters. People will be judged for their choice regarding Christ, of course, but even Christians will be rewarded in the kingdom based on what they did with the exercise of their free will (1 Corinthians 3:8). Equal opportunity is worth pursuing in the name of justice, but what people do with opportunity can also create inequality.

Is inequality a function of systemic injustice or what people do with their opportunities? Both. A worldly system committed to unequal opportunity or individuals failing to take moral responsibility for their lives? Both. Human systems and structures driven by power and profit resist equal opportunity. They will always cater to one group at the expense of another. But human free will means people get to make choices, and choices matter in outcomes. Thus, inequality results from *both* unjust systems and unwise or immoral choices, and both need to be examined carefully. Walker, who happens to be African American, took both the systemic nature of evil and the weight of personal responsibility seriously, a combination I've rarely experienced in Christians, regardless of racial background.

You'll almost never hear someone representing a CRT perspective talk about personal responsibility. Is it because they don't affirm the power of personal agency? That may be the case for some, but CRT exists to confront people who give little weight to structural and systemic sin as a reality. The "Critical" aspect of CRT tries to expose structural inequalities created by racial injustice, past and present. If they're reticent to recognize personal responsibility, it's because of a history of people using "choice" to explain away structural problems. They want people to acknowledge systemic complications.

When I hear someone touting personal choice, it's usually because they don't believe systemic racism exists, or if it does it's so rare as to be irrelevant, an excuse used by underachievers to justify their existence. In some cases, it's coming from someone who takes pride in their own narrative of overcoming, someone who feels they earned their current success status without handouts. White folks in this camp love to hear black intellectuals say, "Systemic racism isn't the reason the black community struggles today. We need to take care of our own business and quit blaming white folks for our personal and communal decline." They want people to acknowledge personal responsibility.

But Christians should resist this binary trap. The Bible recognizes how people suffer because of evil, godless systemic realities. It also warns every man and woman of their individual responsibility before God regardless of systemic realities. Depending on the specific situation, sometimes the problem is mostly systemic, and sometimes it's more a function of poor choices and a lack of responsible action. Christians who understand the profound nature of sin should have the capacity to affirm both while applying discernment to the particulars in question.

As a Christian, if you align with those who point out systemic and structural evil such that you're unable to declare the need for responsible, moral, ethical decisions, you've been compromised. If you champion responsibility but can't admit that systemic realities load the deck against certain people groups, you've been compromised. In either case, you've succumbed to a worldly lens, shaped more by political prejudices than the mind of Christ. Political discipleship forces us to take a side, but the theology of sin holds both structure and agency in tension. We need to think through this tension like Christians, not partisans.

"CRT UNDERMINES THE AUTHORITY OF SCRIPTURE BY PRESENTING 'BIBLE + CRT' LOGIC"

Do some people in the Christian racial justice camp take their cues more from sociology books than the Bible? Certainly. I know people on both sides of the antiracism/anti-antiracism aisle who need more Bible and less social media in their toolbox, but that doesn't mean everyone quoting Beverly Tatum or Robin DiAngelo is guilty of using "external sources of authority" as lenses through which to improperly interpret the Bible.[7] Nor does it mean they are putting those or other sources above the Bible as a final word. I remain partial to people who say, "The Bible is all we need to fix our race problem within the church. We don't need any additional lenses or sociological books to teach us." But since the Bible *should* be all we need both to make things right and to relate as the body of Christ, we need to ask why it hasn't been.

We can know our Bible without ever having thought about why all the black kids sit together in the cafeteria.[8] We may recite a list of passages yet not realize how we've been conditioned to never talk about race or confront difficult truths about American history.[9] We may be seminary trained but not recognize how structural patterns continue to negatively affect BIPOC. Ignorance about these realities impacts the cultural competency and effectiveness of Christians as both missionaries and human beings. Acquiring more education about racial truths aids our ability to connect with people, love them better, and see what they see. They should help us live biblical truth more effectively, not replace it.

"The Bible is all we need" sounds like a noble statement, but it's often being proclaimed by someone who can't articulate what the Bible teaches about oppression or racial partiality or demonic structural realities. When it comes to race, too many in this camp seem to have mastered the art of hiding behind the truth of certain Bible verses while ignoring crucial others, or, if they do know what the Bible says about those things, they either don't recognize the relevance of those teachings for this cultural moment or they've been discipled by political culture to such an extent that the Bible loses its power to challenge their thinking.

This reaction to CRT surfaces a few other problems. To begin with, American racism was created and maintained by people who knew their Bibles. Their Bible knowledge didn't help them refute racism—it helped them strengthen it. "Knowing" the Bible isn't enough. History shows us that regarding race, knowing whether the Bible is a positive thing or not depends on one's interpretation and how they apply it.

Further, it seems rare to find a white pastor or Bible study leader who teaches on both individual and structural racial sin. Unless people are doing work on their own, most Bible-taught congregations full of people who "know their Bibles" remain biblically ignorant regarding these topics. The Bible doesn't pretend to teach us everything regarding life under the sun. It's true that it provides everything we need for life and godliness (2 Peter 1:3), but it does not provide us with exhaustive knowledge about every subject relevant to humanity.

Why would Christians conclude we have little to learn from books on racism or racial justice or social injustice, especially since most of our formal education poorly addresses these subjects? Why shouldn't we learn from people who make it their life's work to study the social effects of racial sin? I don't reject the oncologist's diagnosis of cancer just because the Bible never talks directly about the disease, nor do I assume he's right or wrong without hearing the details. So why do I reject the sociologist's diagnosis of social cancer?

Humility should at least allow for the possibility that someone else's perspective might help me see the world more accurately, even if it never appeals to the Bible. But if you don't want to read books on race written by folks who do not submit to Christ as an authority, are you open to reading Christians who will write many of the same things instead of immediately dismissing them as "woke"? Assuming a person using CRT language considers it superior or even equal to Scripture is unfair and impossible to prove apart from significant discussion.

Nor should we pull one or two lines from an article or talk as evidence that someone is "using CRT above the Bible." I once received a call about a talk given by one of our ministry staff to a group of college students. The caller heard this speaker say that ethnic identity is more important than, or even equal to, our identity in Christ, and he saw this as an obvious example of our ministry replacing scriptural truth with CRT. But I know this teacher and knew that even if his teaching could have been clearer, what this concerned caller heard isn't what he meant.

The Bible teaches us that identity in Christ matters more than any other identity, but it does not say that other God-created identities don't matter at all. This teacher was exhorting his mostly white audience to not let their commitment to colorblindness keep them from appreciating the differences created by God-purposed ethnicity or allowing their majority culture norms to blind them to minority culture concerns. Unfortunately, the caller assumed the speaker he'd heard was compromising the faith based on a couple of words.

When people promote secular voices and their solutions above Scripture, we should resist them and allow the Bible to have final say. But even this conclusion should be approached with some measure of fear and trembling since submitting to the Bible in this way can't be accomplished in real time apart from sinful humans doing the interpreting and applying. When it comes to racial realities, white folks have a checkered history regarding what they choose to see in their Bibles and how they choose to apply it.

Using Critical Theory to dissect society is different from using it to dissect Scripture. Evangelicals maintain the infallibility of Scripture despite God using humans in its transmission while still acknowledging that every social action includes human sin and prejudice. We can't just assume that a conclusion derived from looking through a CRT lens is necessarily competing with Scripture or being held above it.

"CRT CREATES MISSION DRIFT OR COMPROMISES THE GOSPEL"

Talking about biblical social justice issues only represents mission drift if your conception of discipleship has always excluded teaching parts of the Bible concerned with biblical social justice. Or if you talk about social issues but never talk about how the Bible addresses them. Or if you talk about justice but wind up sounding more like a politician or talk show host and less like a Christian preacher. Those are legitimate concerns that represent "drift."

Concern with issues of justice should make up one part of Christian discipleship. If you *only* talk about justice, that's a problem. If you *never* talk about justice, that's also a problem. If you feel forced to choose sides, recognize that both need an adjustment. But if you've been brought up in one strand of evangelicalism, you've been taught that an overemphasis on issues of justice will pull you away from the real work of missions, which involves sharing the transactional message of salvation with people who don't know God.

I say one strand of evangelicalism because most people don't realize there's always been a minority position present during the rise of late-twentieth-century evangelicalism that was concerned with bringing the gospel message to bear on social issues. Most of my friends who are products of the Religious Right brand of evangelicalism have never heard of the Chicago Declaration of Evangelical Social Concern (1973).[10] They don't know of the evangelical faith leaders who gathered specifically to call Christians to reject racism, economic materialism and inequality, militarism, and sexism as an extension of their commitment to both Scripture and evangelistic ministry. As Carl Henry sounded alarms about divorcing redemption from social action in 1947, it's worth considering how this concern became a "minority" position within our expression of Christianity today.[11]

If you're aligned with a church or parachurch ministry that foregrounds evangelism and discipleship as your Christian priorities, anything that prevents you from sharing about the crucified and risen Christ might be considered "drift." But there's no drifting involved in explaining the social implications of receiving the crucified and risen Christ. One side believes the gospel is compromised by those who prioritize social issues, while the other suggests it was compromised decades ago when we stopped attending to them at all. Both sides share concerns that different forms of secular ideology are infiltrating the church. Both are concerned with mission drift, manifested either by de-emphasizing the cross or minimizing the effects of the cross.

Maybe you've heard the question framed this way: Is the Christian's primary role in the world to preach a crucified and risen Christ or to speak against injustice and the ways people get trampled by abusive power? But bracketing it this way creates an unnecessary binary. These are not mutually exclusive ideas. Preach Christ and, in alignment with his heavenly kingdom, intercede on behalf of mistreatment, injustice, and abuse of power. What are you being asked to do? Share Jesus. Live Jesus. One way you do both is by standing with those who are suffering because of living in a broken world. If your Jesus doesn't care about social evil beyond abortion, he's much less compelling for those who live each day under the weight of legitimate oppression.

WHAT NEXT?

Developing a Christian consciousness regarding race doesn't mean we have to embrace radical expressions of CRT to get there, but when it comes to racial theory, I'm convinced more damage has been done by my white brothers and sisters who have, as Rasool Berry calls it, an "uncritical race theory" than by anything CRT brings to our attention. I'm more concerned about the gap in awareness and empathy between those who rarely think about the racial component of life in America and those who live each day trying to make sense of their own racialization. That gap is more real than any threat posed by those supposedly encouraging Marxism in the church.

People regularly send me content sounding alarms about CRT. Most of it seems to serve the dual purposes of confronting the "woke" Christian crowd while simultaneously comforting the deeply concerned anti-progressive-politics, anti-Marxist, anti-antiracist crowd. It warns about pastors who've drunk the "woke" Kool-Aid, organizations trying to be seen as cool among progressives, and individual believers who've fallen prey to neo-Marxist ideology. There are some out there who fall into these categories, but I don't believe that's the case for most of the people being accused of trying to merge Marxist-inspired CRT with Christianity. In my experience, most of the time, people talking about race in the evangelical world—even those who may be using Marxist terms—are trying to call people deeper into the Bible, not away from it.

Don't immediately assume that people pressing for consideration of "systemic" issues, power stewardship, or patterns of social negligence are trying to reconcile CRT with Christianity. They may just be talking about parts of the Bible you're less familiar with. Don't assume when you hear similar terms or language that they're necessarily being used the way non-Christians use them. Slandering people trying to become more racially redemptive doesn't help the situation, and the last thing I need as a white person already averse to talking about race is another way out, another excuse to dismiss the race tension either as someone else's problem or just a cover for worldly ideologies.

I have a friend who says she knows listening is taking place when she's investing more energy in trying to understand than in trying to be understood, and that wisdom could serve us here. What if we separated ourselves from the insult-filled madness of social feeds, dropped the hostile rhetoric, and instead listened in the pursuit of genuine understanding? Let's reject the spirit of the age, which Carl Trueman provocatively describes as "eschew[ing] thoughtful argument about difficult issues for moronic and often malicious soundbites."[12] We desperately need to develop our instincts for active listening and learning from perceived opponents and "others," instead of recklessly fueling incivility. Let's get more understanding and do less assuming.

CRT is not trying to usher in God's kingdom. It's trying to adjust power imbalance and inequality in this one. As Derrick Bell said, CRT is "the response to a need for expressing views that cannot be communicated effectively through existing techniques."[13] The first CRT scholars wrote out of their own lived experience and the practical challenges they faced because of race. But if I don't share the same experiences or face the same challenges, my default response when in conversation with those who do should be *generating many questions in an effort to understand*, not immediately offering corrective instruction, citing a Thomas Sowell article, or silently disdaining them for being a victim and wishing *their* people would worry more about making better decisions. The scholars responsible for crafting the first documents had ideas they thought would make the world less unjust. Obviously, they thought someone needed to be challenged in their thinking, and it's ironic that today the people most needing this challenge are often the quickest to shut it down.

13

REDEEMING "SOCIAL JUSTICE" FROM INJUSTICE

Well, if one really wishes to know how justice is administered in a country, one does not question the policemen, the lawyers, the judges, or the protected members of the middle class. One goes to the unprotected—those, precisely, who need the law's protection most!—and listens to their testimony. Ask any Mexican, any Puerto Rican, any black man, any poor person—ask the wretched how they fare in the halls of justice, and then you will know, not whether or not the country is just, but whether or not it has any love for justice, or any concept of it. It is certain, in any case, that ignorance, allied with power, is the most ferocious enemy justice can have.

James Baldwin, No Name in the Street

Fundamentalism in revolting against the Social Gospel seemed also to revolt against the Christian social imperative.

Carl F. H. Henry, The Uneasy Conscience of Modern Fundamentalism

"Justice was discipled out of me."

My Asian American co-minister friend tossed those words out as an afterthought, but they echoed in my head. We were talking about the exasperation we felt while trying to motivate fellow ministers in our parachurch organization to wrestle with the biblical theme of justice instead of offhandedly rejecting it as Marxist. He explained how justice never came up in years of people teaching him the Bible. If "social justice" was ever mentioned, it was pejoratively. A concern for matters of societal justice was seen, at best, as a distraction from the work of evangelism and disciple making and at worst as the heretical playing field of liberal theologians or secular ideologues.

His lament reminded me of a story I'd read decades earlier in a book called *Discovering an Evangelical Heritage*. At the height of the Vietnam War, some church leaders asked Billy Graham to use his influence with President Richard Nixon to curtail US bombing of North Vietnam. Graham replied by saying, "I am convinced that God has called me to be a New Testament evangelist, not an Old Testament prophet!"[1] Statements like this from major evangelical figures fueled the justification to ignore, or at least downplay, words like *justice* and *social justice*. They had their place on the fringes of Christianity, but it wasn't part of *our* kind of ministry.

My own history with social justice is all over the place. In the early years of my discipleship, shaped by voices like Graham's, social justice was a rejected term for theological reasons. In seminary a decade later, exposed to the saturating expectation on God's people to protect those in society who needed it, social justice became a necessary phrase for biblical reasons. Later, in a PhD program at a secular school, social justice was appropriated to mean something far beyond the biblical vision, a corrupted phrase for ideological reasons. And across those seasons, social justice was always an acceptable phrase for racial reasons, especially in those instances where the Bible and secular ideology overlapped.

Of course, the reason people fret about social justice in the church today has to do with a concern for "wokeness" and "Critical Social Justice."[2] The critique of social justice coming from evangelicals is largely in reaction to the secular, non-Christian, cultural Marxist implementation of Critical theory. Voddie Baucham suggested that a "worthy goal" would be "to make [Christian] speakers and writers everywhere ashamed to use the term 'social justice' ever again."[3] But is that right? Should we consign social justice to a radical slogan dustbin? Or should we reclaim it and infuse it with the biblical intentions it started with?

The term *social justice* is used by different groups of people with different definitions. As Christians, we need a biblical understanding of social justice so we can discern both when Christian versions go off the rails and when progressive versions overlap with things we can affirm.[4] What a person means when referring to social justice depends entirely on their starting point. Where a person lands, whether they know it or not, comes on the heels of a war of ideas surrounding those two words both inside and outside the church for at least the last 150 years.

SOCIAL JUSTICE AND ITS CHRISTIAN ORIGINS

The original use of the term *social justice* has biblical roots.[5] In fact, a Jesuit priest named Luigi Taparelli (D'Azeglio) gets credited for first merging the words *social* and *justice* in the 1840s.[6] The idea of social justice in the Bible grows primarily out of two Hebrew words. *Mishpat*, used over two hundred times in the Old Testament, means to treat people equitably or fairly in accordance with the righteous standard of God's moral law. As Tim Keller explains, "It means acquitting or punishing every person on the merits of the case, regardless of race or social status."[7] *Mishpat* confronts situations where wrong is being done, where one party is taking advantage of another in a harmful way, but it goes beyond just punishing wrongdoing. In a positive sense it means giving people what they have coming to them. So *mishpat* means giving people their due, whether that is punishment for a transgressor or giving those transgressed against what they are owed.

Follow this word and you'll see a handful of populations showing up around it repeatedly: widows, orphans, immigrants, and the poor. Why? All these groups lack social power, leaving them most vulnerable to being mistreated. *Mishpat* ensures both those acting treacherously and those trod upon get what they deserve.

A second word runs closely alongside *mishpat* in helping us understand the social side of biblical justice. *Tsedaqah* can be translated as either "being just" or "being righteous," but in both cases it refers to right or proper living in relationships. Beyond personal moral righteousness, *tsedaqah* refers to "day-to-day living in which a person conducts all relationships in family and society with fairness, generosity and equity."[8] When these two words, *mishpat* and *tsedaqah*, are used together, the English expression that best conveys the meaning is "social justice." *Mishpat* demands accountability for wrongdoers and recompense for those wronged, while *tsedaqah*, a posture properly lived out across all social relationships, reduces the need for *mishpat*.[9]

For example, in Jeremiah 7:5-7, God says, "If you really change your ways and your actions and deal with each other justly, if you do not oppress the foreigner, the fatherless or the widow and do not shed innocent blood in this place, and if you do not follow other gods to your own harm, then I will let you live in this place, in the land I gave your ancestors for ever and ever." Throughout the Bible, social justice isn't portrayed as a secondary luxury or as outlier acts of benevolence. It's fundamentally necessary as part of one's worship before God. Don't coddle false gods, and don't allow people to be mistreated on your watch. Then you can enjoy the benefits of God's blessing.

Unless you are trained to miss it, the concern for the accountability of God's people toward others drips from the pages of Scripture, especially for vulnerable populations, irrespective of whether those groups exist inside or outside the family of God. You can barely turn a page without being confronted by it.

Biblical social justice involves righting wrongs and balancing unjust scales, but it also requires the initiation of generous behavior and social concern toward those most vulnerable and in need of it. Social justice, then, may come through personal interaction or civil structures, through conversation or courts. It focuses on both vulnerable groups of people and, obviously, individuals within those groups.[10]

SOCIAL JUSTICE AS SOCIAL GOSPEL AND LIBERATION THEOLOGY

In the late nineteenth and early twentieth centuries, veins of Protestant liberalism replaced the gospel of Jesus Christ with a "social" gospel that focused on the improvement of human society and social progress. In seeking to compensate for the neglect of people's physical well-being, they watered down the bad news of people's spiritual condition and the solution offered by the cross, replacing it with a political mission for the church devoid of spiritual salvation.

Another version of social justice that caused people to disparage the term arose in 1960s Latin America, when liberation theology became a reaction to the deep poverty and brutal injustices experienced there. By combining biblical ideas with Marxist language, calls to repentance were sacrificed on the altar of freedom from oppression. Jesus became less a spiritual Savior leading the rebellion against Satan and more a political revolutionary leading the rebellion against corrupt government.

There's always a danger that a legitimate corrective might go too far and become heretical, emphasizing what's been missing to such an extent that we create a new idolatry. That happened with both the social gospel and liberation theology. But note that both the social gospel and liberation theology are the result of Christians not taking biblical social justice seriously enough in their sphere of influence.

Both arose in response to orthodox teaching lacking the teeth of real-world aid on behalf of oppressed people.

Ironically, one reason both became attractive to masses of people is that conservative and orthodox believers put comfort over kingdom, protecting their own conveniences while neglecting and ignoring the injustice of others. Where these movements took root, Christians either failed to respond or responded so slowly to the plight of the marginalized, dispossessed, and neglected that eventually someone felt the need to overcorrect.

I'm not suggesting we ignore heretical teaching, but social justice heresies don't arise out of thin air. They are responding to an imbalance. As Carl Henry warned, Christians ignoring injustice and failing to adequately provide care for vulnerable populations make it that much easier for secular perversions of social justice to exist.

SOCIAL JUSTICE AS CRITICAL SOCIAL JUSTICE

So some Christians are leery of "social justice" because of these gospel-drained applications of the idea done in the name of Christ in the last century. However, most church people today resist the term because of something being done with it in *this* century—the onset of Critical Social Justice (CSJ). Scott David Allen refers to this form of ideologically driven justice as fixated on "deconstructing traditional systems and structures deemed to be oppressive, and redistributing power and resources from oppressors to their victims in the pursuit of equality of outcome."[11]

In their book, *Is Everyone Really Equal?*, Özlem Sensoy and Robin DiAngelo clearly define what is meant by Critical Social Justice and how it differs from other uses of the term *social justice.* They start by describing the common, philosophically liberal understanding of social justice that focuses on principles like fairness, equality, and protecting basic human rights.[12] Then they explain how a Critical approach differs:

A critical approach to social justice refers to specific theoretical perspectives that recognize that society is *stratified* (i.e., divided and unequal) in significant and far-reaching ways along social group lines that include race, class, gender, sexuality, and ability. Critical social justice recognizes inequality as deeply embedded in the fabric of society (i.e., as structural), and actively seeks to change this.[13]

So Critical Social Justice relies on a constant interrogation of inequality and systems of power. Its endgame is access to resources, but there's much more going on than just resource acquisition. CSJ works to confront the groups holding power in hopes of redistributing both power and the resources it produces across society. At its best, CSJ protects human rights, removes restrictions to accessing essentials like shelter, food, education, and health care, and champions the voices of those being left out.

But CSJ advocates also assume a governing authority should be endowed with the power to impose their version of a fair and equal society, and this authority should be entrusted to redistribute advantages and resources to disadvantaged groups of their choosing to realize equal social and economic outcomes. Thus, one group of fallen people using power to their own advantage gets replaced by another group doing the same. They assume that inequality is always the result of discriminatory structures and social evil at work while virtually ignoring personal agency and the serendipitous nature of God's created world.

Plenty has been written explaining why this approach to social justice isn't justice at all.[14] I appreciate CSJ's intended desire to protect and elevate marginalized populations, but attaching the word *justice* to an act or behavior does not indicate that the act or behavior is just according to kingdom standards, ethics, or virtues. Every socially offended group of human beings makes declarations about justice, but if these grievances contradict the Word of God, they aren't justice. They just affirm the spirit of the current age.

I used to ask my leftist classmates, "You want to tear down the current structures and replace them with . . . what? Who will run your world and guarantee that equality remains intact? Why should I trust that Sensoy and DiAngelo will operate in a more just way than those currently running things?" I was always met with uncomfortable silence. I want the justice that results from an enacted kingdom ethic, but Critical Social Justice only knows of one kingdom, and its ethics are driven by a different god.

Progressive, Critical, or neo-Marxist social justice doesn't appeal to or include any conception of a personal God. Thus, no one from outside the system sets the bar for what justice means, nor do we collectively give an account of ourselves and our treatment of others to anyone above humanity. Christians put the will of a holy God at the center of social justice. Liberals put the choices of individual humans at the center of social justice. Critical theorists put the power of offended groups at the center of social justice. The further a concept of a personal God is removed from the discussion, the more human desires make their way to the center and the worse becomes our analysis and solutions.

WHAT WE MEAN BY SOCIAL JUSTICE

Frankly, most people don't have enough knowledge of either Marxism or the Bible to rush to hasty conclusions in these discussions. When lazy demonization takes the place of real understanding, we get the hostile outrage culture we're now experiencing from both directions. It's not wise to make assumptions when someone references social justice. Instead, seek clarification. When it derives from a Marxism that rejects Christ and seeks to erase all moral lines, that's unbiblical. When social justice derives from Christian theology that examines sinfully produced disparity to bring righteous correction, that's biblical.

Thus, we need to clearly delineate what we mean by social justice, especially when it comes to race. White Christians have spent so much time debunking a secular notion of social justice. What if we redirected that effort toward understanding what black Christians have been calling out for literally hundreds of years now with unsatisfying results? Social justice is paying attention to how people get taken advantage of because they lack money, or education, or social capital. It is about bringing God's kingdom to bear on individual and corporate circumstances in this world because that's part of our calling as salt and light. Here are a few ways we as Christians should adjust our thinking about social justice in the context of race.

Separate race from gender and sexuality. We need to separate the conversation around racial injustice from claims of gender or sexuality oppression—they are not the same thing. Critical Social Justice says all three must be considered together, but we don't have to accept that packaging. I'm not suggesting there's no overlap regarding the shared mistreatment of all these labels as minority groups, but the racial conversation is less cluttered when kept separate from these other incendiary topics.

Recognize the confusion created when progressive and conservative groups frame racial justice in their own terms. People with a politically driven desire to overthrow the foundations of this country took up the mantle of civil rights alongside BIPOC folks and, in effect, used their plight as an all-purpose battering ram against the establishment. Meanwhile, evangelicalism hitched itself to Republican political positions in the form of the Religious Right, which dealt with race by focusing on individual choice, minimizing structural and systemic problems, and overlooking biblical themes calling attention to marginalized and oppressed populations.

When both of these political positions borrow from Christian tradition and use Christian language, it creates confusion for people trying to think biblically about racial justice. Political discourse these days doesn't offer nuance. One side speaks as though structural racism accounts for every racial disparity, while the other denies any such systemic evil exists. One side recognizes the importance of personal agency regardless of circumstances, while the other rarely talks about choices at all. One believes financial reparation will cure much inequality, while the other says money doesn't change hearts. And on it goes. Neither side of the political continuum concerns itself with biblical justice. Both prioritize partisan loyalty and platform consistency. Recognizing this is a helpful step in untangling the race web.

Grow in your curiosity about why people are attracted to distortions. I've spent enough time around proponents of Critical Social Justice to conclude that many of them genuinely long for the kind of justice promoted by the Bible. They've rejected Jesus and everything to do with the formal aspects of organized Christianity, but common grace leaves them yearning for biblical kingdom justice, especially when they see people being harmed by structures and policies. They take American ideals of "life, liberty, and the pursuit of justice" seriously enough to despise those who trample and violate them, even if they don't explicitly believe in the *imago Dei*. People within the Christian world who become attracted to variations of the social gospel and liberation theologies want the same—more humane living conditions, more opportunities, less hoarding of resources, and less mean-spiritedness.

BIPOC and white Christians I encounter who employ Critical Theory or Progressive language are doing so not because they want to embrace Marxist ideology or replace their orthodox theology with something heterodox, but because they've found helpful language supporting the kind of change that Christian teaching and action should have already addressed. Because Christian folks have so easily aligned themselves with secular conservative politics, they now make themselves a target for the language of Critical Theory, which challenges entrenched hierarchies and social patterns that oppress people. They're trying to bring a corrective to Christian indifference, not a replacement for Christian belief.

When it comes to race, Critical Social Justice isn't the answer to realizing God's justice on earth, but sometimes Critical Social Justice proposes questions and legitimate concern for people being mistreated—people we, as God's people, *should* be engaging but aren't.

Recognize that justice and equality aren't the same thing. Sometimes inequality occurs because of bad choices; other times inequality exists because of longstanding systemic problems. Usually, it's a mixture of both, and it seems prudent that we start asking how both choices and structures contribute to racial inequality found in specific situations.

From a Christian perspective, equality isn't the final goal, but misuses of power, partiality based on status or socially constructed labels, and mistreatment of people because of skin color are inequalities that not only affect outcomes but also create dividing walls of hostility between the races. Power *is* always at work, but power isn't always to blame for inequality.

Groups of people benefit from and are hindered by structural evil, but they also benefit from and are hindered by personal choices and a host of other circumstantial realities. Individuals within named groups should take seriously their social benefits from being associated with that group and reflect on how other groups may experience disadvantages simply for their association with an outlier group. There really are victims of mistreatment at the hands of bullies in this country, but just because I'm encouraged to feel bad about some aspect of myself or find myself in a social minority doesn't mean I'm experiencing a violence that needs governmental correction.

WHAT ABOUT THE CHURCH?

How should we address race-based social injustice as the church? What do BIPOC brothers and sisters wish we knew? Consider this from attorney and political strategist Justin Giboney:

At best, many white evangelicals treat racial justice like an extra-curricular activity. At worst, racial justice is framed as a distraction to proclaiming the gospel of Jesus Christ. When mentions of race and justice surface, too many evangelical leaders roll out distorted and extreme examples to make the case against Christian participation in justice efforts. They've resigned themselves to being skeptical commentators, experts at finding fault in the efforts of others and unwilling to find inspiration or courage to attack the problem more biblically.[15]

Why do white folks struggle so much with being the hands and feet of Jesus when it comes to racial justice? We've already seen at least several of the main culprits, but how did we allow the word *justice* to become so bastardized by politicians and ideologues that we've all but dropped it as a Christian responsibility?

Racial justice is our concern because real justice is an enemy of Satan. Real justice protects the *imago Dei*, promotes human flourishing, and reflects God's shalom. On the other hand, social injustice is like oxygen for the principalities and powers of this present darkness. Given that "the whole world lies in the power of the evil one" (1 John 5:19 ESV), we should expect various expressions of social injustice to be the norm, and Christians should be the quickest to sound alarms for a kingdom-shaped response. Are we fervently *for* biblical justice or just urgently *against* Critical Social Justice? It's far easier to debate justice *in theory* than to reflect on how our Christian responsibility to do justice *in reality* influences our practices and behavior.

When I think about social justice and the church, my imagination often takes me back to September 23, 1955, thirteen years before I was born. In the street outside a courthouse in Tallahatchie County, Mississippi, people file out after a five-day sham trial produced the acquittal of two men in the murder of fourteen-year-old Emmett Till. Weeks earlier, photographs of Till's mutilated body lying in his open casket became a lightning rod for the burgeoning, justice-seeking civil rights movement, but there's no evidence of "justice" in Sumner right now. The all-white jury needed only sixty-seven minutes to reach their verdict, and four months later the two men brazenly confessed to the murder in stark detail for four thousand dollars and an article in *Look Magazine*.[16] Maybe it's naive, but as I think about the day of the acquittal, I wonder, *Where are the white church people? Why are they letting this happen? Why doesn't their biblical view of justice compel them to speak against this?*

What if white evangelical congregations had shown up at the court-house to protest both Emmett's murder and the coddling of the men who did it? What if they had verbally confronted this obvious and heinous injustice of a little boy tortured and murdered for supposedly talking sassy to a white woman in their county, which, as it turns out, he never actually did?[17] Online, I can find the picture of a "Garment Center Labor Rally" taking place a month later in New York City protesting "the murder of Emmett Till" and "racial terror in Mississippi," organized by the NAACP and local labor unions, but I can't find evidence of a rally held anywhere by white Christians representing the church of Jesus Christ.[18]

If Christians can't show us what justice looks like when Emmett Till gets murdered, someone else will. Examples like this explain why Marxism, Communism, Socialism, or any "ism" often appear more attractive to people affected by race and racial injustice. The greatest threat to the strength of the church isn't secular ideology; it's the vacuum created by our own indifference toward social evil the Bible plainly condemns. It takes work to separate out the political from the biblical, the cultural from the theological—the most predominant forms of discipleship happening simultaneously in most people's lives.

But it should disturb us when legitimate cries for justice get "lost in an echo chamber of bad theology, excuses, and bad faith deflections."[19] I recognize that biblical justice isn't the true concern of either political party, but it should always be the concern of Christians who, while "foreigners and exiles" (1 Peter 2:11) in this world, protect a kingdom vision for justice on behalf of people being hurt by others and the systems they create. Jesus cares about justice, and it's the people who've claimed the name of Jesus whose silence in the face of racial injustice causes the universe to shudder. Why would a heart changed by Jesus give only scraps of attention to those considered marginalized in their midst?

We should be more highly sensitized to satanic marring of the *imago Dei* and less prone to politicize it away. The last thing we need is another excuse not to think deeply about what justice means in our time. In social pockets where it's lacking, what if more conservative-minded folks restored an emphasis on social concern? Not as a prerequisite to the gospel, but because of the transformation the gospel produces.

White silence need not be corrected with words. Silence is best filled with action. With intentional movement toward people. With effort toward relationship building. With humble acknowledgment of blind spots. With confronting self-deception that underappreciates injustice, suffering, and disparity with roots in past policies and decisions. Much work has been done to set and cast our national racial fracture, but how do we continue to help it heal? We know what politicians from both sides propose, but what does a kingdom response look like in your corner of the world?

14

HEALING FROM THE PERSISTENCE OF WHITE SUPREMACY

Racism is not about how you look,
it's about how people assign meaning to how you look.

ROBIN D. G. KELLEY,
"RACE—THE POWER OF AN ILLUSION"

In this country, American means white.
Everybody else has to hyphenate.

TONI MORRISON, THE BLUEST EYE

NOTHING GETS WHITE-SKINNED PEOPLE more riled up than asking them to talk about being white. I didn't need Robin DiAngelo to teach me that. It's been my consistent experience throughout life. Some people consider this kind of discussion divisive, unhelpful, and even theologically problematic, and it certainly can be all three. I've read anecdotes of people reporting that their pastors want them to repent of their "whiteness," as though having white skin is now a sin needing salvation. People hear "white supremacy," imagine hooded riders on horses, and naturally want to distance themselves from the image. I can certainly understand why talk of "whiteness studies" and "white supremacy" puts people on edge.

But can we separate ourselves from those emotions long enough to consider what it means to be white in a culture that, for centuries, said it mattered if you weren't? Because without a steely-eyed look at how race and racial difference developed in America, we'll always lack perspective on why skin color continues to matter in this country, even though so many tell us it doesn't. Race doesn't matter because leftists say it does—it matters because history says it does. A racial hierarchy was created, and it helps to appreciate how white folks wound up at the top of it.

I was talking with my friend James, one of the most thoughtful and intellectually stimulating people I've ever known. James happens to be African American, and when I told him I was considering writing a book trying to help white folks sort through the race conflict, he scoffed. "Why in the world would you do that? White people don't want to hear any of that. They don't want to think about race. You'll do nothing but get yourself in trouble." He went on to say, without a hint of hyperbole, that white supremacy has become neurological for white folks. It's so seared into our psyche that a literal rewiring of our brains would have to take place for us to view black folks differently. James isn't given to making over-the-top statements like this. It caught me off guard, but he meant it.

When white people sit down to study race, they assume their topic of study will be black folks or Asians, Natives, or Latinos and their experience relative to white populations. They rarely consider studying the white population because most white folks don't consider white a race. But "black" and "white" racial classifications were created at the same time and in opposition to one another. The only way to really understand how race works in this country is to pay more attention to the color all other colors are compared to and the ideology behind it: "whiteness."

HOW DO YOU CREATE RACE?

The word *race* has a complicated history for many reasons, one simply being the different ways the term gets used across disciplines and centuries. At one time, race involved grouping people according to language. At others, it distinguished national origin or the part of the world a person came from, virtually synonymous with ethnicity. Used this way, race is just an observation, a way of recognizing distinguishing characteristics of people based on their demographic history.

But race becomes more problematic when we add values to those otherwise neutral physical differences. Skin color doesn't *mean* anything on its own. Humans declare why one color denotes virtue and another does not.[1] We call the process of developing and maintaining those meanings "constructing race." Calling race a social construct is just a fancy academic way of saying it's a made-up idea to distinguish among groups of people based largely on some aspect of their outward appearance. It's a labeling system flowing from the prejudices of a society, a tool used by people with a vested interest in creating separation between themselves and another group of people. When we create a hierarchy based on those added meanings, we entertain demons, and the work is no longer just social, it's also spiritual.

Appreciating how race gets constructed in this sense is a deeply theological issue and needs to be understood as such. When race starts to mean something, human value doesn't come from being created in the image of God; it comes from where a person lands on a fabricated hierarchy. We might conclude that's just the way the world works, but for Christians, that's a problem.

I think most people who believe in a sin nature assume racial animosity is innate, but it isn't. While it's true that broken humans will always find a reason not to like one another, racial disdain must be cultivated. It's not natural to us. White and black kids play together and can plainly see they look different, but they're unaware that skin color has meaning until they learn it from somewhere else, and that teaching flows from a racial construction devised somewhere in the past. At first, they just have a friend with different skin color, but once they learn different skin color has distinct meanings associated with it, they are experiencing the effects of race being constructed.

Put an African, Native American, and European in a room with each other in the year 1400. In their own minds, each of them imagines themselves no less than equal to everyone else in the room, and perhaps even superior to the other two, but no one in the room thinks themselves inferior. They have pride in their own heritage, feel justified in their history, secure in whatever their religious faith teaches. Establishing an oppressive hierarchy of superiority and inferiority among this group requires physical and psychological struggle.

The group making it to the top needs technological power to assert their will, but they also need psychological shortsightedness about the humanity of the others as well as their own treachery. The other groups need to be broken physically, mentally, spiritually. They need to relinquish the belief in their own equality and any claims they had to superiority. Put simply, the raw work of colonialism demands the simultaneous effort to elevate one group while breaking all others.

Martin Luther King Jr. explained the justifying psychology of colonizers like this:

> It seems a fact of life that human beings cannot continue to do wrong without eventually reaching out for some rationalization to clothe their acts in the garments of righteousness. And so, with the growth of slavery, men had to convince themselves that a system which was so economically profitable was morally justifiable. The attempt to give moral sanction to a profitable system gave birth to the doctrine of white supremacy.[2]

Our European predecessors came to this land inhabited by dark-skinned people and made race-based differences a thing. They intentionally gave value to skin color, arguing for the goodness of white folks and the inferiority of everyone else. Once the decision was made to colonize and conquer, what option did they have? If they knew in advance that peaceful coexistence wasn't part of the expansion plan, they had to demonize, degrade, and dehumanize those they were replacing.

Good Christians and humanists couldn't tolerate blatant participation in defacing the *imago Dei* in other humans, so they made non-whites something less than human. Using religion, they made them expendable for not knowing Jesus. Then, even after many of them came to Jesus, politics made them expendable because they might rebel. Finally, science made them expendable by developing the "truth" that dark-skinned people are biologically and mentally inferior to white-skinned people.[3] Creating and reifying race categories allowed the belief in separate, distinct, and exclusive groups of people made unequal by either God or nature and thus deserving to be treated as inferior beings. They created white supremacy.

The colonizing work done in the fifteenth through the eighteenth centuries by Britain, France, Portugal, Spain, and the Netherlands—self-identified "Christian" empires—all required the formal and legal development of whiteness as a superlative. In the pursuit of creating countries and governments by and for those deemed "white"—a racial caste system C. R. Boxer called a "pigmentocracy"—the idea of whiteness had to be taken seriously. An impressive amount of legislative intentionality went into creating "whiteness" across four centuries. It's against this backdrop that "white supremacy" becomes inevitable and "whiteness" becomes a problem to be explored.

THE DEPTHS OF WHITE SUPREMACY

White supremacy only exists as a category for us because race was constructed in a particular way in America. Indeed, those few parts of the world lying outside the reach of European colonization would hardly understand those two words together. But what do *we* mean when we use that phrase? I hear it used in at least three different ways depending on context, and it's important to appreciate the differences.

White supremacy as hate. This form of supremacy promotes unapologetic malice, gets fueled by a noxious combination of fear and disdain, and seeks total separation from both non-white-skinned people and others they consider inferior, like Jews, LGBTQ individuals, and immigrants. When people hear the term *white supremacy*, I think this is the caricature they imagine most often. It's also why people recoil at the possibility of being implicated with it. It not only views white-skinned humans as superior but despises those with dark skin, seeing them as an ever-present threat.

White supremacy as normativity/hierarchy. This is white supremacy without dependence on hate. It's the intuitive sense that white people make better leaders, are more innately moral, are better interpreters of history, make the most important contributions to civilization, are intellectually superior, the heroes of liberalism and global progress, and so on. Euro-American inclinations are not just *preferred*, they are *superior*. That's the key to this manifestation of supremacy. Part of what makes this form of white supremacy most insidious is that it's invisible. It's racism without racists. It's sanitized and acceptable and has none of the messiness of overt hate. It's hegemonic, so assumed and absorbed into our collective consciousness we don't have to think about it.

Europeans came to this land with a superiority complex, baked it into every level of society, and used it to dominate everyone in their way. Our American predecessors worked hard not only to create a racial hierarchy but also to preserve it for future generations. Until the recent push to tell American history from "below," American national identity has always been constructed from the top of that hierarchy and almost entirely as white. This is simply a historical and sociological truth. American history gets told from the white perspective.

Our education bleeds European. Our national holidays predominantly celebrate the lives and behavior of white men. Most of our politicians and business leaders are white. Except for momentary trends, advertising speaks to and promotes white standards of beauty and the "good life." Other than professional sports, our entertainment industry is run and dominated by white faces. Whether you're conscious of it or not, this is the air we breathe. But racial theorists note another form that quietly goes a step beyond just affirming the hierarchy.

White supremacy as ideological/cultural power. Since the inception of CRT in the late 1980s, scholars started using "white supremacy" to include more than just racial hatred and racial superiority. They expanded it to describe the way those attitudes result in social and structural dominance. Law scholar Frances Lee Ansley put it this way in 1989:

> By "white supremacy" I do not mean to allude only to the self-conscious racism of white supremacist hate groups. I refer instead to *a political, economic and cultural system in which whites overwhelmingly control power and material resources,* conscious and unconscious ideas of white superiority and entitlement are widespread, and *relations of white dominance and non-white subordination are daily reenacted across a broad array of institutions and social settings.*[4]

As such, white supremacy describes the ongoing racial power structure of the United States, where the economic, legal, educational, housing, entertainment, and financial systems continue to be controlled primarily by white people. It presumes we've all been situated in an historically racist hierarchy and in varying degrees are still experiencing the consequences of a social system created to favor one race at the expense of others.

This view of white supremacy flows from a global history of white countries dominating nonwhite countries and people, suppressing or erasing their cultures and autonomy. It's a response to European countries invading, oppressing, and superimposing white cultural laws, morals, and social standards on colonized people. Even after centuries of assimilation into whatever it means to be American, people with non-Euro cultural backgrounds feel a need to fight for their own cultures and identities, rebuilding their original culture free from white influence and control.[5] Jim Crow no longer rules the land, but when white folks control the levers, make the decisions, experience the benefits of financial privilege set in motion decades ago, control the courtroom, and determine the history, what reason is there to believe nonwhite interests will be protected?

WHAT DOES IT MEAN TO STUDY "WHITENESS"?

Studying "whiteness" involves the practice of understanding and critiquing a particular cultural perspective, a way of being situated in the world relative to others that winds up producing racial inequalities. Given their historical backdrop, whiteness studies usually veer toward the negative, but they don't have to be disparaging. Nor are they primarily about skin color. Having white skin isn't a problem, but having white skin gives me a ticket to absorb discriminatory cultural ideas that are a problem without even realizing it, and whiteness studies focus on the embodiment, manifestation, and effect of those ideas.

The National Museum of African American History and Culture summarizes it like this:

> *Whiteness* and white racialized identity refer to the way that white people, their customs, culture, and beliefs operate as the standard by which all other groups are compared. Whiteness is also at the core of understanding race in America. Whiteness and the normalization of white racial identity throughout America's history have created a culture where nonwhite persons are seen as inferior or abnormal. This white-dominant culture also operates as a social mechanism that grants advantages to white people, since they can navigate society by feeling *normal.* Persons who identify as white rarely have to think about their racial identity because they live within a culture where whiteness has been *normalized.*[6]

Andrew T. Draper describes it as the study of "an idolatrous system of embedded norms intricately arranged to prefer, esteem, and profit white people by any means necessary."[7]

So whiteness is a constellation of patterns, ideas, beliefs, attitudes, policies, structures, and resourcing that creates inequities and injustices along racial lines. It's a way of seeing the world, originating in the way race has been constructed throughout the history of the United States.

When people advocate for the dismantling of white supremacy, they're attacking a posture more than a color, the embodiment of ideas more than a group itself. Hate groups are a product of whiteness ideology, and we can easily see them, but invisible attitudes of superiority producing more easily camouflaged bigotry or discrimination can be far more problematic. It's those attitudes that need to be exposed, discussed, and sometimes neutralized.

Within the context of a talk, I've asked a mixed, black/white audience, "When did you become conscious of being black or white?" Inevitably, regardless of background, black folks have a story describing the moment they realized they lived in a racialized culture that put stock in skin color. White folks almost never have one. Until the moment I asked, they'd never considered themselves part of a race or given thought to what it means to be white in a culture that has always taken racial differences seriously. Why?

BIPOC folks have a story because at some point they are confronted with whiteness, and it usually comes to them through a person with white skin. It's not that they didn't realize they had dark skin while living in a country full of people with white skin. It's the realization that something in their soul has been judged, something in their psyche has been compared and crushed, something from the palette of their own cultural preference has been deemed less than and dismissed. They had a direct encounter with racism, or they simply felt smothered by the dominant cultural ethos.

But white folks only have that feeling if they're placed in a situation where they are the minority for a time. Otherwise, their racial preference is usually the standard. Not so for nonwhite folks and their cultures. They're usually abandoning or stripping their preferences. Realizing this is happening matters. It helps me to be more careful and sensitive when it comes to other people's cultural desires. We should do this for everybody, of course, but especially when we're in a mixed-race situation given the historical damage created from not doing this.

Thinking about whiteness is complicated. Not all white people helplessly subscribe to the exact same thinking about themselves or others. But maybe most literature on whiteness sounds leftist because conservative-minded people won't allow themselves to consider whiteness as a thing at all. It's confounding that for centuries white-skinned people had no problem saying, "This is what it means to be white and you're not it," but now the suggestion that we study the history of an ideology called "whiteness" offends. Whiteness is a sociological reality stemming from an intentionally created hierarchy-based racism. It serves Marxists but really isn't the property of Marxists. We don't need to be afraid of it, and we really shouldn't ignore it.

What patterns or norms have I developed from being around mostly white-skinned people my whole life? I don't need to repent for having cultural preferences, but I do need to check myself and ask whether I've allowed those preferences to become an idol or hinder my ability to appreciate and value the differences and preferences God created in others, especially those labeled by another race.

WHY DOES ANY OF THIS MATTER FOR THE CHURCH?

I hear white Christians complaining they are tired of talking about race, but being tired of *hearing* about race and *talking* about race aren't the same thing. Unfortunately, many people who say it's time to stop talking about race never really started talking about it in the first place, or at least not in a productive way with people different from them. Race talk, if it happens at all, is usually about others, not about my place in the racial majority and how I relate to others.

As a Christian, I don't study the details of the construction of race in this country because of some "woke" agenda encouraged by the political left. I do it because I want to understand my own situatedness in the American racial narrative and the lived experience of my nonwhite brothers and sisters. I do it so I can love better.

It's important to learn about the past because having a vague sense that bad things happened around race isn't the same as knowing the specific dynamics of the construction of American racialization or understanding its ramifications for today. Even if it's difficult, we can start by expanding our education regarding the origins of race and how race works on our minds today. Then we can determine whether we need to talk about it in a specific social space.

Austin Channing Brown suggests there's a connection among knowledge, understanding, and justice when she says,

> Our only chance at dismantling racial injustice is being more curious about its origins than we are worried about our comfort. It's not a comfortable conversation for any of us. It is risky and messy. It is haunting work to recall the sins of our past. But is this not the work we have been called to anyway? Is this not the work of the Holy Spirit to illuminate truth and inspire transformation? It's haunting. But it's also holy.[8]

Obviously, whiteness leading to hate-driven white supremacy is sinful evil. Apart from some forms of extremist Christian nationalism, most people with a basic Bible education see this clearly and reject it.[9] But what about white supremacy packaged as preferential norms leading to hierarchy? What about when white supremacy becomes a cover for protecting power dynamics and maintaining control of leadership levers within Christian fellowships? Do I need to repent of my preferences becoming idols? What do I do with whatever amount of God-given racial power I'm entrusted to steward?

When Christian hip-hop artist Lecrae announced he was leaving "white evangelicalism," Christians reacted with a biblical explanation for the wrongness of it without seriously digging into the "whiteness" of it.[10] Out came accusations of wokeness and suggestions he'd fallen into the Leftist abyss. Instead of asking questions, empathizing, or expressing any sort of grief, people declared their own racial innocence, took issue with his blanket condemnation of white evangelicals, questioned his theology, and warned those who still supported him of their complicity in wokeness. The prevailing Christian response to Lecrae seems flavored more by an antagonistic political ethos than by Christians steeped in love. What is his perception of the group or his experience among those who make up the group that causes him to say he doesn't want to be a part of it anymore? I wish our collective default would be to explore the hurt and frustration behind his words instead of immediately correcting his ecclesiology.

When POC abandon evangelicalism as a movement, they're usually rejecting its anthropology, not its theology. They're leaving because too many white people they encounter refuse to consider the possibility that their cultural norms lend structural support to walls of hostility. They leave because abortion is the only social injustice that gets attention or energy from most conservative-leaning, white evangelicals despite racial justice issues making headlines on a regular basis. They leave because of a stubborn unwillingness to think about racial injustice as being systemic or structural or anything other than poor personal choices. Perhaps this explains Carl Ellis Jr.'s reaction to the firestorm: "Evangelicalism is as much of a culture as it is a theological movement."[11]

Is it fair to condemn *all* of white evangelicalism for anything, given the diversity of belief and behavior that exists under the umbrella of white evangelicalism? Of course not. Blanket condemnation of entire groups is rarely helpful. But there's also damage when we judge Lecrae's public departure without concern for the stories behind it. He feels disillusioned. He feels pain. He feels resentment. What experiences with white-dominant culture contributed to those negative emotions? In a case like this, we have an obligation to grieve with those who grieve.

HOW PERSONAL PREFERENCES HINDER LOVE

Most people I interact with confidently assume personal objectivity when it comes to race. I hear people flippantly testify to their color-blindness and adamant commitment to accept all people as equal, but how can anyone know what they think about different races until they submit to a person of color at work or in church or in a boardroom? How can I know my biases and racial attitudes until they've been challenged? Not until I become the minority does my racialization get tested.

In my early twenties, I remember being at a conference run entirely by black folks. I'd been to many Christian retreats and conferences by this time but never one with black people making every decision. When several things went wrong, I remember thinking to myself, *Black people don't know how to run things like this.*

The previous five years, I'd spent as much time with black and Hispanic folks as I had white folks and I was comfortable in all crowds, but in two decades I'd never been under black people in leadership, which conditioned me to be suspicious of their credibility in these spaces. I questioned their ability to lead, their access to knowledge and training, and whatever else it took to pull off a successful event. In my experience to that point, white people ran these events, and without white input it probably wouldn't be as good. Of course, that's an ignorant assessment that I'm embarrassed to admit now, but I don't think it's all that uncommon among white folks who've rarely or never been under black leadership in any context of their life.

Was I a white supremacist? Not in all social arenas, but I certainly was in this one. Simply by living in dominant culture, we're predisposed to assume that our normal is right. Something feels slightly off with non-white theologians, pastors, styles of worship, orders of service, and so on. We don't naturally concern ourselves with the concerns of different subcultures of people around us unless we're in relationship with them and start to see the world through their eyes, even as we continue to look through our own.

If I need to repent, it's not for having white skin. Nor is it for having cultural preferences. If I need to repent, it's for allowing those norms to become idols. It's for weaponizing my norms, for measuring others against them and judging their preferences as less than. Here, preferences and norms have nothing to do with sexual ethics, women in leadership, or soteriology. I'm talking about different aesthetic styles. Ways of handling and inhabiting time. The role of storytelling in acquiring truth. What stories get told. Which moments and people of history get remembered. How significant cultural moments are framed and talked about. Which parts of our local community get served and what it means to serve them. Which Bible verses and theological concepts get prioritized.

As such, repenting of whiteness has more to do with attitude and posture toward others than the color of my skin. It's a recognition that unless I've been intentional to break free from demonic racialization and the ways we're taught to ascribe meaning to skin color, I'm probably guilty of accepting the racial hierarchy implicitly fed to me throughout society.

THE PRODUCTS AND CONSEQUENCES OF RACIAL FORMATION

Race and racial meaning are products of cultural dynamics. Both get learned and passed on through content delivery systems: family, friends, mass media and entertainment, schools, church, and social media. Racial meaning is reflective of the values and interests of those who produce it, and that can look quite different in diverse contexts. Instead of assuming moral immunity, what if we asked, "What have I learned about people different from me through these sources? Even if I've rejected them, what messages about POC do the content producers in my life promote?"

At a recent ministry training conference, I saw three promotional videos for a worldwide organization serving people in poverty. Each video featured white-skinned people in the position of helping dark-skinned people. I met with a group of friends after the session, and they all had the same question: Why don't we ever see three minutes of happy and flourishing dark-skinned people helping poor white people? Why do white people always wind up in the helping role, with nonwhite people usually being helped? How do videos like these subtly shape our thinking? You don't need to be "woke" to recognize the potential problems this creates over time in meaning formation related to skin color. I'm not interested in whether the video producers are themselves racist or harboring some form of antibiblical partiality in their soul. I'm more interested in the small but consequential effect this discourse has on racial formation in those who watch it.

Right into the 1960s, white people were constructing racial categories in a deliberate attempt to make skin color significant when black folks just wanted colorblindness. For decades now, black people have been affirming their cultural differences and identifying positively with skin color, but now white folks don't want to see color anymore. Such irony. For Christians, color and all other social labels take a back seat to identity in Christ, but we're "in Christ" living in a culture where racialization in the forms of supremacy and inferiority are already in play. The degree might be contested, but failing to acknowledge it exists at all or not recognizing many are still acutely affected by it fuels the problems we're experiencing in the church today.

So I want to grow up in my thinking about whiteness and racialization, even if it's not always easy to pin down. Whiteness has identifiable, socially derived meanings, and it's helpful to recognize the effect of those meanings in crosscultural encounters. This doesn't mean the themes are consistently shared or visible among everybody with the same skin color. Indeed, skin color isn't really the issue at all. It's discourse, it's ideology. It's how people operate toward one another. It's racial formation already in place.

Christopher Rufo warns America about CRT training in government and schools, concerned that "these trainings, based on neo-Marxist notions, treat 'whiteness' as a moral blight and malign all members of that racial group as complicit in oppression." He cautions that "universities, corporations, churches and nonprofit organizations across the country have adopted them."[12] But talking about whiteness in my parachurch organization is a very different conversation than the one I was having in my PhD program. Whiteness *is* a product of neo-Marxist analysis. Properly understood as a colonialist, idolatrous mindset, whiteness *is* a moral blight, but none of this necessitates "malign(ing) all members of that racial group as complicit in oppression." All members of that racial group may benefit from not being aligned with the group being oppressed, but that doesn't mean they're complicit in oppression. That's the conclusion of progressive and leftist extremists, but not one I have to accept, and certainly not how the discussion should manifest itself in the church. A person can study the problems associated with whiteness without having to condemn all white-skinned people as co-conspirators in oppression.

Do most white-skinned Americans adhere to the ideology being challenged? I don't know. No one can say for certain. One constituency declares all white people guilty while another holds that none are, and both end up wrong at the extremes. But the goal isn't to condemn a racial group; it's to weed out an ideology leading to hate, idolatrous preferences, and the maintenance of power to the detriment of people. Within the church, it's self-reflection and institutional audits producing reparation-motivated manifestations of love toward others, not navel-gazing disdain for my skin color. It's not just assuming we're all one in Christ but doing the ideological work to get there.

15

HOW SHOULD WE THEN LIVE?

There is ecstasy in paying attention . . .
if you start to look around, you will start to see.

ANNE LAMOTT, BIRD BY BIRD

The past may live inside the present, but it does not govern
our growth. However sordid or sublime, our origins are not
our destinies; our daily journey into the future is not fixed
by moral arcs or genetic instructions.

MATTHEW KARP, "HISTORY AS END"

SEVERAL YEARS BEFORE HIS DEATH, Derrick Bell admitted in an essay, "Even Solomon with all his wisdom would be hard pressed to resolve the racial challenges facing our society. Deep down, most of us working in civil rights know that there is no real salvation in the racial field."[1] In my Christian world, leaders avoid public honesty like this. Positivity over pessimism for the sake of morale rules the day, so I appreciate his naked confession. I'm guessing his words only reflect what most people engaged in justice work always feel intuitively in their bones. In this world, there's no relief from injustice. Fight against it all you want, but it's not going away.

When I read Bell's words, I immediately wanted to offer him the hope of the church, but then I imagined him looking at me with a mix of pity and disgust. "You mean the church that's firing pastors for speaking about race? The church pulling their financial support from ministries after a podcast calls them Marxist? The church dismissing CRT as demonic with no discussion? That church?" I've experienced "that church." I know he's right. But I also know another church. I know people with a deep appreciation for the already/not yet nature of the kingdom of God.

Like Bell, these people don't expect that racism or injustice will be eliminated until Jesus returns, but they're also not constantly rehearsing how things are better now than they used to be. They take responsibility for racial healing, whatever that means in their context. As part of the dominant culture, they know the limits of their own experience with racial injustice and don't project it onto everyone else's journey, but even more importantly, they don't do race work because it is trending, popular, or socially profitable. They do it because the gospel compels them to move outside relational comfort zones, the Great Commission compels them to love like missionaries, and sanctification compels them to grow in areas that hurt. Their efforts are imperfect, but they're *trying*.

That's the church I want to be associated with, and if you're still reading, I'm guessing it describes what you want as well. I didn't write this book to prescribe a strategy for wiping out racism. I'm not trying to get people aligned with a list of political ideals or gather a mob to attack enemies within the camp. I wrote it to look more like the church of Jesus Christ in the way we think about and act toward one another in race spaces. I want more Christians consistently embracing both the history and consequences of racial evil without being thrown off by extreme rhetoric coming from either the political right or left. I want more white evangelicals developing their powers of discernment, recognizing when an idea conflicts or overlaps with

the Bible, cultivating a different reputation in our relationship with
racial injustice.

I know these pockets of Christians already exist across the country.
They don't make the news, but I hear about them all the time. They're
part of organizations and churches in different contexts who share
similar ways of operating. I want to follow in their footsteps. I don't
have earth-shattering advice for what to do next other than to em-
ulate what I think the best are already doing.

WHAT DOES THEIR PATH LOOK LIKE?

The best evangelical leaders and their organizations aren't spending
much time responding to the danger of CRT or CT or Marxism. Instead, they are trying to understand both the historic and current
experiences of POC that make the language and insights of those
movements attractive for both Christians and non-Christians. You
won't find them trying to figure out who the racists are in the room
or obsessing over their own racial awareness. Instead, they're addressing cultural patterns and ways of operating that work against
being the people of God. They're removing hindrances so believers
from every race and ethnicity can experience a culturally confounding fellowship together. They're inspecting their processes and
seeking input from a wide demographic to better understand how
the way they've structured themselves affects the different people
they influence.[2]

They push toward these conversations even if their population is
monocultural. In the end, they want to be Christians with crosscultural competence, so they're not satisfied with either their education
or engagement with people different from them and take intentional
steps to swim upstream. They don't assume all POC have the same
experience with race or racism and know not to be surprised when
people land on different points of the racial pain continuum. They
hold stories of successful upward mobility alongside those of crippling

poverty and systemic abuse, seeking to understand how both reflect something of the total racial picture in the US.

Justice isn't an add-on but rather a central part of their discipleship, flowing out of a holistic biblical theology. Their view of justice inspires them to treat racism and poverty with the same intensity as abortion and human trafficking. Partisanship doesn't determine the issues they care about. They recognize how sin works in individuals and becomes hardwired into social systems, and their discipleship includes concern and action on behalf of marginalized people as a function of salvation and sanctification. They help their people understand how the gospel intersects a range of headlining social issues, not just the ones they are most comfortable addressing.

They maintain a high view of truth when it comes to biblical principles but also recognize how binary simplicity fails us. Sin shows up in people and systems. Oppression is a significant category in Marxism and Christianity. The church provides the answer to racism and contributes to it. They recognize our role as peacemakers (Matthew 5:9) and the dangerous hypocrisy of declaring peace while remaining apathetic toward injustice (Jeremiah 6:14).[3]

They pursue crosscultural competency in all the ways it's acquired. They ask questions of their Bible they haven't asked before. They regularly audit their own community and pursue experiences that expose them not only to racial history but also to stories of people they don't know.[4] They listen to podcasts. They watch documentaries and feature-length movies, deepening their racial sensibility. They read and discuss racially insightful books, especially biographies and autobiographies of people who've overcome obstacles to live exemplary lives. As Christians, they don't agree with every perspective they read or hear but compare it all against what they know from the Bible.

Finally, and perhaps most importantly, they're practicing how to be in relationship with people different from themselves. They take relationship building seriously, and not just the ones that come easily.

WHY RELATIONSHIPS MATTER IN CROSSCULTURAL COMPETENCY

Given the tone and posture associated with most of the anti-CRT content sent to me, I don't sense it's produced by people in meaningful relationships with those trying to address race in the church. By relationship, I mean eating meals, sharing life stories, exchanging reactions to current events, seeking understanding. I don't mean arguing with at conferences, debating on podcasts, confronting online, or talking about in classrooms. These pieces usually lack the kind of understanding that only comes through relationship and context.

Exchanging stories opens a door to crosscultural depth and understanding, transforming my imagination into how the world is for people not living inside my own head. There's no other way. Ideas have consequences and debate is important, but racial understanding comes to us packaged in relationships, not arguments. Being in relationship helps me to stop excusing, dismissing, or explaining away other peoples' experience of racism. I stop worrying about whether racism is still a problem and gradually appreciate that the racial climate for folks not in dominant culture is never as comfortable as white folks like to think. It's never productive to haggle over whether a specific social incident is racially motivated, but the world changes as I become more skilled at connecting with the feelings it produces in the person sitting across from me. When I can feel what they feel, that's when change happens.

Relationships expose my insecurities, my blind spots, and my ignorance, and a safe relationship turns vulnerability into opportunity. It allows for give and take, for follow-up questions, for the communication of nonverbals, for quick apologies. Being in relationship gives me an opportunity to exercise what Paul considered the most important Christian muscle. Agape love covers a multitude of sins in every direction—personal, communal, and historical—doing what's best for others regardless what it costs me. Agape love looks past an out-of-place statement for the sake of the conversation. Agape love transforms defensiveness into sympathy.

Filled with the Holy Spirit, we can do all of this with whatever time we have remaining. We can be people who bring love to bear in those moments when race intersects our lives and requires it. We can't do away with racism, but we can step into each day with humility and intentionality, praying that in our corner of the world, the kingdom might manifest itself a little more clearly, its colors and contours becoming a little more distinct against the backdrop of a world under the spell of the powers of darkness.

That's the church I want for Derrick Bell. That's the church I want to be. God help us to that end.

EPILOGUE

SEEING THE WORLD A LITTLE DIFFERENTLY

I don't mind walking through a museum and thinking about someone else's sin, but I don't want to go through one and be reminded of my own.

BRIAN GOINS, CONVERSATION WITH THE AUTHOR

I'M STANDING IN A LEXINGTON, Kentucky, park with twelve other white ministers across the street from a rundown row of brick homes in a predominantly black neighborhood. This stop is part of an ethnic diversity training our ministry forces us to attend, and we're all here grudgingly, self-conscious and waiting for the facilitators to arrive.

It's not been made clear exactly what we're doing at this location, but I already don't want to be here. I hate the feeling that I'm being set up, and the more people drive by and see us standing here looking like a museum tour, the more I want to hide in a tree or get run over by one of the many cop cars that pass while we wait. I grew up playing ball in parks like this and managed to fit in well enough, but it seems so foreign to me now, especially as I stand with this pack of people who obviously don't live in the sandstones across the street. The people who do live in them are on their porches looking at us while wary men in the park keep watch. We stand, glowing like neon church lights, and I want to get out of here without talking to anyone.

But of course two guys walk up to us. The lead guy has a mouthful of gold teeth, a Boston Celtics jersey down to his thighs, and arms blanketed with tattoos literally covering bullet scars. The other guy is shorter and walks behind him. I'm a little nervous about what they're about to do, but amid the fear I'm thinking, *Fellas, please don't come over here and ask us for money. Don't start our time here like that.* Before I finish the thought, Celtics Jersey asks if we're a church group, and I know—he's going to need "just a couple dollars." He represents exactly what I'm already afraid is the unspoken view shared by this group about how *they* are—inner-city welfare, lowlife, vagrant dudes. The whole scene reeks of stereotypes, and as much as I can't stand it, now even I'm breathing life into them. I feel myself hating him for creating this stress, and I resent our leaders—who show up just as he's asking—for making us come here.

Then one of the guys who's just arrived steps up and offers to give him some money, and I'm thinking, *Well all right, man, God bless you for not letting this drag on,* and before I can ask, "How do you know he's not just playing you?" Celtics Jersey speaks directly to another guy in our group, saying, "Bret, you gotta have some money too, man . . . don't you have some money for me?" Now I'm seriously disoriented and feeling really vulnerable. He's not a gangbanger in a park squeezing us for money. He's our instructor, our guide for the rest of the time. He tricked us, but I'm feeling hot shame for different reasons.

His name is Corey, and for the next ninety minutes he drops a semester's worth of knowledge on us. During his monologue he cites Shakespeare and *The Odyssey* and his dependence on the library, explains the bureaucracy of the drug culture on this and surrounding streets, offers political perspective on the history and development of the neighborhood, shares openly and honestly about his own father wounds, depicts himself as both a former drug dealer and a current role model, outlines the psychology of being a cop on this particular block, uses the word *gentrification* multiple times while describing the practical effect of whites ruining the community while trying to save it, sketches the church's role in helping and hurting the situation, and has multiple drive-bys wave and call out to him over the course of his lecture. It's amazing. He's a verbal artist, a "professor" in the truest sense, a walking advanced degree, and now I absolutely love him, seriously distracted by his brilliance and wishing I could talk with him alone.

He starts fielding questions from our group, and now he's serving us profound insights about ministry, politics, and theology. I love what he's doing, but for some reason I'm also irritated by it, and it takes a while before I recognize why. The social power dynamic between us has flipped, and I'm suddenly aware of how uncomfortable I am with it. He came up asking us for money, but now I'm waiting in line to ask him a question. When we met, he was reaching out to me, but now I'm reaching up to him. I entered the park thinking I was the teacher, but now he's the one dropping knowledge. He's the one expanding our theological horizons. He's the one helping us understand what it means for the gospel to live amid the treachery of this neighborhood's red-lined, racist history and its ongoing attempts to cleanse it away.

He's got all the power. He goes from thug beggar to street professor, from welfare requester to Don Corleone. He doesn't need us—at least not in the way I anticipated. He wants us to get out of his park too. But he practically lowers himself to spend time with us, enduring the white zoo troupe game because he knows that if he invests in us, there's a chance we'll grow up and be part of solutions. He's living redemptively in his community and inviting us to do the same. Somehow, with the power flipped, I start to see myself as I really am, stained with social prejudices and hierarchies and judgment. I'm surprised to be learning from Corey, but I'm even more surprised at what's rising to my surface, and it's not pretty.

Finally, it's over. I'm still unsettled as I leave the park, but I'm also laughing to myself. No one else knows, but I'm leaving these two hours feeling exposed yet enriched. I see my pharisaical heart toward the "beggar," toward the people I stood with, toward cops and the random people who passed by, toward church people, toward black and white intellectuals, toward Christian school people, toward my family. Indeed, I despise *myself* in a clarifying way and yet somehow, after tasting the invisible ugliness of my heart, after spending two hours with and carefully listening to a man I'd never met nor cared about before, I realize he's given me the gift of a chance to grow. Brokenness and grace coalesce in my heart to rehabilitate and refine, repairing an unknown-to-the-world-but-rotten part of my inner self.

Corey didn't shame me with anything he said. He shamed me by his loving persistence in this place contrasted with my apathetic judgment toward it. In this urban neighborhood, he saw people to love through the eyes of Jesus, but I saw problems to judge through the eyes of a politician. I feel embarrassed and gross, and yet I know full well the cross and its power to make something of the sewage that's been exposed to my mind. I'm the one who is messed up—not the people I'm with, not the guys pretending to ask for money, not the people on the porches. I walked into the park secure and justified in my self-righteousness and left unraveled and convicted in my heartless hypocrisy.

I'm guilty, not because I did anything to these folks but because I really didn't care about them at all. If the news or other media should bring them to mind, they'd be processed as avatar-like caricatures experiencing self-induced consequences, not as manifestations of the image of God needing agape love. We can easily write off someone's struggling corner of the world as the cumulative effect of thousands of empty choices made by those living there, shaded perhaps by a few unfortunate decisions thrust on them by others. But in slowing down long enough to try understanding the multilayered, historically complex details of their lives—and perhaps even starting to feel the challenge of navigating them—I face the possibility that the real emptiness, the place most needing moral reformation, actually hides inside me.

ACKNOWLEDGMENTS

The cultural and ethnic melting pot of the Elyria/Lorain nexus: You laid the foundation. You shaped the lenses. You made me value crosscultural ministry before I knew what it was, and I appreciate you far more now than I did when kicking it in your streets.

My sisters, Susie Gerlak and Jenni Janis, because we grew up through it all, and anything I do or write or say is an overflow of our lives together back in the day. I love you both.

Cecil Shorts: You not only poured into my life and opened me to yours but also introduced me to men who taught me to think about race and the gospel across the social and theological spectrum. Thank you, Bishop Joey Johnson, Pastor Richard Walker, Pastor Dennis Butts, Marc Greenwood, Kevin McIntyre, Al McIntosh, Phil Hodge, Rev. Henry Payden, James Hicks, Theo Woods, Lucien Stephenson, Ben Torres, Tony Miller, Aaron Barkley, and Dr. Bob Sturkey. Everything looks different because of you.

Dr. E. Timothy Moore: You welcomed "white brothers and sisters" into your 1980s classes when that wasn't a popular idea among your Pan-African studies colleagues. You believed racial healing came through education and relationship, not retaliation and separation, and I understand better now what your graciousness toward me and others might have cost you. Racism blurred your vision of the faith back then, but I hope you trusted Jesus before the end.

Elder Gilbert Carter: You taught me black American church history, let me tag along to your brother's church in the Bronx, answered my persistent questions late into the night, and drew a line with John 14:6 when I needed it most. Our time was short but transformative.

James White and Dr. Crawford Loritts: In our sporadic encounters across the decades, you've both trusted me with far more of yourselves than I deserve, and your thoughts about ministry, race, leadership, and the gospel cast an inescapable but welcome shadow across every part of my mind. Thank you for your friendship, mentorship, and wisdom from a distance through the years.

Alethea Lamberson and Emma Tautolo: Your leadership challenges me to ask clearer questions, to not accept excuses, and to direct more energy toward people trying instead of fixating on those who aren't. Keep going. He'll make everything right in the end.

Dr. Tim Muehlhoff: You not only opened the door to IVP, but your constant encouragement, feedback, and lift also got me to the finish line. This doesn't happen without you.

Judd Burke, Matt Hardy, Steve Koproski, Steve Lane, Ron Touby, David Thompson, and Brian Smith: Nobody writes a book without friends, and you are mine. Your belief fuels me. Your belief motivated me from the beginning of this process to the end.

Chris Fields, Eric Clayton, Jason Williams, Bill and Paula Pugh, Michael Porter Sr., Bruce Fields, James Pittman, Erik Thoennes, Ben and Janet Burns, Preston Sprinkle, David Myles, David Rose, and Schelli Kronk: In different seasons of life you all provided hours of conversation about race and the gospel, helping me clarify my own thoughts.

Elizabeth Koproski: Before you left us, I promised you I'd try. Your contagious crosscultural love motivates these pages from cover to cover. I needed your push, and I hope you know it's done.

Brian Goins: You help me think better about everything. I appreciate you freeing my head to meet this deadline amid other ones squeezing us both.

Al Hsu: Thank you for your unwavering confidence in this project, for your patience toward me, and for turning the mess into something we could both feel good about. I hope we work together again soon.

Amy, Erik, Maria, Jack, and Trey: We do life together, and mine is immeasurably richer because of you. When it comes to loving people different from us, thinking the gospel precedes living the gospel. I hope the perspective in this book helps us all get better at both.

QUESTIONS FOR REFLECTION AND DISCUSSION

1. What judgments and assumptions do I make about individuals/ groups that are different from me? What partiality has made its way into my subconscious in the way that I deal with people?

2. What responsibility do I/we have to intercede on behalf of those who are vulnerable, marginalized, or taken advantage of? What do these categories look like in our community?

3. What can I learn about God, myself, and the brokenness of the world by listening to the lived experience of others who are different from me?

4. "God helps those who help themselves" isn't in the Bible, but how does this quasi-religious idea shape my expectations for other people and the way I judge them?

5. How should my congregation care for the specific needs of the broader community outside our church walls?

6. Are people of color represented in our leadership spaces? If not, what dynamics are in play and what changes would we need to make to have a more representative table?

7. How can I use my forms of capital (social, financial, cultural) to help those who have less of them for whatever reason?

8. What written or unwritten "laws" might be creating inequality or perpetuating some unnecessary power imbalance for those in my organizational community?

9. When thinking about the way we operate as an institution, where did our racial "normals" come from? Are there people among us who have different ones?

10. Why does _____ matter to my denomination but not other social issues? How do we determine what we're going to raise our voice about or lend support to?

NOTES

INTRODUCTION

[1]Throughout this book, I will variously use "non-white," "black," "POC" (person(s) of color), and "BIPOC" (black, indigenous, people of color). I will try to use them intentionally where necessary, and while recognizing that each brings its own history and complications, I may just be using one or another to generically constitute a contrast with "white evangelical." Please forgive any unintentional misuses of these terms.

[2]Examples abound: the unrecorded "citizens arrest" murder of Trayvon Martin was followed by a deluge of videoed black deaths at the hands of police officers; the racial triggers represented by the presidencies of Barack Obama and Donald Trump; the academy with its language and concerns suddenly becoming part of popular culture, seen especially in curriculums developed out of the 1619 Project arguing that the country started in 1619 with the arrival of the first slave ships, not in 1692 with the Pilgrim landing.

[3]Douglas Murray says, "Although the foundations had been laid for several decades, it is only since the financial crash of 2008 that there has been a march into the mainstream of ideas that were previously known solely on the obscurest fringes of academia." Elsewhere, Greg Lukanoff and Johathan Haidt cite 2013 as the year phrases like "triggered," "feeling unsafe," and "social justice" spiked in popular culture. See Douglas Murray, *The Madness of Crowds: Gender, Race and Identity* (London: Bloomsbury Publishing, 2019), 1-10, and Greg Lukanoff and Jonathan Haidt, *The Coddling of the American Mind: How Good Intentions and Bad Ideas Are Setting Up a Generation for Failure* (New York: Penguin, 2018), 5-7.

[4]Read the full memorandum sent to "the heads of executive departments and agencies" here: Executive Office of the President: Office of Management and Budget, "Training in the Federal Government," September 4, 2020, www.whitehouse.gov/wp-content/uploads/2020/09/M-20-34.pdf. For the SBC Seminary president's statement, see George Schroeder, "Seminary Presidents Reaffirm BFM, Declare CRT Incompatible," *Baptist Press*, November 30, 2020, www.baptistpress.com/resource-library/news/seminary-presidents-reaffirm-bfm-declare-crt-incompatible/.

[5]Michael O. Emerson and Christian Smith, *Divided by Faith: Evangelical Religion and the Problem of Race in America* (New York: Oxford University Press, 2000), 7.

[6]Robert Chao Romero and Jeff M. Liou published an excellent, theologically rich exception as this book was in final edits. See Robert Chao Romero and Jeff M. Liou, *Christianity and Critical Race Theory: A Faithful and Constructive Conversation* (Grand Rapids, MI: Baker Academic, 2023).

[7]See EFCA, "Where We Stand in the EFCA: Denials and Affirmations," June 21, 2023, www.efca.org/where-we-stand-in-the-efca-denials-and-affirmations, as a representative example.

1. A WHITE GUY'S JOURNEY INTO RACIAL CONTROVERSY

[1]Most church folk today probably aren't familiar with Carl Henry, though he helped found Fuller Seminary, started and edited *Christianity Today* for many years, organized the

Evangelical Theological Society, wrote a massive five-book systematic theology, and has his name carved in stone above the chapel entrance at Trinity Evangelical Divinity School. Henry is arguably the dean of evangelical theologians who worked in the latter half of the twentieth century. Carl F. H. Henry, *The Uneasy Conscience of Modern Fundamentalism* (Grand Rapids, MI: Eerdmans, [1947] 2003).

[2]Carl F. H. Henry, *God, Revelation, and Authority*, vol. 4, *God Who Speaks and Shows* (Wheaton, IL: Crossway, [1979] 1999), 551.

[3]Henry, *Uneasy Conscience*, 16-23. Also, see Tim Keller's commentary on first-century Christianity in Tim Keller, *Generous Justice: How God's Grace Makes Us Just* (New York: Dutton, 2010), 148-53.

[4]Henry, *God*, vol. 4, 542-54.

[5]Henry, *Uneasy Conscience*, 35.

[6]Henry, *Uneasy Conscience*, 39. "Today, Protestant Fundamentalism although heir-apparent to the supernaturalist gospel of the Biblical and Reformation minds, is a stranger, in its predominant spirit, to the vigorous social interest of its ideological forebears. Modern Fundamentalism does not explicitly sketch the social implications of its message for the non-Christian world; it does not challenge the injustice of the totalitarianisms, the secularisms of modern education, the evils of racial hatred, the wrongs of current labor-management relations, the inadequate bases of international dealings. It has ceased to challenge Caesar and Rome, as though in futile resignation and submission to the triumphant Renaissance mood. The apostolic gospel stands divorced from a passion to right the world. The Christian social imperative is today in the hands of those who understand it in sub-Christian terms."

[7]For examples see Thabiti Anyabwile, *The Faithful Preacher: Recapturing the Vision of Three Pioneering African-American Pastors* (Wheaton, IL: Crossway, 2007) and Mary Beth Swetnam Mathews, *Doctrine and Race: African American Evangelicals and Fundamentalism between the Wars* (Tuscaloosa: University of Alabama Press, 2017).

[8]Voddie T. Baucham Jr., *Fault Lines: The Social Justice Movement and Evangelicalism's Looming Catastrophe* (Washington, DC: Salem Books, 2021).

[9]Examples include the Babylonian ransacking of Jerusalem depicted in Daniel 1, the four-hundred-year Egyptian captivity, and the Roman occupation of Israel. See also Deuteronomy 28: 25, 36, and 49 and Habakkuk 1:5-11 as examples of God using pagans to judge his people.

[10]For an excellent overview of the term's origin and historic usage, see Aja Romano, "A History of "Wokeness," Vox, October 9, 2020, www.vox.com/culture/21437879/stay-woke-wokeness-history-origin-evolution-controversy.

[11]See Ellis Cose, "The Saga of the Scottsboro Boys," ACLU, July 27, 2020, www.aclu.org/issues/racial-justice/saga-scottsboro-boys.

[12]Nur Ibrahim, "What Are the Origins of the Term 'Stay Woke'?" Snopes, June 1, 2023, www.snopes.com/articles/464795/origins-term-stay-woke/.

[13]William Melvin Kelley, "If You're Woke You Dig It: No Mickey Mouse Can Be Expected to Follow Today's Negro Idiom Without a Hip Assist," *New York Times*, May 20, 1962, www.nytimes.com/1962/05/20/archives/if-youre-woke-you-dig-it-no-mickey-mouse-can-be-expected-to-follow.html.

[14]See excellent article summarizing the contrasting usage at Julie Mastrine, Henry Brechter, and Andrew Weinzierl, "Woke," AllSides, accessed December 11, 2023, www.allsides.com/translator/woke.

2. WHAT DO WE NEED TO UNDERSTAND ABOUT MARXISM?

[1]David Breese, *Seven Men Who Rule the World from the Grave* (Chicago: Moody Publishers, 1990).

[2]As found in Karl Marx and Friedrich Engels, *On Religion* (New York: Schocken Books, 1964).

[3]"A revolution is required because the ruling class cannot be overthrown in any other way, but also because the working class that dislodges it needs a revolution itself . . . a revolution that will purge the proletariat of the accumulated trash of its past. Only thus can the workers rebuild society." In Karl Marx (with Friedrich Engels), *The German Ideology* (Amherst, NY: Prometheus Books, 1998).

[4]See Karl Marx and Friedrich Engels, trans. Samuel Moore, *The Communist Manifesto* (New York: Penguin, 2011).

[5]Marx had several reasons for believing Christianity was an enemy of the people. First, he believed that by teaching that citizens should submit to authorities and live a quiet, peaceful life, Christian theology becomes a mechanism to keep them controlled. Remember, in Marx's world, religion bolsters groups of power-hungry people controlling others in the name of God from within it. Religion works to convince you that everything is all right, to go about the business of caring for your own soul so you don't notice the ways others are trying to kill it. Second, religion snuggles up to government for its own protection, then prostitutes itself by protecting that same government using spiritual language as a cover. Marx saw the power relationship between church and state as a detrimental social ill. Finally, Christianity supports family units that function autonomously from the state. Families with a patriarchal hierarchy become little "states" living under their own rule and thus act as a block to communal utopia. For socialism to work, families must lose their independent power as units and submit to the communist flattening of all for the supposed betterment of all.

[6]Ironically, some of the most successful experiments in communal living happened among the hippie-driven, Christian-based Jesus People movement of the 1970s. See Richard A. Bustraan, *The Jesus People Movement: A Story of Spiritual Revolution among the Hippies* (Eugene, OR: Pickwick, 2014), and Larry Eskridge, *God's Forever Family: The Jesus People Movement in America* (New York: Oxford University Press, 2013).

3. THINKING CRITICALLY ABOUT CRITICAL THEORY

[1]See Paulo A. Bolanos, "What Is Critical Theory?: Max Horkheimer and the Makings of the Frankfurt School Tradition," *Mabini Review: Polytechnic University of the Philippines* 2, no. 1 (2013): 1-19, www.academia.edu/9844158/What_is_Critical_Theory_Max _Horkheimer_and_the_Makings_of_the_Frankfurt_School_Tradition; Philip Smith and Alexander Riley, *Cultural Theory: An Introduction* 2nd ed. (Malden, MA: Blackwell Publishing, 2009); also, Michael J. Thompson, "Introduction: What Is Critical Theory?" in Michael J. Thompson, ed., *The Palgrave Handbook of Critical Theory* (New York: Palgrave Macmillan, 2017), 1-14. For the best overview I've read, see Robert S. Smith, "Cultural Marxism: Imaginary Conspiracy or Revolutionary Reality?", *themelios* 44, no. 3, www .thegospelcoalition.org/themelios/article/cultural-marxism-imaginary-conspiracy-or -revolutionary-reality/.

[2]*The Matrix*, directed by Lilly Wachowski (Burbank, CA: Warner Home Video, 2001), 29:00-29:35.

[3]For a simple overview of "Conservative" political history, see Terence Ball, Richard Dagger, and Peter Viereck, "Conservatism," *Encylopaedia Britannica*, updated November 22, 2023, www.britannica.com/topic/conservatism. See also Russell Kirk, "Ten Conservative Principles," Kirk Center, https://kirkcenter.org/conservatism/ten-conservative-principles/;

and Russell Kirk, *The Politics of Prudence* (Bryn Mawr, PA: Intercollegiate Studies Institute, 1994).

[4]Much of this language comes directly from a class syllabus of philosophy professor Daniel Koltonski.

[5]*The Truman Show*, directed by Peter Weir (Los Angeles, CA: Paramount Pictures, 1998), 1:06:00-1:06:17.

[6]Thomas Kuhn scandalously argued that even objectivity couldn't separate itself from these processes in Thomas Kuhn, *The Structure of Scientific Revolutions* (Chicago: Chicago University Press, 1970).

[7]The interplay between power and knowledge—and how power gets used to control and define knowledge—flows through all of Michel Foucault's work. In summarizing Foucault's arguments, philosopher Philip Stokes observes, "What authorities claim as 'scientific knowledge' are really just means of social control. Foucault shows how, for instance, in the eighteenth century 'madness' was used to categorize and stigmatize not just the mentally ill but the poor, the sick, the homeless, and indeed, anyone whose expressions of individuality were unwelcome." Philip Stokes, *Philosophy: 100 Essential Thinkers* (Kettering, UK: Index Books, 2004), 187.

[8]"What becomes of humanity when the summation of profit-driven social life amounts to 'the decline of *being* into *having*, and *having* into merely *appearing*?'" See Thesis 17 in Guy Debord, *The Society of the Spectacle* (New York: Zone Books, 1995).

[9]More than just a science, Capitalism depends on a psychology that keeps people thinking in a certain direction, and hegemony is the path by which that ideology gets distributed, absorbed, and maintained. See Stuart Hall, "The Rediscovery of 'Ideology': Return of the Repressed in Media Studies," in John Storey, ed., *Cultural Theory and Popular Culture: A Reader*,4th ed. (Essex, UK: Pearson Education, 2009), 111-41, and Kevin J. Vanhoozer, Charles A. Anderson, and Michael J. Sleasman, eds., *Everyday Theology: How to Read Cultural Texts and Interpret Trends* (Grand Rapids, MI: Baker Academic, 2007), 39.

[10]See Hannah Arendt, *The Human Condition* (Chicago: The University of Chicago Press, 1958).

[11]Some early Critical theorists would still hold to a Modernist universalist moral framework where principles of right and wrong can be used to evaluate systems. See Douglas Kellner, *Critical Theory, Marxism, and Modernity* (Cambridge: Polity Press, 1989). Also, Georges Van Den Abbeele, "Postmodernism and Critical Theory," in Stuart Sim, ed., *The Routledge Companion to Postmodernism*, 3rd ed. (New York: Routledge, 2011), 15-24.

[12]Charles Lemert, *Postmodernism Is Not What You Think* (Oxford: Blackwell, 1997), xii.

[13]From "The Second Coming" in W. B. Yeats, *The Collected Poems of W. B. Yeats* (New York: Macmillan, 1949).

[14]Ironically, reversing this thinking is what CT is trying to do. CT says, "You should be critical of Capitalism *precisely* because you've been systematically programmed *not* to be. *They* don't want you to think about your role as a cog in their machine or how your life has been absorbed into a system. They *want* you to associate Capitalism with positive and any alternative with negative."

4. CAN A CHRISTIAN GAIN ANYTHING FROM CRITICAL THEORY?

[1]They started by challenging the historic distinction between "high" art and "low" art, recognizing that technology was changing the rules of how art functioned within society.

[2]Michael Ryan, ed., *Cultural Studies: An Anthology* (Malden, MA: Blackwell Publishing, 2008), xvi.

[3]"The power of those who control a society culturally, economically, politically, and socially is best secured by the pretense that the projection of their values, choices, assumptions, and ideals into the world constitutes 'reality.'" Ryan, *An Anthology*, xvi.

[4]For classic texts representing the merging, see John Storey, ed., *Cultural Theory and Popular Culture: A Reader*, 4th ed. (Essex, UK: Pearson Education Limited, 2009), and Simon During, ed., *The Cultural Studies Reader*, 3rd ed. (New York: Routledge, 2007).

[5]Caron Staff, "Alcohol Use Disorder Statistics and Demographics," Caron, accessed December 11, 2023, www.caron.org/addiction-101/alcohol-addiction/alcohol-use-disorder -statistics-and-demographics.

[6]Judith Butler, *Gender Trouble: Feminism and the Subversion of Identity* (New York: Routledge, 1990), 1-46.

[7]Blaise Pascal, *Pensées* (London: J.M. Dent, 1943).

[8]C. S. Lewis, *A Grief Observed* (London: Faber & Faber, 1968).

[9]Many of the observations being made by godless Critical theorists in the middle of the last century were simultaneously being made by Christian social critics whose books already sat on my shelf, like Carl Henry, Neil Postman, Hannah Arendt, Os Guinness, Francis Schaeffer, and Robert Bellah. They used different vocabulary and certainly proposed different paths toward social healing, but they had the same concerns about life untethered from a theistic worldview and the human wreckage that accompanies living in a consumer society.

[10]Ryan Bomberger, "Critical Race Theory: It's a Cancer, Not a Cure," *The Christian Post*, May 4, 2021, www.christianpost.com/news/critical-race-theory-its-a-cancer-not-a-cure .html.

[11]Neil Shenvi and Pat Sawyer, "The Incompatibility of Critical Theory and Christianity," The Gospel Coalition, May 15, 2019, www.thegospelcoalition.org/article/incompatibility -critical-theory-christianity/.

[12]Shenvi and Sawyer, "The Incompatibility of Critical Theory and Christianity."

[13]Shenvi and Sawyer, "The Incompatibility of Critical Theory and Christianity."

[14]In 1972 Marcuse wrote, "To extend the base of the student movement, Rudi Dutscheke has proposed the strategy of the *long march through the institutions:* working against the established institutions while working within them, but not simply by 'boring from within,' rather by 'doing the job,' learning (how to program and read computers, how to teach at all levels of education, how to use the mass media, how to organize production, how to recognize and eschew planned obsolescence, how to design, et cetera), and at the same time preserving one's own consciousness in working with others" (italics his). Though Marcuse appreciated the value of "working against the established institutions while working within them," he also saw the futility of hoping masses of people would awaken to the crippling effects of Capitalism. They were too comfortable in it and had learned to be satisfied within the personal and social limits it set. Revolution, if it was to come, would originate with those already "uncomfortable" in society. See Herbert Marcuse, *Counterrevolution and Revolt* (Boston: Beacon Press, 1972), 55-56.

[15]"Underneath the conservative popular base is the substratum of the outcasts and outsiders, the exploited and persecuted of other races and other colors, the unemployed and the unemployable. They exist outside the democratic process; their life is the most immediate and the most real need for ending intolerable conditions and institutions. Thus their opposition is revolutionary even if their consciousness is not." See Herbert Marcuse, *One Dimensional Man: Studies in the Ideology of Advanced Industrial Society* (Boston: Beacon Press, 1964), 256-57.

[16]Robinson traces the history of what he called "racial capitalism," the form of Capitalism that depended on slavery, violence, imperialism, and genocide for its growth. He argued that Marx and his acolytes didn't account enough for these conditions, nor did they have categories for the history of the black radical tradition existing as an addendum to or completely apart from white Marxist leadership. See Cedric Robinson, *Black Marxism: The Making of the Black Radical Tradition* (Chapel Hill: University of North Carolina Press, 1983).

[17]See David Levering Lewis, *W. E. B. DuBois: A Biography* (New York: Henry Holt, 2009), 1-10, 646-95.

5. WHAT IS CRITICAL RACE THEORY, REALLY?

[1]Note the important distinction made between "Critical Race Theory" (the body of legal scholarship developed in the 1970s, '80s, and '90s) and "critical race studies" (a broader, more loosely affiliated array of academic work). See David Theo Goldberg, "The War on Critical Race Theory," *Boston Review*, May 7, 2021, www.bostonreview.net/articles/the-war-on-critical-race-theory/.

[2]Francisco Valdes, Jerome McCristal Culp, and Angela P. Harris, eds., *Crossroads, Directions, and a New Critical Race Theory* (Philadelphia: Temple University Press, 2002), 9-31.

[3]Adam Harris, "The GOP's 'Critical Race Theory' Obsession," *The Atlantic*, May 7, 2021, www.theatlantic.com/politics/archive/2021/05/gops-critical-race-theory-fixation-explained/618828/.

[4]"Critical race theory sprang up in the 1970s, as a number of lawyers, activists, and legal scholars across the country realized, more or less simultaneously, that the heady advances of the civil rights era of the 1960s had stalled and, in many respects, were being rolled back. Realizing that new theories and strategies were needed to combat the subtler forms of racism that were gaining ground, early writers, such as Derrick Bell, Alan Freeman, and Richard Delgado, put their minds to the task." Richard Delgado and Jean Stefancic, *Critical Race Theory: An Introduction*, 3rd ed. (New York: New York University Press, 2017), 4.

[5]Nathan Luis Cartagena, "What Christians Get Wrong About Critical Race Theory—Part 1," *Faithfully Magazine*, February 27, 2020, https://faithfullymagazine.com/critical-race-theory-christians/.

[6]Part of what's caused confusion for people is the lack of a singular definition, even among the legal scholars who initially developed it.

[7]Bradley Mason rightly argues that "racism has and can structure systems, institutions, and ideologies to the disadvantage of historically marginalized peoples" whether people are consciously aware this is happening or not, and CRT started by considering how law works in conjunction with latent racist assumptions/effects to produce unjust inequality. Bradley Mason, "Introducing Critical Race Theory," *Also a Carpenter*, September 13, 2021, https://alsoacarpenter.com/2021/09/13/introducing-critical-race-theory/.

[8]The American Bar Association calls CRT "a practice of interrogating the role of race and racism in society," primarily in the context of law and its practical implications for everyday life. It's an interpretive posture armed with precepts that challenge the assumptions of *dominant cultural modes of expression*, which in America means the way white people set up society through law and how that continues to work against non-white people. See Janel George, "A Lesson on Critical Race Theory," ABA, January, 11, 2021, www.americanbar.org/groups/crsj/publications/human_rights_magazine_home/civil-rights-reimagining-policing/a-lesson-on-critical-race-theory.

[9]Kimberlé Williams Crenshaw, "Twenty Years of Critical Race Theory: Looking Back to Move Forward Commentary: Critical Race Theory: A Commemoration: Lead Article," *Connecticut Law Review* 3, no. 5 (2011): 1253-1353, https://digitalcommons.lib.uconn.edu /law_review/117/.

[10]Delgado and Stefancic, *Introduction*, 1-4.

[11]Systemic problems may not be nearly as pervasive today as they were in 1970, but they still exist, and some institutions remain just as blind to them now as ever. Debating the *extent* of systemic problems distracts us from asking ourselves whether an issue is a systemic problem or something else. It also keeps us from interrogating the ways a situation could be a result of *both* systemic problems and something else. See Valdes, Culp, and Harris, *Crossroads*, 11-15.

[12]Devon Carbado says CRT "rejects the standard racial progress narrative that characterizes mainstream civil rights discourse—namely, that the history of race relations in the United States is a history of linear uplift and improvement." Slavery ends and Reconstruction, Jim Crow, and Black Codes fight back. *Brown* confronts school segregation and "with all deliberate speed" opens the door to resistance. MLK's vision of racial cooperation and responsibility brings about the Civil Rights Act, countered by a colorblind doctrine that restricts necessary remediation efforts. See Devon Carbado, "Critical What What? Commentary: Critical Race Theory: A Commemoration: Afterward," *Connecticut Law Review* 43, no. 5 (July 2011): 1607, https://digitalcommons.lib.uconn.edu/cgi/viewcontentcgi?article =1126&context=law_review.

[13]Alan David Freeman, "Legitimizing Racial Discrimination through Antidiscrimination Law: A Critical Review of Supreme Court Doctrine," *Minnesota Law Review* 62 (1978): 1049-50, https://scholarship.law.umn.edu/mlr/804/.

[14]While an antidiscrimination law may present itself as a solution, it often only covers over deeper, more established racial patterns in society, patterns impervious to the arrival of isolated laws. Law can shape race relations, but it is also shaped by pre-existing race relations at every level of society. What happens in the courtroom affects society, and what happens in society affects the courtroom. See Kimberlé Crenshaw, *Critical Race Theory: The Key Writings that Formed the Movement* (New York: W. W. Norton, 1995), xxv.

[15]As another example, consider how the New Deal, understood as one of the greatest catalysts of intergenerational wealth in the twentieth century, was shaped so that Dixiecrats in the South could prevent Southern blacks from accessing its benefits. So what happens when an entire demographic of people is prevented from accessing those benefits? How do we study the disparate outcomes resulting from the way those resources were allocated?

[16]Delgado and Stefancic, *Introduction*, 100.

6. WHAT ARE SOME TENETS OF CRITICAL RACE THEORY?

[1]They didn't materialize in a vacuum, but instead grew out of "organizationally learned lessons" while reflecting on ethnic studies, traditional civil rights, Critical legal studies, retrenchment politics, the implications of "colorblindness," and the institutional cultures of law schools. See Devon Carbado, "Critical What What? Commentary: Critical Race Theory: A Commemoration: Afterward," *Connecticut Law Review* 43, no. 5 (July 2011): 1607, https://digitalcommons.lib.uconn.edu/cgi/viewcontent.cgi?article=1126&context =law_review.

[2]Gordon Hodson, "Race as a Social Construction," *Psychology Today,* December 5, 2016, www .psychologytoday.com/us/blog/without-prejudice/201612/race-social-construction.

[3]Even today when children with different skin colors get together, those differences don't "mean" anything until the kids are taught they do.

[4]Ian F. Haney Lopez, "The Social Construction of Race: Some Observations on Illusion, Fabrication, and Choice," *Harvard Civil Rights-Civil Liberties Law Review* 29 (1994): 1-62.

[5]Or books like Frederick L. Hoffman's popular 1896 treatise *Race Traits and Tendencies of the American Negro*, a book full of unfounded racist drivel used to justify the expanding reach of Jim Crow terrorism. Frederick L. Hoffman, *Race Traits and Tendencies of the American Negro* (New York: Macmillan, 1896).

[6]Carbado, "Critical What What?," 1613. "The drafters of the Constitution took a sober second look at the rhetoric of radical egalitarianism in the Declaration of Independence, and they blinked. The adoption of the Constitution in 1787 and its ratification one year later depended on a compromise, one that integrated slavery into the very fabric of American democracy."

[7]Derrick Bell, *Faces at the Bottom of the Well: The Permanence of Racism* (New York: Basic Books, 1992).

[8]See Richard Delgado, "Words that Wound: A Tort Action for Racial Insults, Epithets, and Name-Calling," in Timothy Davis, Kevin R. Johnson, and George A. Mártinez, *A Reader on Race, Civil Rights, and American Law: A Multiracial Approach* (Durham, NC: Carolina Academic Press, 2001), 507-13. Also Mari J. Matsuda, ed., *Words that Wound* (Boulder, CO: Westview Press, 1993).

[9]See Derrick Bell, "Who's Afraid of Critical Race Theory," 78-84, in Richard Delgado and Jean Stefancic, *The Derrick Bell Reader* (New York: New York University Press, 2005).

[10]See Susan M. Shaw and Regina McClinton, "Want to Understand Critical Race Theory? Read the Good Samaritan Story," *Baptist News Global*, December 11, 2020, https://baptistnews.com/article/want-to-understand-critical-race-theory-read-the-good-samaritan-story.

[11]Bell, "Who's Afraid," 78-84.

[12]See Mark Coppenger, *Moral Apologetics for Contemporary Christians: Pushing Back Against Cultural and Religious Critics* (Nashville, TN: B&H, 2011).

[13]Bell, "Who's Afraid," 78-84.

[14]Bell, "Who's Afraid," 78-84.

[15]Jeffrey Rosen, "The Bloods and the Crits: O. J. Simpson, Critical Race Theory, the Law, and the Triumph of Color in America," the *New Republic*, December 9, 1996, https://newrepublic.com/article/74070/the-bloods-and-the-crits.

[16]Over a century ago Frederick Douglass offered this insight into how power works that still holds true today: "If there is no struggle, there is no progress. . . . Power concedes nothing without a demand. It never did, and it never will." From Frederick Douglass, "Speech Before the West Indian Emancipation Society (August 4, 1857)," in Philip S. Foner, *The Life and Writings of Frederick Douglass*, vol. 2 (New York: International Publishers, 1950), 426.

[17]Mary L. Dudziak, "Desegregation as a Cold War Imperative," *Stanford Law Review* 41 (1988): 61.

[18]Kimberlé Williams Crenshaw, "Mapping the Margins: Intersectionality, Identity Politics, and Violence Against Women of Color," in Kimberlé Crenshaw, et.al., *Critical Race Theory: The Key Writings That Formed the Movement* (New York: The New Press, 1995): 357-83; and Kimberlé Crenshaw, "Demarginalizing the Intersection of Race and Sex: A Black Feminist Critique of Antidiscrimination Doctrine, Feminist Theory and Antiracist Politics," *University of Chicago Legal Forum*: Vol. 1989, article 8.

[19]Mike Hixenbaugh and Antonia Hylton, "Southlake Episode 4 Transcript: The Circus Comes to Town," NBC News, January 12, 2022, www.nbcnews.com/podcast/southlake/transcript-circus-comes-town-n1283149.

7. WHY CRT MEANS DIFFERENT THINGS TO DIFFERENT PEOPLE

[1]William Murrell asks readers to consider the difference between Critical Theory as method (looking at particular bits of social life through new glasses), Critical Theory as metanarrative (looking at all of life through a set of contact lenses), and Critical Theory as mood (looking at the world through one's tears). See William Murrell, "Critical Theory as Method, Metanarrative, and Mood," *Mere Orthodoxy*, May 3, 2021, https://mereorthodoxy.com/critical-theory-mood/.

[2]It's important to recognize that while CRT owes its posture and line of questioning to the Critical Legal Theory tradition—for example, unmasking how power protects its own, questioning the role of social bias in the formation of law, and exposing the influence of capital—the movement is actually a reaction *against* Critical theorists for not taking the racial component seriously enough in their theorizing. Though CRT has Marxist ancestry and can be used to further Marxist or Progressivist ends, early Critical Race theorists pointed out how someone could be both Marxist/Progressivist and still be racist. CRT arose precisely because white Progressivism had largely ignored racial injustice into the later decades of the twentieth century. CRT is the child who embarrasses his parents by reaching adulthood and publicly pointing out the hypocrisy and neglect he lived with at home. He may share their DNA, but he spends his life opposing them, trying to get them to see their faults while provoking them to change. People might say CRT and CT are part of the same family, and that would be accurate, but not recognizing their conflicted relational status causes us to misunderstand fundamental differences.

[3]Most of my classmates seemed to be in the process of constructing their own worldview, pulling from various traditions, philosophies, and ideologies to make sense of life. Aspects of CRT could contribute to that process.

[4]Each of these words is intentional and significant. *Radical* implies extreme. *Secular* acknowledges no appeal to divine authority like the Bible. *Progressive* recognizes a desire to trade what is for what could be.

[5]To be sure, the "race-plus" approach is contested among CRT proponents, recognizing both a potential watering down of the black/white specific project and a hypocrisy for not standing with other minoritized groups.

[6]In other words, behind closed doors it's not difficult to find black folks fully aligned with CRT who do not support the LGBTQ agenda, and plenty of white LGBTQ folks who would not support a racial emphasis. They may support one another publicly for consistency's sake, but in my own experience, I've seen examples of disagreement between those different identity groups.

[7]Though theorists in other disciplines may borrow language from CRT, they aren't *necessarily* trying to present a totalizing approach to life either. Through their own discipline, they're just trying to make people aware of how race and racialization work in a world where white people have historically made the rules.

[8]Benjamin Wallace-Wells, "How a Conservative Activist Invented the Conflict Over Critical Race Theory," *New Yorker*, June 18, 2021, www.newyorker.com/news/annals-of-inquiry/how-a-conservative-activist-invented-the-conflict-over-critical-race-theory.

[9]Christopher Rufo, "What Critical Race Theory Is Really About," *New York Post*, May 6, 2021, https://nypost.com/2021/05/06/what-critical-race-theory-is-really-about. As already noted, CRT is birthed from "radical roots," but it's only a "distinct ideology" when combined with Progressivism. Only distorted applications, not the theories themselves, could produce an "existential threat," and CRT as "America's new institutional orthodoxy" could have no meaning apart from the tenets being combined with something else.

[10]Dripping with irony, President Trump's executive order banning any teaching containing "divisive concepts," "race or sex stereotyping," or "race or sex scapegoating" from federal contracts demonstrates why CRT exists in the first place. The policy he enacted suppresses the conversation CRT exists to encourage! As white people, how do we talk about American racial history without potentially feeling scapegoated? Who decides what is divisive? Does racial scapegoating mean I can't talk about experiences where racial power was intentionally used to suppress someone in real time?

[11]Charlie Sykes, "Scenes from the Culture War: Yoga, the 1619 Project, and Critical Race Theory," *The Bulwark*, May 24, 2021, https://plus.thebulwark.com/p/scenes-from-the-culture-war. Rufo wanted the phrase "Critical Race Theory" to connote "hostile, academic, divisive, race-obsessed, poisonous, elitist, anti-American." This uproar isn't a new experience for those familiar with the ideas of CRT. Kristina Crenshaw wrote in 2002, "Our critics' reconstruction of who we are and what we do is so complete that we can barely recognize ourselves in the mass media." Long before Rufo's strategic attack, Crenshaw described a common and effective strategy, which includes "identify(ing) some threat to our cherished institutions or way of life, tie it to some 'pointy-headed intellectuals,' and then claim that ruthless suppression is the only way to be sure the threat has been contained." She wrote this two decades earlier, but it's literally how Rufo described his approach to blocking all that he references as CRT in 2021. Francisco Valdes, Jerome McCristal Culp, and Angela P. Harris, eds., *Crossroads, Directions, and a New Critical Race Theory* (Philadelphia: Temple University Press, 2002), 23, 24.

[12]Wallace-Wells, "Conservative Activist." Ironically, this strategy parallels Marxian strategies—if you can control the ideas and how people perceive ideas, you'll control the culture that develops around them.

[13]"The exact targets of CRT's critics vary wildly, but it is obvious that most critics simply do not know what they are talking about. Instead, CRT functions for the right today primarily as an empty signifier for any talk of race and racism at all, a catch-all specter lumping together 'multiculturalism,' 'wokeism,' 'antiracism,' and 'identity politics'—or indeed any suggestion that racial inequalities in the United States are anything but fair outcomes, the result of choices made by equally positioned individuals in a free society. They are simply against any talk, discussion, mention, analysis, or intimation of race—except to say we shouldn't talk about it." See David Theo Goldberg, "The War on Critical Race Theory," *Boston Review*, May 7, 2021, www.bostonreview.net/articles/the-war-on-critical-race-theory/.

[14]In some cases people with good hearts but lacking skills at leading discussions about race are doing more damage rather than being redemptive, clumsily pouring shame on white participants or causing minority folks to feel even more misunderstood. I've been in groups where both of these happened simply because the facilitator was unprepared to manage where conversations went or because emotions erupted before even a competent facilitator could reel the group in.

[15]For example, see Daniel Bergner, "'White Fragility' Is Everywhere. But Does Antiracism Training Work?," *New York Times Magazine*, July 15, 2020, www.nytimes.com/2020/07/15/magazine/white-fragility-robin-diangelo.html, and Jesse Singal, "What If Diversity Training Is Doing More Harm Than Good?," *New York Times*, January 17, 2023, www.nytimes.com/2023/01/17/opinion/dei-trainings-effective.html.

[16]"George Floyd: Timeline of Black Deaths and Protests," BBC, April 22, 2021, www.bbc.com/news/world-us-canada-52905408.

[17]For example, there were Cru staff training conferences in July 2015, 2017, and 2019. Both the T4G (Together for the Gospel) and MLK50 conferences took place in April 2018, and the SBC annual conference was in June 2019.

¹⁸See Phil Johnson, "The Rise of 'Woker-Than-Thou' Evangelicalism," Sovereign Nations, July 10, 2018, https://sovereignnations.com/2018/07/10/the-rise-of-woker-than-thou -evangelicalism/.

¹⁹See David French, "On the Use and Abuse of Critical Race Theory in American Christianity," *French Press*, The Dispatch, September 13, 2020, https://thedispatch.com/newsletter /frenchpress/on-the-use-and-abuse-of-critical/.

²⁰See SBTS Communications, "The Church Must Remain Holy, Urge Evangelical Leaders at T4G," The Southern Baptist Theological Seminary, April 16, 2018, https://news.sbts. edu/2018/04/16/church-must-remain-holy-urge-evangelical-leaders-t4g/.

²¹Watch his full message here: www.youtube.com/watch?v=9o9uHTmnzdY&t=308s.

²²Michael O. Emerson and Christian Smith, *Divided by Faith: Evangelical Religion and the Problem of Race in America* (New York: Oxford University Press, 2000).

²³Eric Mason, *Woke Church: An Urgent Call for Christians in America to Confront Racism and Injustice* (Chicago: Moody Publishers, 2018), 15-20.

²⁴See Cody Libolt, "Are Albert Mohler, Ligon Duncan, and Mark Dever Compromised?," *Medium*, March 9, 2019, https://medium.com/christian-intellectual/are-albert-mohler -ligon-duncan-and-mark-dever-apostate-be8080527dfa, and Staff Writer, "Critical Race Theory Advocate Ligon Duncan is Teaching at John MacArthur's Seminary. Why?," Protestia, September 14, 2022, https://protestia.com/2022/09/14/crt-advocate-ligon-duncan -is-teaching-at-john-macarthurs-seminary-why/.

²⁵Iris Dimmick, "Pastor Max Lucado Asks Forgiveness for Christian White Supremacy," *San Antonio Report*, August 9, 2020, https://sanantonioreport.org/pastor-max-lucado-asks -forgiveness-for-christian-white-supremacy/.

²⁶For example, see Spencer Smith, "Max Lucado Bows to the Woke Mob," YouTube, February 16, 2021, 27:59, www.youtube.com/watch?v=Qme-bUkwfPY.

8. HOW CHRISTIANS GET RACE WRONG: WHY CRT ISN'T THE PROBLEM

¹These groups are further defined in Michael Graham, "The Six Way Fracturing of Evangelicalism," *Mere Orthodoxy*, June 7, 2021, https://mereorthodoxy.com/six-way-fracturing -evangelicalism.

²Graham, "Six Way Fracturing."

³Various, "The Statement on Social Justice and the Gospel," SJ&G, September 4, 2018, https://statementonsocialjustice.com/. The statement grew out of a meeting of fourteen evangelicals in Dallas, Texas, on June 19, 2018.

⁴The use of "postmodern, intersectional equivalent" perfectly captures why these videos prove less than helpful other than to rally already hyped tribes. I'd never heard these words conflated in this way before and have no idea exactly what either means in this context. It sounds important and cites two big words, but it's a meaningless phrase created on the spot to make a point and only adds to the confusion people experience in this conversation.

⁵For example, see Monique Duson, "5 Signs Your Church May Be Going 'Woke,'" The Center for Biblical Unity, August 17, 2020, www.centerforbiblicalunity.com/post/5 -signs-your-church-may-be-going-woke.

⁶David Kinnaman and Gabe Lyons, *Unchristian: What a New Generation Really Thinks about Christianity—and Why It Matters* (Grand Rapids, MI: Baker Books, 2007).

⁷Whether one agrees with his conclusions or not, Kendi studies the history of race in America deeply and wrestles over its effect on his own life. See Ibram X. Kendi, *Stamped from the Beginning: The Definitive History of Racist Ideas in America* (New York: Nation Books, 2016).

[8]John MacArthur: "The New Testament never speaks of our unity in Christ as a far-off goal to be pursued or a provisional experiment to be trifled with. Our union with Christ (and therefore with one another) is an eternal spiritual reality that must be embraced, carefully maintained, and guarded against any possible threat. That's why I'm deeply troubled by the recent torrent of rhetoric about 'social justice' in evangelical circles. The jargon is borrowed from secular culture, and it is being employed purposely, irresponsibly in order to segment the church into competing groups—the oppressed and disenfranchised versus the powerful and privileged." But this assumes that there's been a unity throughout the ages just now being messed with, that a true unity exists between races. That's exactly why the language of Critical Theory is having its turn at the plate, because a comprehensive corporate unity doesn't exist and hasn't through the centuries. Just the opposite, and white people need to get their minds around the actual history of separation to perhaps remove the naive way statements like this come across. Did black churches come to exist because of a commitment to ethnic solidarity? Of course not. They arose because white people wouldn't let them in their doors. John MacArthur, "No Division in the Body," SJ&G, September 4, 2018, https://statementonsocialjustice.com/articles/no-division-in-the-body/.

9. FIVE STUMBLING BLOCKS TO THINKING CHRISTIANLY ABOUT RACE

[1]From the original, unpublished transcript of her July 2019 main session. As of this writing, the sessions from Cru 15, 17, and 19 are no longer available to the public because of backlash from those opposed to their content. I created a transcript of Latasha's talk while the sessions were still available.

[2]Bob Shirock, "Conversations Series Follow-Up: A Letter from Pastor Bob," Oak Pointe Church, July 11, 2020, www.oakpointe.org/conversations-series-follow-up-a-letter-from -pastor-bob/.

[3]John Stott, *Between Two Worlds: The Art of Preaching in the Twentieth Century* (Grand Rapids, MI: Eerdmans, 1982), 192.

[4]McCaulley shows how "the instincts and habits of *black biblical interpretation* can help us use the Bible to address the issues of the day." See Esau McCaulley, *Reading While Black: African American Biblical Interpretation as an Exercise in Hope* (Downers Grove, IL: IVP Academic, 2020), 23, 71-95.

[5]For the Tom Skinner message, listen at Urbana Missions, "Urbana 70: Tom Skinner, 'Racism and World Evangelism' (Audio)," YouTube, January 29, 1915, 58:10, www.youtube.com /watch?v=bvKQx4ycTmA. For the history of the Impact Movement, see Bill Hunt, "How The Impact Movement Began," Cru, 2023, www.cru.org/us/en/communities/ministries /the-impact-movement/impact-history.html or https://impactmovement.org/. For Promise Keepers, read Daniel Silliman, "Promise Keepers Tried to End Racism 25 Years Ago. It Almost Worked," *Christianity Today*, June 21, 2021, www.christianitytoday.com/ct/2021/july -august/promise-keepers-racial-reconciliation-reconsidered.html.

[6]See Dave Hunt and T. A. McMahon, *The Seduction of Christianity: Spiritual Discernment in the Last Days* (Eugene, OR: Harvest House, 1985) and Gary DeMar, *The Reduction of Christianity: Dave Hunt's Theology of Cultural Surrender* (Fort Worth, TX: Dominion Press, 1988), 23.

[7]Theology combined with political partisanship produces even more blind spots. I have Christian friends who know how to speak out against the immorality of Leftism but have almost zero language for the failures of Capitalism. Others can plainly see the ways radical Conservatism crushes peoples' souls but then have no discernment when ecumenical charity shifts into the dilution of gospel truth. Most of the people I've gone to church with through the years know Bible verses to condemn abortion but aren't nearly as proficient in Bible literacy when it comes to race or poverty or systemic forms of oppression, and that's a

problem evangelical POC have been drawing attention to for decades. See Preston Sprinkle, *Exiles: The Church in the Shadow of Empire* (Colorado Springs: David C. Cook, 2024).

[8]See Deuteronomy 10:19; 27:19; Psalm 146:9; Isaiah 1:17; Amos 5:24; Micah 6:8; Zechariah 7:9-10; Matthew 23:23.

[9]Jon Harris, "CRU Goes Down the Woke Hole," Conversations That Matter, YouTube, Sept 27, 2019, 38:37, www.youtube.com/watch?v=3qC9jx7Xnpg.

[10]From my original transcript of Latasha's talk.

10. CAN CRT BE OF USE?

[1]Tom Ascol, "Resolution 9 and the Southern Baptist Convention 2019," Founders Ministries, https://founders.org/2019/06/15/resolution-9-and-the-southern-baptist -convention-2019/.

[2]See 2019 Annual Meeting, "On Critical Race Theory And Intersectionality," SBC, June 1, 2019, www.sbc.net/resource-library/resolutions/on-critical-race-theory-and -intersectionality/.

[3]George Schroeder, "Seminary Presidents Reaffirm BFM, Declare CRT Incompatible," *Baptist Press*, November 30, 2020, www.baptistpress.com/resource-library/news /seminary-presidents-reaffirm-bfm-declare-crt-incompatible/.

[4]See Sarah Pulliam Bailey and Michelle Boorstein, "Several Black Pastors Break with the Southern Baptist Convention over a Statement on Race," *Washington Post*, December 23, 2020, www.washingtonpost.com/religion/2020/12/23/black-pastors-break-southern -baptist-critical-race-theory/, and Kate Shellnutt, "Two Prominent Pastors Break with SBC after Critical Race Theory Statement," *Christianity Today*, December 18, 2020, www .christianitytoday.com/news/2020/december/charlie-dates-ralph-west-southern -baptist-sbc-crt.html.

[5]From an internal Cru staff update letter not available to the public.

[6]Michael Emerson and Christian Smith, *Divided by Faith* (New York: Oxford University Press, 2000), ix.

[7]Ecclesiastes 4:1; 5:8.

[8]Theology in the Raw, "Race, CRT, the Gospel, Social Justice, Evangelicalism, Systematic Racism: Thabiti Anyabwile," YouTube, February 23, 2021, 1:12:05, www.youtube.com /watch?v=LNLST0kMzic.

[9]Cooper Thompson, "Can White Men Understand Oppression?," in Maurianne Adams et al., *Readings for Diversity and Social Justice* (New York: Routledge, 2000), 478.

[10]Joseph Backholm, "Critical Race Theory and the Path to Truth," Family Research Council, August 25, 2021, www.frc.org/blog/2021/08/critical-race-theory-and-path-truth. The front of this paragraph is included in the article: "Heterosexual white men in this society tend to have a dualistic view of the world: we are either right or wrong, winners or losers. There is only one truth, and we will fight with one another to determine whose truth is right."

[11]Ashe Schow, "Washington Post Issues 'Clarifications' to Story Trying to Discredit Christopher Rufo and Critical Race Theory Critics," Daily Wire, June 22, 2021, www .dailywire.com/news/washington-post-issues-clarifications-to-story-trying-to -discredit-christopher-rufo-and-critical-race-theory-critics.

[12]Bacon's Rebellion is widely accepted as the triggering event that accelerated division based on race and skin color in colonial America. See Staff, "Inventing Black and White," Facing History & Ourselves, August 2, 2016, www.facinghistory.org/resource-library /inventing-black-white.

[13]A conflict Christian historian Mark Noll describes in Mark Noll, *The Civil War as a Theological Crisis* (Chapel Hill: University of North Carolina Press, 2006).

[14]Frankly, intersectionality as a concept should add little to controversial conversations that have already been going on in churches across the country for decades. If you're among leaders who are already conscious of body-life dynamics, what intersectionality illuminates isn't anything new, but for those who aren't, intersectionality could be a wake-up call to notice the complications of identity many people face. That's how it can work as a tool.

11. RESPONDING TO CONCERNS ABOUT CRT, PART 1

[1]See Jemar Tisby, "The People Who Don't Have Any Questions," Footnotes by Jemar Tisby, September 22, 2022, https://jemartisby.substack.com/p/the-people-who-dont-have -any-questions.

[2]Duke L. Kwon and Gregory Thompson, *Reparations: A Christian Call for Repentance and Repair* (Grand Rapids, MI: Brazos, 2021), 39-43.

[3]Denny Burk, "Dealing with Resolution 9 at the SBC," A Commentary on Theology, Politics, and Culture, May 28, 2021, www.dennyburk.com/dealing-with-resolution-9-at -the-sbc/.

[4]Oxford Languages, s.v. "Racism," Google Dictionary, accessed December 11, 2023, www .google.com/search?q=racism.

[5]George Yancy, *Backlash: What Happens When We Talk Honestly About Racism in America* (Lanham, MD: Rowman and Littlefield, 2018), 95-126. For a helpful take on the mutual responsibility required by sinners of all races, see the similarly named but different George Yancey, *Beyond Racial Gridlock: Embracing Mutual Responsibility* (Downers Grove, IL: InterVarsity Press, 2006).

[6]For example, see Ibram X. Kendi, *How to Be an Antiracist* (New York: One World, 2019).

[7]Merrill F. Unger and R. K. Harrison, eds., *The New Unger's Bible Dictionary* (Chicago: Moody Press, 1988), s.v. "Samaritan."

[8]See Bradly Mason, "Critical Theory, Dr. Levinson, Dr. Shenvi, and Evangelicalism: Final Thoughts," *Bradley Mason* (blog), November 26, 2019, https://alsoacarpenter. com/2019/11/26/critical-theory-dr-levinson-dr-shenvi-and-evangelicalism-final -thoughts/. Perhaps ironic given the usual pushback about "groups," Critical theorists are trying to dismantle the binary separations pre-established by Enlightenment sensibilities. In *Modernity and Ambivalence* (1991), Zygmunt Bauman says that Modernity was all about controlling chance and diversity; that is, it sought to bring order through control and classification, using regulations, institutions, laws, and moral codes. It sought universal standards for truth, justice, and reason while erasing relativism, uncertainty, and ambiguity. But in the process of this ordering, Modernity relied on binary oppositions, leading to the identification of the "other"—anything not fitting into the positive side of the binary and therefore requiring subjection to power and control. Critical Theorists took up the side of the "negative," attempting to dissolve the binary by flipping it upside down.

[9]Malcolm X, with the assistance of Alex Haley, *The Autobiography of Malcolm X* (New York: Ballantine Books, 1992).

[10]Christian sociologists regularly use fabricated divisions to think about faith: denominational distinctions, movements within the grander narrative, theological traditions, celebrity theologians who develop followings, and so on. We understand how to step away from the whole to consider a slice in order to gain insights, draw conclusions, suggest change, and measure all these topical substacks against the plumb line of orthodoxy.

[11]Bradley A. Levinson, "Does Critical Theory Matter for the Evangelical Church to Act for Social Justice?: A Response to Neil Shenvi," *The Aquila Report*, November 14, 2019, https://

theaquilareport.com/does-critical-theory-matter-for-the-evangelical-church-to-act
-for-social-justice-a-response-to-neil-shenvi/.

[12]See for example Noel Ignatiev, *How the Irish Became White* (New York: Routledge, 1995), or Brent Staples, "How Italians Became 'White,'" *New York Times*, October 12, 2019, www .nytimes.com/interactive/2019/10/12/opinion/columbus-day-italian-american-racism .html.

[13]See Lori L. Tharps, *Same Family, Different Colors: Confronting Colorism in America's Diverse Families* (Boston: Beacon Press, 2016) and Ekeoma E. Uzogara et al., "A Comparison of Skin Tone Discrimination among African American Men: 1995 and 2003," *Psychology of Men & Masculinity* 15, no. 2 (2014): 201-12.

12. RESPONDING TO CONCERNS ABOUT CRT, PART 2

[1]"'Say Their Names' Cemetery in Minneapolis Memorializes Black Americans Killed by Police," KSTP-TV, June 6, 2020, updated March 1, 2021, https://kstp.com/special-coverag e/george-floyd/say-their-names-cemetery-in-minneapolis-memorializes-black-americans -killed-by-police.

[2]Ezekiel 18:20 says, "The child will not share the guilt of the parent, nor will the parent share the guilt of the child. The righteousness of the righteous will be credited to them, and the wickedness of the wicked will be charged against them." See also Nehemiah 9:2; Jeremiah 14:20; Daniel 9:16.

[3]In writing on the one-hundredth anniversary of the Tulsa Race Massacre, David French nails this heart attitude when he says, "Thank God that we do not live in the America of 1921. Thank God that we do not have the church of 1921. But we do live in an America that was shaped by 1921. We live with the legacy of 1921. And the posture of the present American church should not be some version of 'how dare you try to make me feel bad for crimes I did not commit.'" David French, "When Our Forefathers Fail: On the Moral Imperative of Mourning the Tulsa Race Massacre Today," *The Dispatch*, May 30, 2021, https://thedispatch.com/newsletter/frenchpress/when-our-forefathers-fail/.

[4]Devon W. Carbado, "Critical What What Commentary: Critical Race Theory: A Commemoration: Afterword," *Connecticut Law Review* 127 43, no. 5 (July 2011): 1608.

[5]For an insightful consideration, see Jonathan Church, "White Privilege, the Law of Large Numbers, and a Little Bit of Bayes," *The Good Men Project*, August 14, 2016, https:// goodmenproject.com/featured-content/white-privilege-law-large-numbers-little-bit -bayes-wcz/.

[6]Lawrence Blum, "'White Privilege': A Mild Critique," *Theory and Research in Education* 6, no. 3 (November 2008): 309-21.

[7]For an example of this conclusion, watch Dr. James White, "An Exegetical & Historical Examination of the Woke Church Movement," Sovereign Nations, YouTube, January 30, 2019, 43:40, www.youtube.com/watch?v=Jz6vD6Jr3FM.

[8]Beverly Daniel Tatum, *Why Are All the Black Kids Sitting Together in the Cafeteria: And Other Conversations About Race* (New York: Basic Books, 1997/2017).

[9]Robin DiAngelo, *White Fragility: Why It's So Hard for White People to Talk About Racism* (Boston: Beacon Press, 2018).

[10]See Ronald J. Sider, *The Chicago Declaration* (Eugene, OR: Wipf and Stock Publishers, 1974), or find the full body of the text at Jemar Tisby, "A Better Statement on Christianity and Justice: The Chicago Declaration of Evangelical Social Concern," *The Witness*, September 10, 2018, https://thewitnessbcc.com/a-better-statement-on-christianity-and -justice-the-chicago-declaration-of-evangelical-social-concern/.

[11]For an excellent history of how the separation developed in the last half of the twentieth century, see David Swartz, *Moral Minority: The Evangelical Left in an Age of Conservatism* (Philadelphia: University of Pennsylvania Press, 2012).

[12]Carl R. Trueman, "Is Tim Keller a Marxist?," *Modern Reformation*, October 8, 2018, www .modernreformation.org/resources/articles/the-mod-is-tim-keller-a-marxist.

[13]Derrick Bell, "Who's Afraid of Critical Race Theory?," *University of Illinois Law Review* 1995, no. 4 (1995): 893-910.

13. REDEEMING "SOCIAL JUSTICE" FROM INJUSTICE

[1]Donald W. Dayton, *Discovering an Evangelical Heritage* (Grand Rapids, MI: Baker Academic, 1976), 121-36.

[2]For example, see James Lindsay, "Naming the Enemy: Critical Social Justice," *New Discourses*, February 28, 2020, https://newdiscourses.com/2020/02/naming-enemy-critical -social-justice/, or Neil Shenvi and Pat Sawyer, *Critical Dilemma: The Rise of Critical Theories and Social Justice Ideology: Implications for the Church and Society* (Eugene, OR: Harvest House, 2023).

[3]Voddie Baucham, "Biblical Justice vs. Social Justice," Coral Ridge, YouTube, February 18, 2021, 55:49, www.youtube.com/watch?v=i60eQZPG5XM.

[4]On a biblical understanding of social justice, see Joe Carter, "The FAQs: What Christians Should Know About Social Justice," The Gospel Coalition, August 17, 2018, https://www .thegospelcoalition.org/article/faqs-christians-know-social-justice/; and Tim Keller, "What is Biblical Justice?," *Relevant*, August 23, 2012, https://relevantmagazine.com/faith /what-biblical-justice.

[5]As a Catholic theologian and social philosopher, he spent portions of his vocational life taking the traditional conception of biblical justice and applying it to the arrangements of social life. For Father Taparelli, the connection between "social" and "justice" arose predominantly from his understanding of Thomistic philosophy. See Joe Carter, "The FAQ's," The Gospel Coalition. Also, Thomas Patrick Burke, "The Origins of Social Justice: Taparelli D'Azeglio," Intercollegiate Studies Institute, October 8, 2014, https://isi.org /intercollegiate-review/the-origins-of-social-justice-taparelli-dazeglio/.

[6]Thomas Patrick Burke, *The Concept of Justice: Is Social Justice Just?* (New York: Continuum International Publishing Group, 2011).

[7]Keller, "Biblical Justice." For a more complete treatment, see Tim Keller, *Generous Justice: How God's Grace Makes Us Just* (New York: Dutton, 2010), 3-5.

[8]Keller, "Biblical Justice."

[9]Keller distinguishes between rectifying justice (*mishpat*) and primary justice (*tsedaqah*) and gives modern examples of each. "Rectifying justice, or *mishpat*, in our world could mean prosecuting the men who batter, exploit, and rob poor women. It could also mean respectfully putting pressure on a local police department until they respond to calls and crimes as quickly in the poor part of town as in the prosperous part. Another example would be to form an organization that both prosecutes and seeks justice against loan companies that prey on the poor and the elderly with dishonest and exploitive practices. Primary justice, or *tsedaqah*, may mean taking the time personally to meet the needs of the handicapped, the elderly or the hungry in our neighborhoods. Or it could mean the establishment of new nonprofits to serve the interests of these classes of persons. It could also mean a group of families from the more prosperous side of town adopting the public school in a poor community and making generous donations of money and pro bono work in order to improve the quality of education there."

[10]Scott David Allen makes the distinction between *communitive justice* (living in right relationship with God and others as image bearers of God) and *distributive justice* (impartially

rendering judgment, punishment, and the righting of wrongs). Both of these are components of how "love God and keep His commandments" and "love your neighbor as yourself" get played out in society. See Scott David Allen, *Why Social Justice Is Not Biblical Justice: An Urgent Appeal to Fellow Christians in a Time of Social Crisis* (Grand Rapids, MI: Credo House, 2020).

[11]Allen, *Not Biblical Justice*, 1-6.

[12]"Liberal" here doesn't mean politically liberal, but rather appeals to the man-centered Liberalism of humanist ideology. "Liberals take social justice to mean the right of individuals to be treated neutrally and objectively when subject to collective power (through law or any other state act). The liberal conception of justice is one of transcending bias and prejudice in the name of rationality, one of neutral and 'equal rights.'" See Gary Peller, "History, Identity, and Alienation Commentary: Critical Race Theory: A Commemoration: Response," *Connecticut Law Review* 43, no. 5 (July 2011): 1483.

[13]Özlem Sensoy and Robin DiAngelo, *Is Everyone Really Equal?: An Introduction to Key Concepts in Social Justice Education*, 2nd ed., Multicultural Education Series (New York: Teachers College Press, 2017), xx.

[14]Alongside other resources already cited, see Thaddeus J. Williams, *Confronting Injustice without Compromising Truth: 12 Questions Christians Should Ask About Social Justice* (Grand Rapids, MI: Zondervan Academic, 2020).

[15]Justin Giboney, "The Absence of Injustice Is Not Justice," *Christianity Today*, September 11, 2020, www.christianitytoday.com/ct/2020/september-web-only/absence-of-injustice-is-not-justice.html.

[16]History.com editors, "Emmett Till Murderers Make a Magazine Confession," History, updated April 27, 2023, www.history.com/this-day-in-history/emmett-till-murderers-make-magazine-confession.

[17]Richard Perez-Pena, "Woman Linked to 1955 Emmett Till Murder Tells Historian Her Claims Were False," *New York Times*, January 27, 2017, www.nytimes.com/2017/01/27/us/emmett-till-lynching-carolyn-bryant-donham.html. See also Timothy B. Tyson, *The Blood of Emmett Till* (New York: Simon & Schuster, 2017).

[18]To see the picture of the rally and a chronology of events surrounding the trial, see Douglas O. Linder, "The Emmett Till Murder Trial: Chronology," UMKC School of Law: Famous Trials, 1995–2023, https://famous-trials.com/emmetttill/1759-chronology.

[19]Giboney, "Absence of Justice."

14. HEALING FROM THE PERSISTENCE OF WHITE SUPREMACY

[1]In 1790, one of the first laws passed by Congress said that only free white persons could naturalize and become a US citizen, followed by a series of Supreme Court cases which required courts to determine who counted as white and who did not. Thus, courts became directly involved in the legal and social production of racial categories. See Susan Smith Richardson, "What Is Critical Race Theory?," The Center for Public Integrity, September 30, 2020, https://publicintegrity.org/inside-publici/newsletters/what-is-critical-race-theory/; and Ian Haney Lopez, *White by Law: The Legal Construction of Race*, 10th anniv. ed. (New York: New York University Press, 2006).

[2]Martin Luther King Jr., *Where Do We Go From Here: Chaos or Community?* (New York: Harper & Row, 1967), 76-77.

[3]"As scholarship on race science and its kissing cousin, eugenics, has shown, research that sets out to find evidence of racial difference will find it, whether or not it exists." Adolph L. Reed Jr., "Marx, Race, and Neoliberalism," *New Labor Forum* 22 (2013): 51.

[4]Richard Delgado and Jean Stefancic, *Critical White Studies: Looking Behind the Mirror* (Philadelphia: Temple University Press, 1997), 592.

[5]Chad Felix Greene, "Conservatives Must Be Vocal in Opposing Racism—But Not with the Language of the Left," PM., July 10, 2020, https://thepostmillennial.com/conservatives-vocal-opposing-racism-not-language-left.

[6]"Talking About Race: Whiteness," National Museum of African American History & Culture, https://nmaahc.si.edu/learn/talking-about-race/topics/whiteness (italics original).

[7]See Andrew Draper, "The End of 'Mission': Christian Witness and the Decentering of White Identity," in Love L. Sechrest, Johnny Ramirez-Johnson, and Amos Yong, eds., *Can White People Be Saved?: Triangulating Race, Theology, and Mission* (Downers Grove, IL: IVP Academic, 2018).

[8]Austin Channing Brown, *I'm Still Here: Black Dignity in a World Made for Whiteness* (New York: Convergent Books, 2018), 117-18.

[9]For disagreement, see "About Faith & Heritage Webzine," Faith & Heritage: Occidental Christianity for Preserving Western Culture and People, https://faithandheritage.com/about/ as an example.

[10]John Piper, "116 Been Real: Lecrae, 'White Evangelicalism,' and Hope," Desiring God, October 6, 2017, www.desiringgod.org/articles/116-been-real.

[11]CT Editors, "The Significance of Lecrae Leaving Evangelicalism," *Quick to Listen* (podcast), *Christianity Today*, October 12, 2017, www.christianitytoday.com/ct/podcasts/quick-to-listen/significance-of-lecrae-leaving-white-evangelicalism.html.

[12]Christopher Rufo, "Even after Trump Ordered an End, Federal Agencies Still Push Insane 'Critical Race Theory,'" *New York Post*, September 15, 2020, https://nypost.com/2020/09/15/federal-agencies-still-pushing-insane-critical-race-theory/.

15. HOW SHOULD WE THEN LIVE?

[1]Though the hope of Bell's own confession of Christian faith remains unpublicized in evangelical circles: "Particularly in hard times, my Christian faith provides reassurance that is unseen but no less real. It never fails to give me the fortitude I need when opposing injustice despite the almost certain failure of my action to persuade those in authority to alter their plans or policies. For me it is my most powerful resource." See Derrick Bell, *Ethical Ambition: Living a Life of Meaning and Worth* (New York: Bloomsbury, 2002), 76; also, for pessimistic quote, see Marlese Durr, *The New Politics of Race: From DuBois to the 21st Century* (Westport, CT: Praeger, 2002), 178-79.

[2]As an example, see David W. Swanson, *Rediscipling the White Church: From Cheap Diversity to True Solidarity* (Downers Grove, IL: InterVarsity Press, 2020).

[3]Peace is the goal interpersonally and socially both inside and outside the church, but justice is a necessary ingredient that precedes peace. Jennie Allen, "Where Do We Go from Here with Mike Kelsey," *Premiere Speakers Bureau*, June 11, 2020, https://premierespeakers.com/christian/jennie_allen/posts/where_do_we_go_from_here_with_mike_kelsey.

[4]For example, museums dedicated to African American history offer great crash courses in key events, people, and conflicts representing the Black experience in America. Some with the most traffic include the National Underground Railroad Freedom Center (Cincinnati), National Museum of African American History and Culture (Washington, DC), Studio Museum (Harlem), National Civil Rights Museum (Memphis), National Center for Civil and Human Rights (Atlanta), and the National Memorial for Peace and Justice (Montgomery).